COACH'S GUIDE TO
GAME-WINNING
Softball Drills

Developing the Essential Skills in Every Player

Michele Smith

Two-Time Olympic Gold Medal Winner,
and **Lawrence Hsieh**

Ragged Mountain Press/McGraw-Hill

Camden, Maine • New York • Chicago • San Francisco • Lisbon • London • Madrid
Mexico City • Milan • New Delhi • San Juan • Seoul • Singapore • Sydney • Toronto

The McGraw·Hill Companies

Library of Congress Cataloging-in-Publication Data

Smith, Michele, 1967-
    Coach's guide to game-winning softball drills : developing the essential skills in
every player / Michele Smith and Lawrence Hsieh.
        p.   cm.
    Includes index.
    ISBN-13: 978-0-07-148587-6
    ISBN-10:   0-07-148587-2
    1. Softball—Training.   2. Softball—Coaching.   I. Hsieh, Lawrence,
1962-   II. Title.

GV881.4.T72S635   2008
796.357'8—dc22   2007048458

*To my parents, Barbara and Ernest Smith, for teaching me to love the game
of softball as well as the importance of "giving back" in all aspects of life*
Michele

*To my all-star team: my wife, Janice, and my children, Jennifer and Jason,
who inspire and amaze me every day, and to my parents, Mary and J. S.
Hsieh, for their wonderful support*
Lawrence

6 7 8 9 10 11 12 13 14 15 16 17 18 19 20 21   DOC/DOC   1 5 4 3 2

ISBN 978-0-07-148587-6
MHID   0-07-148587-2

Interior photographs by Mike Ramos Commercial Photography except as noted.

McGraw-Hill books are available at special quantity discounts to use as premiums and
sales promotions or for use in corporate training programs. To contact a representative,
please visit the Contact Us pages at www.mhprofessional.com.

This book is printed on acid-free paper.

Contents

Preface

As a two-time Olympic gold medalist, I firmly believe that success is the sum of one's efforts. While certainly my Olympic teammates and I were blessed with natural athletic ability, I've seen time and again how physical superiority alone does not assure success in softball at any level, whether it be international, intercollegiate, interscholastic, or even junior softball. In addition to having supportive parents and knowledgeable coaches, what set me apart was equal parts work ethic (unrelenting), thirst for knowledge (unquenchable), and practice (lots of it!). Practice still is my favorite part of softball. Habits, both good and bad, have a tendency to take over in game situations, so it's difficult during games to "work on your game." The time to get better is during practice.

We've written this book to give coaches, parents, and players the tools to use during practice to maximize every player's potential to be the best she can be. I've always been a stickler on proper mechanics, and I believe that the constant repetition of drill work is very important in establishing good habits. And we've coupled each group of drills with detailed coaching instruction to help give you the proper background for doing the drills. There's something in this book for coaches at every level—from novice junior players to advanced high school players and beyond.

Over the years, I've used, and I continue to use, many of the drills in this book to help make my game the best it can be. Having worked with young softball players for many years through my Michele Smith Gold Camps and Clinics, I realize that drilling is seen by some young athletes as boring, almost "too easy." But each drill in this book is designed to help you diagnose and then challenge your players to work on improving different parts of proper softball mechanics. As they progress, your players will start to realize that each drill they can do successfully and consistently is one more good habit seared into muscle memory—one more good habit that adds to the "sum of their efforts." I recognize that each time I step on the practice field I have the chance to work on my game—to work on my swing, to work on my rise, curve, or drop. Being a winner sometimes has little to do with the score. If your players seize the opportunity to be better today than they were yesterday in softball, in math, in music, in anything worth doing in life, regardless of natural ability, that will make them winners on and off the field.

And mastering these drills will arm your players with one of the biggest intangibles necessary to perform well—confidence. In each Olympic game in which I played, I got a boost in self-confidence because I knew I was better trained and better drilled than my opponents. One of the greatest feelings in the world is knowing that you are prepared. It frees you as an athlete to play uninhibited, and that's when hardworking athletes play to the fullest of their potential.

We truly are the sum of what we do. I am confident that our book will help you and your athletes prepare for the successes that follow. Good luck in everything you do!

Onward,
Michele Smith

"The Team" (left to right): Morgan Hughart, Katelyn Perna, Michele Smith, Julia Brakeman, Lawrence Hsieh, Jennifer Hsieh

Acknowledgments

We would like to thank the following coaches for reviewing and providing helpful comments on the manuscript: Debbie Delahunt, Kathryn Klaassens, and Laura Bravyak of Fairfield Ludlowe High School; Gary Quiricone, Cheryl Covino, and Kristina O'Brien of Fairfield Warde High School; as well as Frank Lapolla.

Special thanks to The JUGS Company for providing the equipment and uniforms, and Sandy Fischer for providing the Tee Stackers, used in the photos in our book. Our appreciation also goes out to Ron Radigonda, Brian McCall, Ronnie Isham, and Holly Krivokapich of USA Softball for their guidance. Kudos for a job well done to the athletes on our demonstration team: Julia Brakeman, Jennifer Hsieh, Morgan Hughart, and Katelyn Perna. Thank you also to the consummate professionals at McGraw-Hill, including Bob Holtzman and Charlie Fisher, and Mike Ramos Commercial Photography for a terrific photo shoot. It's been a pleasure to work with all of you.

Michele would also like to acknowledge Donna Exley, her high school coach; Betty Zwingraf, her first pitching coach, who taught her how to pitch the right way from the start; Joe Crookham and Jeanie Bieri of Musco Lighting for teaching her how to make a positive difference in the lives of young girls off the field; and all the other people too numerous to list who have helped Michele and made a difference in her life. Michele would also like to thank her manager, Wanda Rowland, for her amazing support, and Julie Carder, who created and has run MicheleSmith.com for as long as Michele can remember.

Finally, Lawrence would like to thank coaches Shaun Squier, Rich Bergman, Dennis Whalen, and Frank Lapolla for their mentoring over the years.

Introduction

This book is designed to give fast-pitch softball coaches and parents of players from nine to eighteen years old (grade 4 through high school) all the tools needed to teach the entire range of offensive and defensive softball skills. The chapters of this book are organized as follows: defensive skills (throwing and catching, fielding footwork, infield and outfield defense); offensive skills (hitting, baserunning); and specialist-position skills (pitching, playing the catcher position). All of these skills come together in the final chapter with pregame drills that can be used during the compressed time period before your games.

Fast-Pitch Versus Slow-Pitch

Most youth softball leagues play the fast-pitch variety of softball, which places a premium on pitching and defensive skills. Novice fast-pitch pitchers sometimes don't pitch very fast and therefore create the impression of a slow-pitch contest. But the game they are being taught to play in most youth leagues is definitely fast-pitch. As young pitchers develop their mechanics, they quickly pick up quite a bit of speed, and before too long, you even begin to see some fast-pitch offensive strategies like bunting being used by youth teams to counter dominant pitching. On the other hand, slow-pitch is an offense-oriented game in which the pitcher lobs a comparatively high arc pitch over the plate, basically inviting the batter to put the ball in play.

Young athletes rarely take advantage of the opportunities offered by some youth leagues to play sanctioned slow-pitch. And as the kids get older, they find that if they want to play interscholastic or intercollegiate softball, fast-pitch is the only game in town. While the focus of this book is fast-pitch, slow-pitch players can also use some of the hitting and fielding drills to perfect their game. For example, not all "slow" pitches are the same, and slow-pitch batters, like their fast-pitch counterparts, have to work on their timing skills, making a level swing, and so on. Interestingly, once youth and high school players put their competitive playing days behind them, they often find that there are few opportunities to continue playing fast-pitch as adults, and many former fast-pitch moms and baseball dads end up playing competitive slow-pitch and have a "ball" doing so!

Skills and Drills

Each chapter contains both a skills section and a drills section. The skills section of each chapter is a coaching manual that describes the fundamental skills you need to teach your players and includes helpful coaching tips suitable for all age groups. Movements in softball are the sum of their parts; for example, proper hitting includes both a good stride and proper rotation (among other things, of course). Therefore, the skills sections are organized into skill subcategories focusing on the proper execution of each component. The drills sections contain dozens of softball drills, from beginner to advanced, that you can use in practice so that your players can learn and reinforce the skills described in the skills sections.

Within each chapter is a Drills-Skills Matrix that matches each drill in the chapter with the applicable skills and the components of each skill. This will help you to quickly find drills that will teach specific skills or help correct problems your players are having. In addition, the applicable skill component is noted as the "purpose" of each drill. It's a good idea to read the skills section before proceeding to the drills because many of the drills refer to specific skill sets and terminology that are discussed in the skills section. The skills sections provide all the information necessary to pinpoint and diagnose your players' needs and problems.

Let's look at the chapter on hitting (Chapter 4) as an example. The skills section breaks hitting down into its main components of stance, grip, swing, and follow-through and describes the proper mechanics of each of these—such as the details of the stride, how to rotate the hips, and the precise position and movements of the hands and wrists as the mechanical elements of the swing itself. Once the coach understands the details that contribute to the ideal hitting motion, she can turn to the next section, the hitting drills that will teach and reinforce all of these skills. It is not intended that the coach run through every drill in order. Rather, she should observe the players' swings and select drills that address areas that need development or strengthening.

For example, in order to observe and evaluate your players' hitting skills, you might start with the traditional Coach Pitch—Soft Toss or Coach Pitch—Front Toss drills (drills 76 and 80) during batting practice. If these drills reveal that some of your players are having difficulty making short, compact swings, you could select the Double Tee No Sweep drill (drill 63) or the Extension—No Sweep drill (drill 74) to help them shorten their swing. If some of your players require additional practice with off-speed pitches, you could use the Coach Pitch—Changeup Hesitation drill (drill 86) to work on their timing.

Special Features

Because hitting is so different from pitching, which is so different from position play, etc., we do not take a one-size-fits-all approach. Rather, we've tailored each chapter to present issues unique to the skill sets discussed in an efficient and easy-to-follow format. For example, the chapter on pitching (Chapter 6) not only contains drills that neatly break down the mechanics of pitching into component parts but also features a "pitch menu" of drills for advanced pitchers to practice a wide variety of advanced pitches such as changeups, rise balls, drop balls, curveballs, and screwballs. The chapter on infield and outfield defense (Chapter 3) builds on the skills learned in the building-blocks chapters on throwing and catching (Chapter 1) and fielding footwork (Chapter 2) and contains drills that teach and reinforce a variety of skills, including advanced infield and outfield footwork.

Softball defense involves cognitive skills as well as physical ones. Players have to know what to do if the ball is hit to them and what to do if the ball isn't hit to them. They have to know which base to cover depending on where the ball is hit. Infielders have to know who the cutoff is if the ball is hit into the outfield, and outfielders have to know who has priority when fielding balls hit into the gap between two outfielders. Therefore, we've included drills designed to reinforce the mental aspect of the game, including situation drills and our signature Which Way? drills. These are mental drills that help infielders memorize what to do in a variety of defensive situations. If your players prepare both physically and mentally, then they will play in an uninhibited manner, and their play will flourish!

User-Friendly Drill Format

Diagrams

Accompanied by user-friendly player position diagrams, the steps for each drill take you through one repetition of the drill. Instead of adding a lot of confusing verbiage just to tell you how to rotate your players, we get right to the point and take you through the drill itself. We go straight to the essence of the drill, highlight the skill the drill is supposed to teach, and focus on proper mechanics.

Skill Levels

While even the most advanced players can use all of the drills in this book to revisit and reinforce fundamental skills, we indicate following the title of each drill whether the drill is appropriate for beginner, intermediate, or advanced players. Beginner players are those playing their first year or who are in fourth or fifth grade. Intermediate players have played at least one year and are typically in middle school (sixth, seventh, and eighth grade). We believe that most players in high school (and some middle schoolers) have at least the cognitive ability to understand all the skills discussed in this book. On the other hand, the rate of physical development

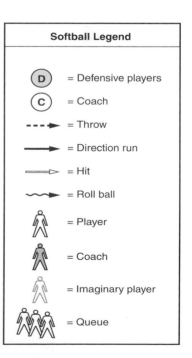

Softball Legend	
D	= Defensive players
C	= Coach
- - - ▶	= Throw
──────▶	= Direction run
═════▷	= Hit
∼∼∼▶	= Roll ball
🧍🧍	= Player
🧍	= Coach
🧍	= Imaginary player
🧍🧍🧍	= Queue

during adolescence varies widely among children, so it will be up to you as a coach and/or parent to determine at what point your player is ready for some of the advanced drills. You should also consider the level of league play. Look to see if the other teams are bunting, or check if the league allows stealing. If many of the kids on other teams in your league have some of the advanced skills discussed in this book, that's a good indicator that the skills are not too advanced, and you should consider teaching your players those skills in order to keep them competitive and progressing at an appropriate rate.

Here are some guidelines to help you determine if a player is ready to do a particular drill.

- Some younger players are simply not physically ready to do an advanced pop-up slide. It's better to first teach them how to do a basic bent-leg slide before they graduate to the more advanced slides.
- Younger pitchers need to learn how to throw a good straight fastball before they should be taught how to throw the more advanced curveball or rise ball. It's not a good idea to teach young pitchers how to throw curveballs or screwballs because the required movements may cause undue stress on the elbow and shoulder and lead to overuse injuries. The soft growth plates in the arm bones typically do not harden until puberty. So first work on proper fastball mechanics, and then the changeup. There will be plenty of time later to work on the breaking balls.
- On the hitting side, it's best for young players to focus on developing strong regular batting skills before they attempt to learn some of the advanced slap hitting skills taught in this book.
- On defense, most young fielders won't throw the ball to a bag until the player covering the bag gets there and sets up (a *static defense*). This is adequate for novice players, but unfortunately many athletes play this way until high school, where all of a sudden they may be expected on day one to already know the advanced fielding footwork to allow them to catch and land on the bag at the same time and throw in the next motion for the double play (a *motion defense*). Our book contains a progression of drills starting in the chapter on fielding footwork (Chapter 2) and moving into the chapter on infield and outfield defense (Chapter 3) to enable you to teach your novice and intermediate-level players how to progress from static defense to advanced motion defense so that eventually they are able to execute advanced infield footwork like the rocker pivot (which is used by second-base players to turn double plays).

On the other hand, players often advance in the sport while missing some of the basics. It is never too late to correct bad habits and instill the proper mechanics of bedrock skills. Therefore, any drill, even one labeled as beginner, should be considered appropriate for any player who lacks the skill that it addresses.

Most of the drills have one or more advanced variations. These are high-octane versions of the basic drill designed to challenge your more advanced players. Sometimes the advanced variations involve live defenders or base runners to infuse the drill with some pressure and make it more gamelike. In some drills, a competitive or contest element is used to create an advanced variation, and in others a stopwatch component is added to encourage more experienced players to execute the skill more quickly. We've named most of the advanced variations to make it easier for you to locate them using the book's index.

Planning

Each drill contains the following information to help you plan your practices:

- **Approximate number of repetitions per player and the approximate time the drill will take.** These are guidelines, and you should feel free to modify based on the number of players and how well your players execute the drill. If a player doesn't "get it," then by all means encourage her to do additional reps. If a player does the drill perfectly, then you can move on to something else. Limit your pitchers to no more than the number of repetitions listed. You don't want your pitchers to overstrain or injure themselves, especially on the advanced pitches that require whiplike movements. If space allows and you have a sufficient number of coaches who can supervise, you can make the drills more efficient by having multiple stations where players are executing the drill or different drills simultaneously. For example, if you have multiple tees, you can have multiple players executing the tee drills if you position the tees a safe distance apart (at least 25 feet apart).
- **Cardio index indicating the relative workout value of the drill.** Each drill has a rating of one to three hearts. One heart is the least strenuous; three hearts the most. Obviously, any drill with a lot of running around will have more workout value. It's important on hot, humid days to watch out for signs of heat exhaustion and dehydration. Familiarize yourself with your local league health and safety guidelines.
- **Number of players.** We list the minimum number of players required to do the drill. You will have the flexibility to form queues of players waiting their turn to do the drill or to run several of the drills simultaneously at stations.
- **Parent-friendly drill indicator.** Very often the most accomplished players are the ones whose parents take a strong proactive role in

their child's development. Thus, we indicate whether the drill can be practiced one-on-one by a child with a parent's supervision or involvement. You'll need to use common sense to make sure your backyard has sufficient space to execute the drill.

All of this information will help you to allocate resources, run simultaneous station drills, and plan your practices. The majority of the drills are designed to be run with one coach present, but some of them require an assistant coach or a motivated, if not knowledgeable, parent to help out.

Hints

Most of the drills contain value-added hints that are based on Michele's years of playing and teaching elite softball. These usually reemphasize key points from the skills section or provide additional player guidance specific to the skill being taught.

A Word on Coaching

Softball mechanics used for skills like hitting and pitching are complex, and if properly executed, happen lightning-quick. So it helps to be able to explain concepts clearly in a way that players understand. This is especially challenging when coaching young players. A fourth grader and a high schooler may interpret the same instruction differently. How often have you heard a coach shout out "too early" or "too late" at a batter? But some junior players will confuse bat *speed* with the real issue—timing (or when to start the swing). Sometimes batters who are too early will compensate by swinging more slowly during their next at bat (and of course still miss the ball) rather than waiting for a millisecond longer before starting the swing. Summon all of your coaching knowledge and try to tailor your explanation to the age and understanding of the player. In this example, you might want to show a fourth grader that the best place to hit the ball is in front of the plate. Then, holding the ball (don't actually throw it), simulate a fast versus a slow pitch by walking at different speeds toward the plate, and explain that the slow pitch takes a little bit longer to get to the front of the plate. At the same time, explain that she's not necessarily going to see results right away; it's going to take some time before the mental part of understanding the concept translates into the hand-eye coordination needed to execute. After all, that's what the drills are for.

Most kids are eager learners; it's truly amazing to see what they can learn and master in just one season. Good luck in all you do, and have a great season!

Throwing and Catching

Great defense starts with good catching and throwing mechanics. When these are executed with speed, precision, and confidence, plus proper fielding footwork (Chapter 2), the defense stands a reasonable chance of making the play. When these skills are executed with improper mechanics and in pedestrian fashion, the defense will be more likely to commit errors and cede extra bases.

Catching Mechanics

Catching is proactive, not passive. Not every ball thrown, and very few hit, will be delivered straight to the fielder's glove. In game situations, players must use proper fielding footwork to hustle to a hit ball or to *get off the bag* to reach errant throws. Assuming the player has gone as far as she can using her feet, then she must be able to move her glove properly into position to catch the ball.

Once her glove is in position, she should do the following:

- Watch the ball into her glove. She should not turn away.
- Keep her glove fingers pointing to the ball. When the ball is thrown above the waist, this means the fingers of the glove will be pointing up, and when the throw is below the waist this means the fingers will be pointing down.
- Catch the ball using two hands—meaning with her glove, of course, but also with her throwing hand right next to or just behind the webbing of her glove.
- Cover the ball with her throwing hand to keep it from popping out of her glove.

- Bring both arms in to her body as she catches the ball. This cushioning action is called *soft hands*. Soft hands will help prevent fumbles and put the fielder in position to make the throw.
- Bring both her glove and throwing hand to her throwing-side ear and transfer the ball to her throwing hand.
- Find the proper grip on the ball (as described later in this section) and make the throw to her target.

Kids' Corner

It is a common tendency for young players to stab at the ball or hold out their gloves stiffly. This will cause them to swat the ball away rather than catch it. On the other hand, soft hands does not mean that a player should let the ball control her. Some young players have a tendency to let the force of the ball fling back their gloves, and this too will result in dropped balls.

If a player's fingers are being hit as she covers the caught ball with her throwing hand because her timing is off, teach her to squeeze the thumb and pinky sides of her glove together after the ball is in the glove.

Throwing Mechanics

Proper *throwing mechanics* are designed to harness the energy needed to quickly and efficiently deliver a fast throw that is on target. When throwing, the player's movements should be quick, smooth, and confident. In a game situation, a player typically throws after catching or fielding the ball. After a smooth transfer of the ball from her glove to her throwing hand, she must execute the proper grip, lower-body movement, arm action, hip and trunk rotation, and release and follow-through as described in the following sections.

Throwing grip

Grip

The player should hold the ball with her fingertips, not her palm. She should grip the ball along its horizontal seams (look for the C—that is, across the "smile" of the ball), with her middle fingertip at about 12 o'clock on the C and her other fingertips on the upper part of the C, and place her thumb on the opposite side of the ball. With practice, this reliable grip will become second nature.

Lower-Body Movement

As she begins her throw, the player should keep her back foot perpendicular to her target and stride forward with her *nondominant* foot, landing it at a 45-degree angle a comfortable distance toward her target. The nondominant foot is the foot opposite the throwing side (the left foot for right-handed throwers, and the right foot for left-handed throwers). The stride will cause her body to turn sideways to the target, in position to make the powerful hip and trunk rotation used to whip her throwing arm forward.

Arm Action/Hip and Trunk Rotation

Simultaneously with her stride, the player should draw her throwing arm back and point her glove arm toward her target. She should keep her throwing-arm elbow high so that her elbow and armpit both form 90-degree angles. She should make sure when the ball is behind her that her hand is on top of the ball (if she looks back, she should see her hand and not the ball). At this point her entire body and extremities should be on a vertical plane in line with her target.

Release

To execute the throw, the player must rotate her hips and trunk while whipping her throwing arm forward. Her back foot will naturally pivot from the original perpendicular position. She must take care not to push the ball like a shot put, but rather use her elbow as a pivot to smoothly fling the ball. The motion should be smooth; some kids have the tendency to "wind up" the arm and then freeze for a split second before throwing—these throws usually end up being overthrown or off target. She will then release the ball and follow through by pointing to her target. Her hands should naturally exchange positions.

Katelyn shows good hip rotation in her throw. Instead of pushing the ball like a shot put, she whips her arm forward using her elbow as a pivot. Note Katelyn's downward follow-through (not a sidearm).

Fielding Mechanics: Ground Balls and Fly Balls

As the ball is pitched, each defensive player should get into an *athletic stance*—with knees flexed and weight slightly forward on the balls of her feet, which are slightly more than shoulder-width apart, **with a slight lean at the waist**. She should position her hands close together in front of her body. She is now in her *ready stance.*

If a *ground ball* is hit, she should do the following:

- Hustle into position using proper fielding footwork (see Chapter 2).
- Resume her athletic stance.
- Put her glove down between her legs, but in front of her body.
- Play the roll, and not the bounce. The default position should be glove on the ground; keeping the glove up in anticipation of a bounce will result in too many balls rolling between her legs.
- Watch the ball into her glove. She should not turn away.
- Cover the ball with her throwing hand to keep it from popping out of her glove.
- Bring both arms in to her body up toward her belly button (another soft hands technique).
- Bring both her glove and throwing hand to her throwing-side ear and transfer the ball to her throwing hand.
- Find the proper grip on the ball as described in the preceding section and make the throw to her target.

If, despite best efforts, she is not able to hustle in front of the ball with proper footwork, she will need to resort to making a *forehand* or *backhand grab.* Forehand and backhand grabs are methods of fielding ground balls to be used when there is no longer enough time to get the body completely in front of and square to the path of the ball. The mechanics of making these grabs are described below.

To make a backhand grab, she should do the following:

- Approach the ball with the glove side of her body so that she will field the ball with her glove-side leg closest to the ball; this will allow her to reach farther, if necessary.
- As she approaches the ball, drop her throwing-side knee toward the ground (her glove-side leg is in front). At the same time, she should rotate her glove-side knee, pointing at the throwing-side foot, which will allow her body and glove to rotate better.
- As she approaches the ball, drop her glove to the ground (thumb and webbing down) and remember to keep the glove open.
- Field the ball in front of her glove-side foot.

Morgan makes a backhand grab. Her glove-side leg is closest to the ball to allow maximum reach. She fields the ball in front of her body.

Forehand grabs are similarly executed but with the thumb part of her glove on top because she still wants to field the ball on the glove side of her body.

If a *fly ball* is hit, she should do the following:

- Hustle into position using proper fielding footwork (Chapter 2).
- Catch the ball above her forehead with two hands (arms not stiff, elbows bent), meaning she should position her throwing hand near the pocket of her glove to keep the ball from falling out of her glove and to facilitate a smooth transfer of the ball to her throwing hand.
- Bring both arms down toward her throwing-arm shoulder (yet another soft hands technique).
- Bring both her glove and throwing hand to her throwing-side ear and transfer the ball to her throwing hand.
- Find the proper grip on the ball as described earlier and make the throw to her target, using the *crow hop* (see Chapter 2) if necessary.

Morgan starts in a good athletic stance, moves her feet to get into position, and fields the ball in front of her body.

Chapter 1 Skills Matrix

Drill Number	Drill Title (Indented drills are "named" Advanced Variations)	Overall Throwing Mechanics	Upper-Body Throwing Mechanics	Arm Throwing Mechanics	Throwing Stride	Catching Mechanics
		Skills Reinforced →				
1.	One-Knee Throwing		⚾	⚾		
2.	90-Degree Throwing		⚾	⚾		
3.	Nondominant Foot				⚾	⚾
4.	Catching—Up/Down Glove Position					⚾
5.	Catching—Left/Right Glove Position					⚾
6.	Catching—Quick Reaction					⚾
7.	Ground Ball/Fly Ball Practice					⚾
8.	One-Hop Fielding					⚾
	One-Hop—Wall					⚾
9.	Partner Throwing	⚾			⚾	⚾
10.	Target Throw—Wall	⚾				
	Target Throw One-Hop	⚾				
11.	Target Throw—Bucket	⚾				⚾
	Target Throw—Where's the Bucket?	⚾				⚾
12.	Speed Throwing—Team Competition	⚾				⚾
	Speed Throwing—Two Ball	⚾				⚾
13.	Speed Throwing—Jump Pivot	⚾				⚾
	Speed Throwing—Reverse	⚾				⚾
	Speed Throwing—Second Option	⚾				⚾
14.	Arm Strength—Partner Throw for Distance	⚾				
15.	Arm Strength—Long/Short Alternate	⚾				
16.	Underhand Flip	⚾				
	Underhand Flip Versus Dart Throw	⚾				
17.	Underhand Flip to Second Base	⚾				
	Backhand Flip	⚾				
18.	Around the Horn	⚾				⚾
19.	Backhand Grounder					
	Backhand Grounder with Runners					
20.	Basic Communication					⚾

Reaction Time	Fielding	Pivot	Throwing Accuracy	Throwing Speed	Throwing Strength	Communication
			●			
			●			
●						
	●					
●	●					
●	●					
			●		●	
			●			
			●			
			●			
●			●			
			●	●		
●			●	●		
		●	●	●		
		●	●	●		●
		●	●	●		
					●	
					●	
			●			
			●			
	●		●			
			●			
			●	●		
	●					
	●					
●	●					●

Throwing and Catching Drills

1. One-Knee Throwing (Beginner)

Purpose: To practice basic upper-body throwing mechanics
Equipment: Safety ball or tennis ball
Number of players: 2
Number of repetitions: 20 reps for 2 sets

Allocated time: 5 minutes
Parent-friendly drill: ✔
Cardio index: ♥

1. Two players kneel on their dominant knee (i.e., throwing side), facing each other, 10 to 15 feet apart.
2. The players throw the ball to each other using proper upper-body throwing mechanics.
3. The players catch the ball using two hands (no glove), thus reinforcing soft hands technique.

Advanced Variation

Increase distance to 20 to 25 feet. Although the throwing mechanics are the same for longer throws, the player must rotate her hips slightly and her shoulder faster and whip her throwing hand faster from behind her throwing-side ear to generate the velocity to cover the longer distance.

Hints

Make sure your players rotate their throwing-side shoulder away from the target and bring their throwing hand past the ear before beginning the forward motion toward the target. Don't take the catching part for granted. Your players should use the soft hands technique to catch the ball.

2. 90-Degree Throwing (Beginner)

Purpose: To practice proper arm position in throwing the ball
Equipment: Safety ball or tennis ball
Number of players: 2
Number of repetitions: 20 reps for 2 sets

Allocated time: 5 minutes
Parent-friendly drill: ✔
Cardio index: ♥

1. Two players stand facing each other 15 feet apart.
2. One player holds the ball so that both her elbow and armpit are at about 90-degree angles.
3. A coach checks position and gives the signal for her to throw to the other player.
4. The player throws the ball to the other player using proper mechanics.
5. The players take turns throwing to each other in this manner.

Advanced Variation

Increase distance to 25 feet.

Hints

This drill will help correct the tendency of many players to "shot put" the ball. Shot-putting a ball will decrease power and accuracy. These drills are also great for warming up the shoulder while working on proper form.

Jenn is in the classic two 90-degree angle position, ready to throw the ball. Her hand is on top of the ball to start, and she's pointing to the target with her glove.

3. Nondominant Foot (Beginner)

Purpose: To practice basic throwing stepping with the nondominant foot	**Number of repetitions:** 15 reps for 2 sets
	Allocated time: 3 to 5 minutes
Equipment: Softball or safety ball	**Parent-friendly drill:** ✔
Number of players: Up to 4	**Cardio index:** ♥

1. Up to four players stand on the foul line facing a coach 15 feet away.
2. The player with the ball stands with her nondominant (glove-side) foot slightly forward.
3. The player then steps forward with her nondominant foot to complete the throw.
4. The coach catches the ball and throws it to the next player in line.
5. The player catches the ball using soft hands and repeats the drill.
6. Repeat until the allocated time elapses.

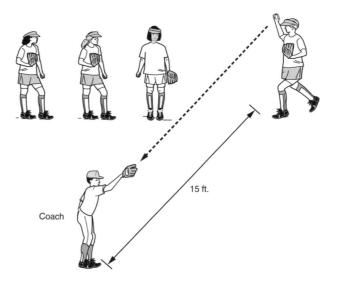

15 ft.

Coach

4. Catching—Up/Down Glove Position (Beginner)

Purpose: To practice catching balls thrown low or high

Equipment: Softball or safety ball

Number of players: 3

Number of repetitions: 10 reps for 2 sets

Allocated time: 3 to 5 minutes

Parent-friendly drill: ✔

Cardio index: ♥

1. Three players line up on the foul line about 5 feet from each other and facing a coach 15 to 20 feet away. Each player assumes her ready stance to catch the ball.
2. A coach throws the ball to each player, alternating throwing above and below waist level.
3. The player rotates her glove hand so her fingers are pointed down to catch balls thrown below her waist and fingers up to catch balls thrown above her waist.
4. Repeat until the allocated time elapses.

Hints

In game situations, fielders should take the explosive first step toward a ball hit in front of them and try to catch the ball with the glove up. If despite best efforts a fielder can't reach the ball before it falls below waist level, then she should turn her glove. In other words, a player should move feet first and hustle to the ball so the catch can be made as close as possible to eye level, where the player can see the ball.

5. Catching—Left/Right Glove Position (Beginner)

Purpose: To practice catching balls thrown to the glove side or throwing side
Equipment: Softball or safety ball
Number of players: 3
Number of repetitions: 10 reps for 2 sets
Allocated time: 3 to 5 minutes
Parent-friendly drill: ✔ Work on this drill one-on-one with your child.

Have her stand in place or sit on a bucket. Throw balls to either side of her. In a game situation, she may need to get off the bag to catch an errant throw to prevent extra bases, but for this drill, encourage her to move her glove to get the ball.
Cardio index: ♥

1. Three players line up on the foul line about 5 to 7 feet from each other and facing a coach 15 feet away. Each player assumes her ready stance to catch the ball.
2. A coach throws the ball to each player, alternating throwing to the glove-side or throwing-arm side.
3. The player's glove crosses the midline of her body to catch balls thrown to her throwing side.

Advanced Variation

Throw some overhead or short hops to really challenge advanced players. Good glove control is important for good fielding.

Hints

Errant throws are common in junior softball. Use this drill to help infielders catch balls thrown to either side. Sometimes an infielder has to get off the bag to catch errant throws, but the feet will only get the player so far, and she may need to maneuver her glove to catch the ball.

Make sure your players start with both hands and fingers spread to make a catch, similar to a good position to catch a basketball.

Hard-hit balls and errant throws don't always allow enough time for a player to use her feet to get in front of the ball to make the catch. After using best efforts to hustle with her feet to get as close as possible to a hard-hit line drive, Jenn still needs to move her glove to catch the ball. (Photo by Lawrence Hsieh)

6. Catching—Quick Reaction (Intermediate)

Purpose: To develop quick reaction time for catching balls
Equipment: Safety ball
Number of players: 1 player or a group of players

Number of repetitions: 15 reps for 2 sets
Allocated time: 5 minutes
Parent-friendly drill: ✔
Cardio index: ♥

1. Players line up facing a coach 30 feet away.
2. The coach signals for the first player to execute the drill.
3. The player steps forward so that she is about 15 feet from the coach and turns around so that she is not facing the coach.
4. The coach calls out "Ready, now!" and throws the ball a reasonable distance on either side of the player.
5. The player turns around and executes proper footwork and glove work to catch the ball and throws it back to the coach.

Advanced Variations

- Have the player sit on the ground facing away from the coach. This makes the drill even more difficult. If at first the player is unable to do this, have her sit on the ground while facing the coach and then advance to facing away from the coach.
- Have the player lie on her stomach facing away from the coach.

Hints

Make sure the athletes are tracking the ball the whole way while moving, getting up, or turning around. Many athletes will take their eyes off the ball when they have to think about other movements. Also, make sure they are running on the balls of their feet; if they run on their heels, it will look to them as though the ball is moving or hopping in the air and make it harder to track and catch.

7. Ground Ball/Fly Ball Practice (Beginner)

Purpose: To practice fielding ground balls and fly balls
Equipment: Softball or safety ball
Number of players: Up to 5
Number of repetitions: 10 reps for 2 sets

Allocated time: 5 minutes
Parent-friendly drill: ✔
Cardio index: ♥

1. Five players stand 10 feet apart from each other and facing a coach 20 feet away. This drill can be practiced in the infield dirt or outfield grass.
2. The coach randomly rolls ground balls at varying speeds and throws fly balls of varying heights directly in front of or slightly to either side of each fielder.
3. The player fields the ball and throws it back to the coach for the next repetition.

Advanced Variations

- Hit the balls so the players have to read the ball off the bat.
- Have the players start on only their dominant leg. This will teach them to put their nondominant leg down and move to the ball. Also have them start on only their nondominant leg.

Hints

Make sure the players are in a good starting position to field both ground balls and line drives or throws.

8. One-Hop Fielding (Beginner)

Purpose: To practice fielding one-hop hits

Equipment: Tennis ball

Number of players: 1

Number of repetitions: 8 to 10 reps for 3 sets

Allocated time: 5 to 7 minutes

Parent-friendly drill: ✔

Cardio index: ♥ ♥

1. A player stands facing a coach 15 to 20 feet away. This drill can be practiced on an asphalt playground or in a gymnasium with a tennis ball. (Players should wear sneakers when doing this drill on asphalt or indoors.)
2. The coach throws a ball about 10 to 12 feet in front of the player so that it takes a bounce.
3. The player sprints to the ball and attempts to catch the ball in the air.
4. The player fields the ball on one bounce and throws it back to the coach for the next repetition.

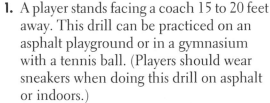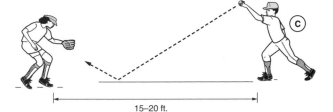

15–20 ft.

Advanced Variations

- Have your players field the ball on the glove side of their body and immediately make a crow-hop throw back to the coach standing about 50 to 60 feet away.
- **One-Hop—Wall.** Have a player face a wall about 15 feet away. Throw a tennis ball or safety ball against the wall so that it hops in front of the player. The player will not be able to see the ball until it hits the wall. To challenge your players even more, have them take one step closer to the wall for every ball they cleanly field. Use common sense in terms of how close you allow your players to stand to the wall. Make a game out of this drill and keep track of the number of steps they are able to take forward.

Hints

Make sure the players are starting with their weight on their toes; this will allow them to react more quickly.

9. Partner Throwing (Beginner)

Purpose: To practice basic throwing mechanics

Equipment: Softball or safety ball

Number of players: 2

Number of repetitions: 10 reps for 2 sets

Allocated time: 3 to 5 minutes

Parent-friendly drill: ✔

Cardio index: ♥

1. Two players stand facing each other 15 feet apart.
2. The players throw the ball to each other using proper throwing mechanics, including stepping forward with the nondominant foot.
3. The players catch the ball using soft hands.
4. A coach observes and, when the players are ready, instructs the players to take a step backward to increase the distance of the throws.

Advanced Variations

- Have the players increase the speed of the drill, catching and immediately throwing the ball using proper mechanics. This will make the drill more gamelike.
- Incorporate the crow hop into the drill for longer-distance throws.
- Make this drill a competition—the pair that completes 20 throws first wins.

Hints

This is a warm-up drill focusing on proper mechanics. Try not to have your players throw farther than they are comfortable doing using proper mechanics. Make sure your players make level throws and avoid throwing high arc throws. If a coach or parent partners with a player, lower yourself to the player's height to encourage level throws.

10. Target Throw — Wall (Beginner)

Purpose: To develop throwing accuracy using proper mechanics
Equipment: Supply of softballs; masking tape, chalk, or plastic sheet and twist ties
Number of players: 1

Number of repetitions: 10 reps for 2 sets
Allocated time: 3 to 5 minutes
Parent-friendly drill: ✔
Cardio index: 💜 💜

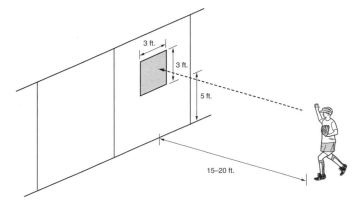

1. A coach draws a 3 feet by 3 feet box about 5 feet above the ground on a wall, fence, or backstop using masking tape or chalk. A piece of plastic of the same size can be substituted by affixing it to the fence or backstop using twist ties.
2. One player stands facing the wall, fence, or backstop 15 to 20 feet away.
3. The player throws the ball and attempts to hit the target area using proper throwing mechanics.
4. Repeat until the allocated time elapses or a certain number of throws is completed.
5. Award points for accurate throws.

Advanced Variations

- Have the player stand farther from the box.
- Make the box smaller—2 feet by 2 feet and then 1 foot by 1 foot.
- Add crow-hop throws for outfielders (increase distance to 50 feet).
- **Target Throw One-Hop.** Lower the box on the fence and have the outfielders throw one-hop throws into the box to simulate throws to home plate on one bounce.

Hints

Make sure the player's head is in proper position after the ball is released. Many young athletes will try to make strong throws and jerk their heads off to the side on the follow-through.

11. Target Throw—Bucket (Intermediate)

Purpose: To develop throwing accuracy using proper mechanics
Equipment: Supply of softballs, five-gallon buckets
Number of players: 2

Number of repetitions: 10 reps for 2 sets
Allocated time: 5 minutes
Parent-friendly drill: ✔
Cardio index: ♥ ♥

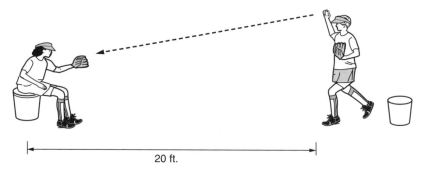

20 ft.

1. Two players sit on large painters' buckets (the kind used to hold softballs) facing each other 20 feet apart.
2. Each player takes her turn standing up and throwing the ball using proper mechanics to the other player sitting on the bucket.
3. The player sitting on the bucket can move her arms to catch the ball but cannot leave the bucket to catch errant throws.

Advanced Variations

- Move the buckets farther apart.
- Have the players work on throwing one-bounce throws that are easy to catch. Too far or too close and it will be a hard catch for the partner on the bucket.
- **Target Throw—Where's the Bucket?** Have the throwing player sit with her back to her partner. Give the receiving partner a couple of seconds to move her bucket to a different location that the throwing partner is not aware of. When the throwing partner turns, there is a good chance she will have her feet in the wrong position to make a good throw. This will help her learn to reset her feet in order to make a good throw to her partner on the bucket.

Hints

Moving and challenging the players will make all drills more gamelike. This is very important for advanced players. Younger athletes should work mechanics first and then build up to gamelike situations.

12. Speed Throwing—Team Competition (Beginner)

Purpose: To develop throwing speed and accuracy using proper mechanics

Equipment: Softball or safety ball

Number of players: 8

Number of repetitions: 6 reps for 5 sets

Allocated time: 5 to 7 minutes

Cardio index: ♥ ♥

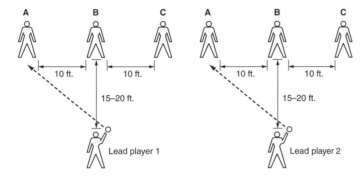

1. Two groups of three players (A, B, and C) stand on the foul line about 10 feet apart, facing a lead player standing about 15 to 20 feet away.
2. On a coach's cue, the lead player starts the drill by throwing the ball to player A using proper throwing mechanics.
3. Player A catches the ball using soft hands and throws the ball back to the lead player, who repeats steps 2 and 3 with players B and C.
4. Each team is awarded one point for every catch; the team with the most points in the allotted time (coach's discretion—1 minute, 2 minutes, etc.) wins.

Advanced Variations

- **Speed Throwing—Two Ball.** Use two balls at the same time. Start by giving the lead player one ball and either A, B, or C the other ball. Be sure that each player only throws when the receiving player is looking at her and giving her a target.
- Move the players farther apart to challenge them more.

Hints

It's important to be able to throw the ball to the receiving player's throwing shoulder. The closer the throw is to the receiving player's throwing shoulder, the more quickly she will be able to catch, transfer the ball, and throw. The time saved in making a throw to the proper location will translate to better fielding in games (double plays, etc.).

13. Speed Throwing—Jump Pivot (Intermediate)

Purpose: To develop throwing speed and accuracy using the jump pivot to turn toward the target

Equipment: Softball

Number of players: 3

Number of repetitions: 8 reps for 2 to 3 sets

Allocated time: 3 to 5 minutes

Cardio index: ♥ ♥

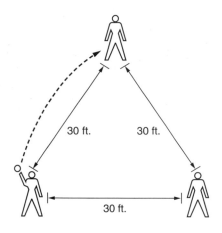

30 ft.   30 ft.

30 ft.

1. Three players stand in a triangle formation about 30 feet apart from each other.
2. The player with the ball starts the drill by throwing the ball to the next player (clockwise or counterclockwise) using proper throwing mechanics.
3. The next player catches the ball and executes a *jump pivot* by jumping and simultaneously turning toward the target (in this case toward the next player).
4. She lands with both feet simultaneously and open to the target and throws the ball to the next player. By landing in an open position she will be able to throw without having to take extra steps.

Advanced Variations

- **Speed Throwing—Reverse.** Have the players reverse the throws when the coach yells, "Reverse!" This will help them learn to think quickly after hearing a verbal cue. This drill will help players learn to filter out ambient noise and listen for the coaches and teammates.
- **Speed Throwing—Second Option.** Have your advanced players jump pivot to a first target but not make the throw, then reset and jump pivot to another target and make the throw. Many times in games, when a teammate is late to a bag or no one is there, the fielder with the ball will have to reset her feet to make a throw to another bag. This will help teach athletes to take the extra split second to make a good throw. Many young players will rush a throw and not set up their feet correctly, almost always resulting in an off-target throw.

Hints

Beginner players may wish to catch the ball and then pivot on the back foot while stepping to the target with the front foot. This type of pivoting is done without jumping at the target.

14. Arm Strength—Partner Throw for Distance (Beginner)

Purpose: To develop arm strength while using basic throwing mechanics

Equipment: Softball

Number of players: 2

Number of repetitions: 25 to 35 throws for 1 set

Allocated time: 5 minutes

Parent-friendly drill: ✔

Cardio index: ♥ ♥

1. Two players stand facing each other 15 feet apart.
2. The players throw the ball to each other using proper throwing mechanics.
3. The players catch the ball using soft hands.
4. For every few successful throws and catches at a certain distance, increase the distance by taking a couple of steps backward.
5. Incorporate the crow hop into the drill for longer-distance throws.

Advanced Variation

Have the players increase the speed of the drill, catching and immediately throwing the ball using proper mechanics. This will make the drill more gamelike.

Hints

This drill is great for outfielders and middle infielders. We often forget that middle infielders also need to have very strong arms. Middle infielders in "cut" play situations are the key to nailing the runners at home plate. The stronger their arms, the greater the chance of making the play at home!

15. Arm Strength—Long/Short Alternate (Beginner)

Purpose: To develop muscle memory to use proper mechanics to make any length throw	**Number of repetitions:** 10 throws to each player for a total of 20, for 1 set per player
Equipment: Softball	**Allocated time:** 5 minutes
Number of players: 3	**Cardio index:** ♥ ♥

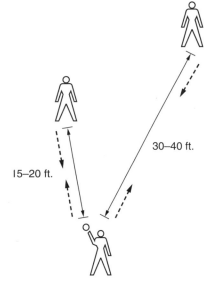

15–20 ft.

30–40 ft.

1. Three players stand in a triangle formation, with one player standing about 15 to 20 feet away from the lead player and the other player standing about 30 to 40 feet away from the lead player.
2. The lead player throws to the player 15 to 20 feet away, who throws it back to the lead player.
3. The lead player throws to the player 30 to 40 feet away, who throws it back to the lead player.
4. The players can switch roles.

Advanced Variations

- Have the players increase the speed of the drill, catching and immediately throwing the ball using proper mechanics. This will make the drill more gamelike.
- Increase or shorten the distances between the players to keep each throw different. This will challenge the athletes to make a good throw regardless of distance.

Hints

The throwing mechanics are the same for short and longer throws, except that the player must rotate her hips and shoulder faster and whip her throwing hand faster from behind her throwing-side ear to generate the velocity to cover the longer distance. Players should also incorporate the *crow hop infield variation* (see Chapter 2) for the longer-distance throw. Alternating between long and short throws will help players develop the muscle memory to use proper mechanics for any distance throw.

16. Underhand Flip (Beginner)

Purpose: To practice *underhand flip* short-distance throws
Equipment: Softball
Number of players: 1
Number of repetitions: 10 reps for 2 sets

Allocated time: 3 to 5 minutes
Parent-friendly drill: ✔
Cardio index: ♥ ♥

1. A player stands facing a coach 10 to 15 feet away.
2. The coach rolls the ball to the player.
3. The player fields the ball and delivers an underhand toss to the coach.
4. The player makes the underhand toss by stepping forward with her nondominant foot and using her upper body, not just her arms, to toss the ball.
5. The player is still moving forward in her follow-through. She completes her follow-through by leaving her hand and fingers pointing toward the target.

Advanced Variation

Underhand Flip Versus Dart Throw. Try varying distances so the player has to decide when to use a "dart" type throw verse a flip toss. *Dart throws* are made when the fielder is too far to make an underhand flip and a bit too close to make a full overhand throw. To make a dart throw, the fielder, who is about 5 to 15 feet from her target, throws the ball like she would throw a dart at a dartboard. In other words, rather than draw the arm all the way back behind her shoulder, she starts the throw at about her shoulder and makes the throw straight out toward the target.

Hints

Remember that flip throws are only used for short distances. It's very rare that an outfielder will have to use a flip. The underhand flip should be done in a smooth manner and while moving forward. Correct the tendency of young players to field the ball, panic, stop in their tracks, and then stiff-arm an underhand toss, which invariably goes awry.

The player should imagine a rope about belt high that she tries to flip the ball under. This will keep the flip on a line toward the target instead of a high arc (like a rainbow) that takes too much time in the air. The follow-through on the flip is very important and should be under this imaginary rope with fingers snapped toward the target.

17. Underhand Flip to Second Base (Intermediate)

Purpose: To practice underhand flip short-distance throws to second base and to develop confidence in throwing decisions
Equipment: Supply of softballs
Number of players: second-base player and shortstop

Number of repetitions: 10 reps for 2 sets
Allocated time: 3 to 5 minutes
Parent-friendly drill: ✔
Cardio index: ♥ ♥

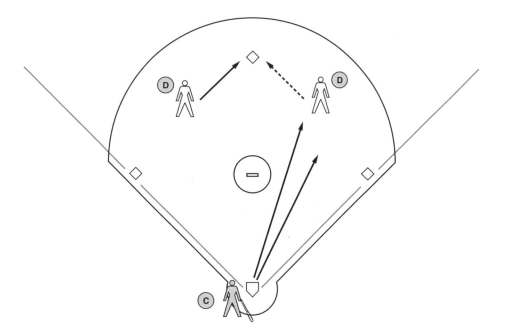

1. A second-base player and shortstop take their positions on the infield.
2. A coach standing at home plate throws (or hits) a grounder to either side of either player.
3. The second-base player or shortstop fields the ball, while the other player covers second base.
4. If the ground ball is "hit" to the far side of the fielder relative to second base, then the fielder makes an overhand throw to second base.
5. If the ground ball is hit to the near side of the fielder relative to second base or within 10 to 12 feet of the second-base bag, then she delivers an underhand toss to second base.

Advanced Variation

Backhand Flip. Sometimes after fielding a ball—for example, a hit up the middle of the infield—a right-handed second-base player may find that she has no time to turn around and make a regular underhand flip toss facing the bag. In this case, she may need to flip the ball behind her body to second base. Practice fielding the ball up the middle so that the second-base player has to *backhand flip* the ball to the shortstop covering second base. The backhand flip (and follow-through) should be made with the thumb in a downward position, pointing toward the ground. This will keep the ball from floating in the air and taking up too much time. Backhand flips are also used for second-base players flipping the ball to first base and for shortstops flipping the ball to third base. Work these bags into the drills as well.

Katelyn has already fielded the ball in the first frame and is now looking at her close-range target. She uses her upper body, not just her arms, to firmly (not stiffly) flip the ball. Even after releasing the ball, Katelyn continues to move forward.

18. Around the Horn (Beginner)

Purpose: To practice throwing and catching at infield distances and to build teamwork
Equipment: Softball
Number of players: 4

Number of repetitions: 5 reps for 3 sets
Allocated time: 5 to 7 minutes
Cardio index: ♥ ♥ ♥

1. Station one player at each base and home plate.
2. The player at home plate starts the drill by throwing the ball to the next base (clockwise or counterclockwise).
3. Each player continues the drill in the same direction "around the horn."
4. Each player catches the ball using soft hands.
5. Each player will need to pivot or, for advanced players, jump pivot after catching the ball in order to throw to the next base using proper throwing mechanics.
6. You can keep score by comparing the number of throws made by teams of four players for a set period of time, for example, number of throws made in one minute. Or you can keep score by comparing the number of throws made by each team until the ball is dropped or a bad throw is made.

Advanced Variations

- Have a base runner run around the bases while the players execute the drill counterclockwise. Experienced players should be able to beat the runner every time.
- Incorporate the crow hop infield variation (see Chapter 2) for players who are ready.

19. Backhand Grounder (Intermediate)

Purpose: To practice fielding ground balls using backhand technique (used where despite best footwork and hustle, the fielder cannot reach the ball in time to field it facing the ball)

Equipment: Supply of softballs

Number of players: 1

Number of repetitions: 10 reps for 3 sets

Allocated time: 5 to 7 minutes

Parent-friendly drill: ✔

Cardio index: ⓥ ⓥ

1. A player stands with her back to a fence and facing a coach 30 feet away. A helper with a glove stands a safe distance away from the coach to help catch returned balls.
2. A coach throws or hits ground balls to the glove side of the player.
3. The player takes a crossover step (see Chapter 2) in the direction of the ball, angling back if necessary in case of a hard-hit ground ball.
4. The player approaches the ball with the glove side of her body so that she will field the ball with her glove-side leg closest to the ball.
5. As she approaches the ball, she drops her throwing-side knee toward the ground (her glove-side leg is in front).
6. She fields the ball in front of her glove-side foot.
7. She brings her glove and throwing hand together in to her body and transfers the ball to her throwing hand.
8. She makes an infield variation crow-hop throw if needed to the helper for the next repetition.

Advanced Variation

Backhand Grounder with Runners. Position infielders and put runners on the bases. Have the fielding players make the play and finish with a good throw to the bag to force out the lead runner.

20. Basic Communication (Beginner)

Purpose: To practice basic fielding communication skills and develop teamwork

Equipment: Supply of softballs

Number of players: 4

Number of repetitions: 10 reps for 2 sets

Allocated time: 5 minutes

Cardio index: ♥ ♥

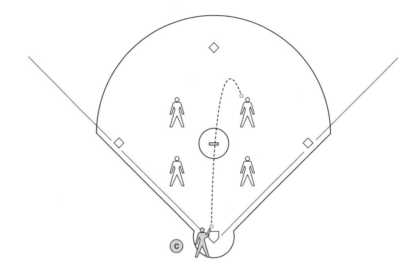

1. Four players position themselves in the infield, each in a quadrant defined by the pitching rubber as the center.
2. A coach standing at home plate throws a pop-up to any of the quadrants (including the boundary areas).
3. The appropriate player calls for the ball by yelling "Ball, ball" or "OK, OK." She should also wave her hands to warn other players away.
4. The fielder throws the ball back to the coach for the next repetition.

Advanced Variation

Assemble the four players in the outfield in a 50-by-50-foot area and execute the drill without the clearly defined boundaries of the basic version of the drill.

Hints

The shortstop is the leader of the infield, the center fielder is the leader of the outfield, and the outfield leads the infield on called-for balls. It is easier for an outfielder to catch a ball while coming in than for an infielder to catch a ball while moving back. However, remind your younger players to exercise common sense. Sometimes it is easier for an infielder to catch a ball hit slightly behind her than for the outfielder to run forward a long distance, especially if the ball is hit in the dirt behind the infielder.

Fielding Footwork

Good defense starts with efficient footwork. Before a defensive player can make a play, she must first get to the ball as quickly as she can. This takes a combination of speed and proper footwork technique. Add a healthy dose of hustle, and even a player with an average arm can save an extra-bases hit from turning into a disaster.

During practice and games, watch how your players react to hit balls, especially that crucial first step. See if your players waste precious time back-pedaling to reach balls hit behind them or lift their leg rather than pivot and then cross over in the direction of balls hit to either side. The drills in this chapter are designed to reinforce the following basic footwork skills for infielders and outfielders of all age groups:

- **Crossover step.** The first move in the direction of balls hit to either side.
- **Drop step.** The first step back before an all-out sprint to catch a ball hit behind the player.
- **Outfield crow hop/infield variation.** Used to add even more distance to long-distance throws.
- **The pivot.** Catch, pivot, and throw to a target in a different direction.
- **Infield footwork progression.** How to catch on the run while stepping on the bag with the correct foot, a prerequisite skill to the advanced footwork drills in Chapter 3.

Before proceeding to the position-specific drills, make sure your players practice these easy-to-learn, but often taken for granted, footwork techniques *until they become second nature*. The repetition will pay great dividends in the defensive development of your players.

Footwork Mechanics

As the pitch is thrown, the defensive player should ready herself in an athletic stance—either square to home plate or with the favored foot slightly in

A Word About Hustle

Missed opportunities happen all the time in life, even in softball. Some opportunities are invisible except to the most prescient people. But many others can be exploited if we only have the conviction to "go for it." How many times in junior softball have you seen fielders defer to hitters—jog and then retrieve pop flies on one hop that could easily have been caught, or sometimes even give the ball the "right of way," literally jogging alongside the hit ball until it slows down? Teach your players that every play of every game is an opportunity for every player to make a contribution. Occasionally, players in game situations choose to allow line drives to one-hop because they're afraid they'll botch the catch. But encourage your players to push the envelope during practice. Eventually, what was once unattainable will become routine.

front of the other. A little bit of swaying movement is recommended; the athlete will react faster if she is moving slightly. We see this often with tennis players awaiting a serve. If the ball is hit, the fielder should immediately gauge where the ball is going. There's no magic to acquiring this skill; it is learned through repetition. But keep in mind that good depth perception is very important for softball players, especially outfielders. If you have athletes who are constantly misjudging balls, recommend that they have their eyes checked, especially their depth perception. Most players with average to poor depth perception will do better as infielders. Infielders have more reference points (the bags, other players, coaches) for the brain to use to calculate where the ball is going. Outfielders don't have this advantage and must rely on depth perception to judge where the ball is going.

Crossover Step

If the ball looks like it will go to her right or left side, the defensive player should do the following:

- Pivot the ball-side foot and cross over with the opposite foot in the direction of the ball, resisting the temptation to lift the ball-side foot as the first step. Lifting the ball-side foot is wasted motion that can mean the difference between a fielded ball and one that gets away.
- Run to the ball and catch or retrieve it in front of the body. A fielder should always try to center the ball up on the midline of the body. This will enable her to be in good position to execute a proper throw to make the play. She should backhand catch the ball only as a last resort. However, backhand fielding is a legitimate technique (as discussed in Chapter 1).

Drop Step

The typical first instinct of a junior outfielder is to step toward the infield upon the crack of the bat, regardless of where the ball is going, and then to backpedal when she realizes that the ball is hit over her head. This can be counterproductive and dangerous because the player:

- Can't see where she's going
- Can't run as fast going backward as she can going forward
- Isn't in position to make a leaping or other desperation catch, if necessary

If the ball is hit over her head, the defensive player should do the following:

- Take a 45-degree step to the rear using the foot on the side the ball is headed. This is called a *drop step*.
- Start running by crossing over with the opposite foot.
- Run like the wind with her body turned sideways directly to where she predicts the ball will fall. Running sideways will allow her to look over her shoulder at the ball while running at full speed.
- Not extend the glove arm until she is ready to make the catch.
- Arrive early on the throwing-arm side of the ball, if possible. This will enable her to reverse momentum toward the infield, catch the ball with two hands in front of her body, and be in position to execute a proper crow-hop throw (discussed in the next section) to make the play. Arriving early will also allow for last-second adjustments for wind, sun, and so on.

Rather than lift her ball-side foot, Morgan pivots it (first frame). Her first step is the crossover, as she crosses over with her other foot in the direction of the ball (second and third frames).

Katelyn's first movement is to drop back with her ball-side foot in the direction of the ball. She then crosses over her other foot in the direction of the ball.

- For lazy fly balls, use the extra time to take a rounded path (but run fast). This will help her get to the ball from behind and make the catch on the throwing-arm side while moving forward toward the infield and so be in a good position to execute a proper throw.

Kids' Corner

For young outfielders less experienced at gauging a ball's flight path, teach them to automatically take a small drop step every time the ball is hit. If it turns out that the ball will fall in front of the player, it's easy to reverse direction. Fielders should never take a step in without knowing where the ball will land. Changing direction after first taking a step in is very awkward and slow.

Crow-Hop Throw

A fielder's job is not done after getting to and fielding the ball. An outfielder must then make the play to the proper infielder or *cutoff*. After fielding balls hit in front of them, make sure your outfielders use the crow hop to harness the required momentum for the long-distance throw. There are two versions of the crow hop—a *traditional crow hop* utilizing a crossover and an *abbreviated crow hop* that utilizes a shuffle. In the traditional version, after fielding the ball, an outfielder should do the following:

- In one smooth motion, step toward the target using her glove-side foot, planting the foot at a 45-degree angle, with her body sideways to the target.
- *Slide hop* forward (no "big air"), crossing her throwing-side foot in front of her glove-side foot. In the meantime, she should smoothly transfer the ball from her glove to her throwing hand.
- Finish the hop by landing on her throwing-side foot perpendicular to the target.
- Make a proper throw to the target.

The traditional version is more common in baseball than in softball because of the longer distances that have to be covered. While the traditional crossover version generates lots of momentum (it's similar to the footwork used by javelin throwers), it's also slower to execute and very difficult for young softball players to learn. Many junior and advanced softball players use the abbreviated version of the crow hop. In the abbreviated version, rather than crossing over her throwing-side foot in front of her glove-side foot, the player lands her throwing-side foot beside her glove-side foot.

In either case, players can only use the crow hop to throw balls hit in front of them (either hit in front, or as the result of the player taking a round

Katelyn has just fielded the ball in the infield (first frame) and does a quick toe-to-heel infield hop (second frame). In the third frame, she plants her rear foot perpendicular to her target and is stepping (not lunging) toward her target with her glove-side foot as she prepares to throw.

path to get in front of the ball). If the ball is hit to either side or behind her, then she will have to plant hard on her opposite side and reverse direction before using the crow hop depending on where she is throwing.

Infielders use the *crow hop infield variation*, which helps them build momentum very quickly in the direction of the target. The infield variation is similar to the outfield version, but the feet stay closer together (no crossover of the back leg). After fielding the ball, the infielder should do the following:

- Push off her back or throwing-side foot and shuffle it toward her front foot, bringing the toe of her rear foot near the heel of her front foot. (Coaches sometimes call this the *toe-to-heel infield hop*.)
- Plant her rear foot perpendicular to the target.
- Make a quick throw stepping forward with her glove-side foot.

Pivot

The fielder uses a pivot when she catches the ball and then has to throw in another direction. For example, if the ball is hit to shallow left-center field with a runner on first base, the outfielder fields the ball and throws to the second-base player covering second base. After the second-base player catches the ball and tags the base, she must execute a basic pivot in order to throw the ball to first base for the double play. To execute a basic pivot, a fielder should do the following:

- Make a proper catch.
- In one smooth motion, pivot on her throwing-side leg (counterclockwise for right-handed players and clockwise for left-handed players) and bring her glove and throwing hand together toward her throwing-side ear.
- Make a proper throw to the target.

Keep in mind that for junior players, the pivot foot is normally the throwing-side foot, but elite athletes have the ability to pivot on either leg. It depends on the direction they are going and the strength of the throwing arm. The younger the arm, the more likely the player will pivot on the throwing-side leg so she can then step with the glove-side leg to make the throw. Elite athletes can pivot and throw while the glove-side leg is down and not have to take a step.

Chapter 2 Skills Matrix

Drill Number	Drill Title	Skills Reinforced										
	(Indented drills are "named" Advanced Variations)	Crossover Step	Drop Step	Crow Hop	Pivot	Dive Fielding	Short-Hop Fielding	Simultaneous Arrive and Catch	Throw to Bag	Throwing	Runner—Tagging Up	Reaction Time
21.	Crossover Grounder	⚾								⚾		
22.	Crossover Wall	⚾								⚾		⚾
23.	Crossover Foul	⚾								⚾		
	Foul Ball Base Runner	⚾								⚾	⚾	⚾
24.	Crossover Interceptor	⚾								⚾		⚾
25.	Drop Step Quarterback		⚾							⚾		
26.	Drop Step with Communication		⚾							⚾		
27.	Crow-Hop Square			⚾						⚾		
28.	Pivot Relay				⚾					⚾		
	Pivot Relay — Stopwatch				⚾					⚾		
29.	Quick Pivot				⚾					⚾		
	Jump Pivot				⚾					⚾		
	Quick Pivot Flip Toss				⚾					⚾		
	Quick Pivot — Stopwatch				⚾					⚾		
30.	Dive for the Ball					⚾	⚾					⚾
	Dive Versus Short Hop					⚾	⚾					⚾
	Dive for Ground Balls					⚾						⚾
31.	Crossover–Drop Step Softball Tennis	⚾	⚾		⚾					⚾		⚾
	Crossover–Drop Step Softball Tennis — Two Ball	⚾	⚾		⚾					⚾		⚾
32.	Infield Footwork Progression							⚾				
	Throw to the Bag, Not the Player								⚾			
	Watch the Incoming Ball							⚾	⚾			

Fielding Footwork Drills

21. Crossover Grounder (Beginner)

Purpose: To practice using the crossover step to field grounders

Equipment: Supply of softballs

Number of players: 1

Number of repetitions: 10 reps for 2 sets

Allocated time: 5 minutes per player

Parent-friendly drill: ✔

Cardio index: ♥

1. A fielder stands facing a coach standing 10 to 15 feet away. This drill can be done on the infield dirt or on the outfield grass.
2. The coach rolls a grounder to either side of the fielder.
3. The fielder uses a crossover step to move toward the ball and fields the ball in the center of her body whenever possible.
4. In one smooth motion, the fielder brings her glove and throwing hand up toward her belly button or the centerline of her body and then to her throwing-side ear and makes a proper throw back to the coach for the next repetition.

Advanced Variations

- Hit grounders instead of rolling or throwing them. This will make the drill more challenging and realistic.
- Vary the speed and angle of each grounder. Deliver some hard-bounce grounders.

Hints

Make sure your players are starting in a good defensive position—knees bent so the rear is low, slight lean at the waist, weight on the balls of the feet, slight rocking motion back and forth from leg to leg. Players who start in this position will react faster to any ball.

22. Crossover Wall (Intermediate)

Purpose: To practice using the crossover step to field line drives and hard bounces

Equipment: Supply of softballs, masking tape or chalk (optional—see Hints)

Number of players: 1

Number of repetitions: 15 reps for 2 sets

Allocated time: 5 minutes per player

Cardio index: ♥ ♥ ♥

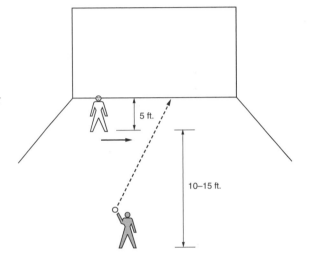

1. A fielder stands 5 or so feet away from and with her back to a fence, the backstop, or a brick wall, facing a coach standing 10 to 15 feet away. (Wear sneakers, not cleats, when executing this drill on asphalt.)
2. The coach throws a line drive or hard bouncer about 4 to 5 feet to either side of the fielder.
3. The fielder uses a crossover step to move toward the ball and fields the ball. (If the fielder misses the ball, the ball will bounce against the wall behind her and roll back to the coach.)
4. In one smooth motion, the fielder brings her glove and throwing hand in to her body and then to her throwing-side ear and makes a proper throw back to the coach for the next repetition.

Advanced Variation

If space permits, have the player stand farther from the wall (15 feet) and execute the drill, but throw more difficult balls to field. This will reinforce the concept that the player may need to "take an angle" using a drop step to field a hard-hit ball. This drill works best indoors in a gymnasium where the walls are padded. (Wear sneakers, not cleats, when executing this drill indoors.) For safety reasons, do not do this variation against a fence, backstop, or brick wall.

Hints

Draw vertical chalk lines or use masking tape on the wall to help you see the boundaries beyond which you should not throw. Expand the boundary lines for advanced players.

23. Crossover Foul (Beginner)

Purpose: To practice using the crossover step to field fly balls and reinforce the concept of crossing the foul line to make the play

Equipment: Supply of softballs

Number of players: 4

Number of repetitions: 20 reps for 2 sets

Allocated time: 8 to 10 minutes per player

Parent-friendly drill: ✔ Indicate imaginary foul line if practicing in the backyard.

Cardio index: ♥

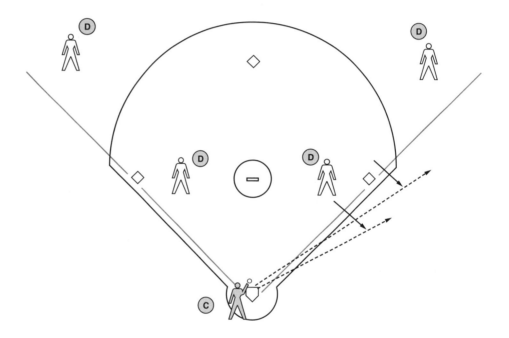

1. The fielders assume position at first and third base and in left and right field.
2. The coach standing at home plate throws a line drive or pop fly on the foul side of the foul line to any of the players.
3. The fielder uses a crossover step to move toward the ball and catches the ball.
4. In one smooth motion, the fielder brings her glove and throwing hand in to her body and then to her throwing-side ear and makes a proper throw back to the coach for the next repetition.

Advanced Variations

- Hit balls instead of throwing them. This will make the drill more challenging and realistic. However, coaches must have the skill to hit the ball to the proper location; otherwise the drill takes too long.
- Vary the speed and angle of each ball thrown.
- Deliver some grounders to the foul side. This will help build the muscle memory needed to "go for it" every time.
- **Foul Ball Base Runner.** Add a shortstop and second-base player, as well as a runner at first. Or execute on only one side of the field and reduce the number of players accordingly. Throw foul balls for the outfielders to field. On a caught pop foul, the runner may advance after she tags up. Have the fielders attempt to get the runner out at second or first base. Remember, if the runner tags up, then it's a tag play at second. If she leaves too soon, then it's a force play back at first.

Hints

This drill is about assertiveness training as much as it is about technique. Young players have a tendency to just stand there if they see a ball go foul. You often hear in life about a person who was "at the right place at the right time." This can be the "luck of the draw," but many times that person puts herself in the right place through hard work. Nine times out of ten, a player makes the correct move and nothing happens. Going for pop or line-drive fouls is one area where there are no negative consequences for trying and being unsuccessful. At worst, the player looks sharp. And if she makes the correct move that tenth time, she just might make the catch she'll tell her grandchildren about.

Base runners should remember that every hit ball, including a foul ball, is a live ball. Execute the Foul Ball Base Runner advanced variation of this drill to reinforce this concept.

24. Crossover Interceptor (Intermediate)

Purpose: To practice using the crossover step to field line drives	**Number of repetitions:** 10 reps for 2 sets
Equipment: Supply of softballs	**Allocated time:** 5 minutes per player
Number of players: 2	**Cardio index:** ♥ ♥ ♥

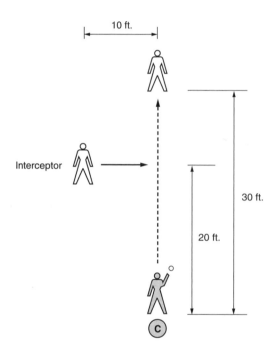

1. The first player stands facing a coach standing 30 feet away. This player will act as backup.
2. The second player stands facing the coach 20 feet away and 10 feet off to the side. This second player is the interceptor.
3. The coach throws a line drive toward the first player.
4. The interceptor uses a crossover step to move toward the ball, crosses the flight path, and catches the ball before it reaches the backup.
5. The interceptor throws the ball back to the coach for the next repetition. She repeats the drill starting from the opposite side since she's already there.
6. The backup catches the ball if the interceptor misses and throws the ball back to the coach for the next repetition.

Advanced Variation

Increase the distance the interceptor has to run to intercept the ball.

Hints

Sometimes when a coach throws to either side of a player in crossover practice, she's not quite certain how hard or how far to the side to throw it. Often the ball just sails away to be collected later. This drill is good because the coach throws it to a target (the backup player)—just like in a game of catch. The coach can throw it as hard as the backup can handle.

25. Drop Step Quarterback (Intermediate)

Purpose: To practice using the drop step to field line drives and pop flies
Equipment: Supply of softballs
Number of players: 1
Number of repetitions: 10 reps for 2 sets

Allocated time: 10 minutes per player
Parent-friendly drill: ✔
Cardio index: ♥ ♥

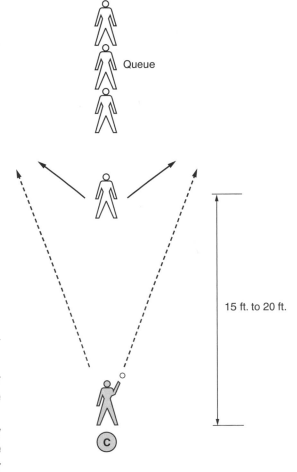

1. A fielder stands facing a coach standing 15 to 20 feet away.
2. The coach throws the ball to either side and a reasonable distance behind the fielder.
3. The fielder uses a drop step to move toward the ball and catches the ball.
4. In one smooth motion, the fielder brings her glove and throwing hand to her throwing-side ear and makes a proper throw back to the coach for the next repetition.

Advanced Variations

- Hit balls instead of throwing them. This will make the drill more challenging and realistic. However, the coach must have the skill to hit the ball to the proper location; otherwise the drill takes too long.
- Vary the speed and angle of each delivery. Deliver some hard-bounce grounders.

Hints

The player should catch the ball with the nondominant foot forward (for right-handed players, this is the left foot), if possible. This will enable the player to go immediately into the crow-hop throw to the target.

Access to a pitching machine would be helpful for this drill. Properly calibrated, the machine can be rigged to deliver the ball to the exact same spot every time. A random toss is more gamelike, but first make sure your players get the movement down using the machine, if possible.

Queue

15 ft. to 20 ft.

26. Drop Step with Communication (Intermediate)

Purpose: To practice using the drop step to field line drives and pop flies and to develop communication among outfielders

Equipment: Supply of softballs

Number of players: 2

Number of repetitions: 10 reps for 2 sets

Allocated time: 5 minutes

Cardio index: 💜 💜

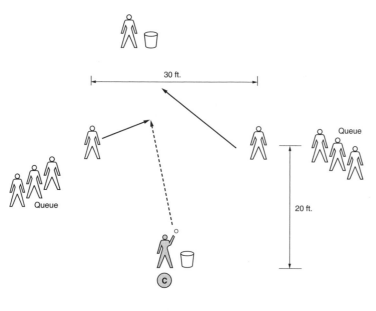

1. Two fielders stand 30 feet from each other and facing a coach standing 20 feet away.
2. The coach throws the ball in between and a reasonable distance behind the fielders.
3. The appropriate fielder calls for the ball, uses a drop step to move toward the ball, and catches the ball. The other fielder backs up the play.
4. In one smooth motion, the fielder brings her glove and throwing hand to her throwing-side ear and makes a proper throw back to the coach for the next repetition.

Advanced Variations

- Hit balls instead of throwing them. This will make the drill more challenging and realistic. However, the coach must have the skill to hit the ball to the proper location; otherwise the drill takes too long.
- Vary the speed and angle of each delivery. Deliver some hard-bounce grounders.

Hints

In game situations, the fielder that is not making the actual catch should back up her teammate and also help communicate to her which bag to throw to after the catch is made.

27. Crow-Hop Square (Beginner)

Purpose: To practice using the crow hop to gain momentum for long-distance throws	**Number of repetitions:** 15 reps per player
Equipment: Softball	**Allocated time:** 5 minutes
Number of players: 4	**Parent-friendly drill:** ✔
	Cardio index: ♥ ♥

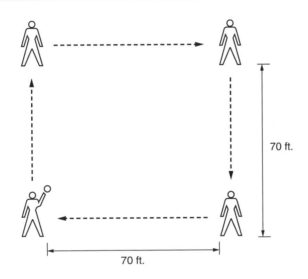

1. Four players stand in a square formation standing 70 feet (less for younger athletes) away from each other.
2. Each player throws the ball to the next player in the square formation using a crow hop.

Advanced Variations

- Increase the distance for advanced players.
- Throw in a clockwise and then a counterclockwise direction.

28. Pivot Relay (Beginner)

Purpose: To practice basic pivot technique

Equipment: Softball

Number of players: Multiple players

Number of repetitions: 8 reps for 3 sets

Allocated time: 5 minutes

Cardio index: ⚫

1. Four or five players line up about 30 feet apart.
2. The player at the end of the line throws the ball to the next player in line.
3. After catching the ball, that player executes a proper pivot and throws the ball to the next player in line.
4. Repeat the drill until each player in the middle of the line has caught the ball (and therefore pivoted) at least eight times.
5. Rotate the players so that the players at the ends of the line have a chance to practice their pivots.

Advanced Variations

- Increase the distance between advanced players.
- **Pivot Relay—Stopwatch.** Give the players a time allotment to finish the drill in; this will make them have to work harder on their glove-to-hand transfer and make more accurate throws.

Hints

Ironically some of your players who complain that this drill is too boring might then proceed to pivot in the wrong direction. Explain to your players that this drill is designed to build muscle memory of the game situation of catching the ball from one direction and having to throw in another.

Form multiple lines of players if needed to maximize the number of pivot repetitions per player in the allotted time. This is a good pregame drill because it doesn't take too much lateral space and it gets the athletes in synch with each other before the game.

Morgan (third from left) has just completed her throw to Julia (second from left). Julia has pivoted and is about to throw to Jenn (left). See how even Katelyn (right), who's four throws away from receiving another throw, is in her athletic stance. The Pivot Relay is an excellent drill if all the players stay engaged.

29. Quick Pivot (Beginner)

Purpose: To practice quick pivot technique
Equipment: 5 softballs
Number of players: Multiple players (1 thrower, multiple players with gloves)

Number of repetitions: 3 reps per player
Allocated time: 3 minutes per player
Cardio index: ♥ ♥

1. Line up five balls in a straight line (use the foul line) about 5 feet apart.
2. Position players with gloves 15 feet away, alternating to the left or right of each ball.
3. The thrower runs up the line, retrieving each ball and executing a quick pivot to throw the ball to the corresponding fielder positioned on the glove or throwing side.

Advanced Variations

- Let the players who catch the balls roll them back to the line. Some of the balls will end up on the foul line, some off to the side. This will add some variation to the drill.
- **Jump Pivot.** Execute this drill by having the player jump pivot 180 degrees and make the throw.
- **Quick Pivot Flip Toss.** Move the receiving players in a bit (7 to 8 feet away instead of 15 feet), and execute the drill by having the player work flip tosses. Tosses across the body to players on the glove side will be easy. For flip tosses to players on the throwing side, make sure when the ball is tossed that the thrower's thumb is always pointed down toward the ground and her palm is to the target with a good firm wrist snap at the end of the toss.
- **Quick Pivot—Stopwatch.** Give the players a time allotment to have to finish the drill in.

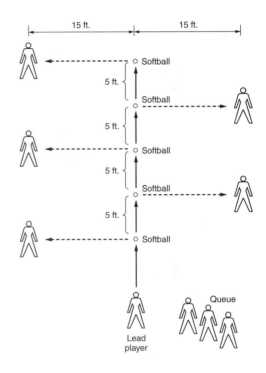

Hints

To make a throw to a player positioned on her throwing-arm side, the thrower will have to pivot on her throwing-side foot 180 degrees toward the player and then make a good throw.

30. Dive for the Ball (Beginner)

Purpose: To practice using last-second diving to catch fly balls or field grounders
Equipment: Supply of softballs
Number of players: 1
Number of repetitions: 10 reps for 2 sets

Allocated time: 5 minutes per player
Parent-friendly drill: ✔
Cardio index: ♥

1. A fielder kneels facing a coach standing 10 to 15 feet away. (This drill can be done on the infield dirt or on the outfield grass.)
2. The coach quick-flips a ball just out of reach to either side of the fielder.
3. The fielder dives to catch or field the ball.

Advanced Variations

- Have the players stand instead of kneel and toss the ball to either side.
- Throw a bit farther away from the player. The player must execute a crossover step or drop step and then try to field the ball before it hits the ground or gets away.
- **Dive Versus Short Hop.** Throw different color balls in front of the player and tell her which colors to dive for and which colors to short hop. However, regardless of the color ball thrown, she may still need to decide which balls to dive for and which balls to short hop because most coaches will not be able to throw a short hop at will. This will help the player work on her decision making.
- **Dive for Ground Balls.** Execute this drill using ground balls, not just fly balls.

Hints

The dive is a maneuver of last resort. So every once in a while, throw the ball straight to the player to keep her alert.

Help build up the player's confidence by quick-flipping the ball (underhand or overhand) instead of throwing too hard. For most coaches, flipping the ball is probably more accurate anyway.

If you have difficulty tossing balls that are just right in terms of being challenging yet fieldable, position a helper about 10 feet behind to either side of the player to act as a target. The helper can also help to retrieve missed balls.

31. Crossover–Drop Step Softball Tennis (Intermediate)

Purpose: Competition-style drill to reinforce footwork technique
Equipment: Softball, cones or other markers
Number of players: 2

Number of repetitions: 2 to 3 sets
Allocated time: 5 minutes
Parent-friendly drill: ✔
Cardio index: ♥ ♥ ♥

1. Mark out a rectangle about 30 feet long by 20 feet wide and mark a line across the middle, similar to a tennis court with an imaginary net.
2. Two players stand in their respective zones facing each other.
3. The first player throws a pop fly or line drive into the second player's zone, and the second player must catch it.
4. The second player then throws a pop fly or line drive into the first player's zone, and the first player must catch it.
5. In each case the fielder uses a crossover step and/or drop step to move toward the ball.
6. In one smooth motion, the fielding player brings her glove and throwing hand to her throwing-side ear and throws the ball into the other player's zone.
7. Repeat until one of the players misses. A missed catch is a point for the thrower, similar to scoring for a game of tennis.
8. The first player to reach 5 points wins.

Advanced Variation

Crossover–Drop Step Softball Tennis—Two Ball. Have two balls going at once. Both players will make the throw to their partner and then have to immediately look for the ball being thrown by the partner.

Hints

While this is a competition-style drill, it's still best for middle school players to execute the drill playing coach/parent versus player. The coach is in a better position to customize the throws in a way that makes the drill fun and challenging without being frustrating for players. The object of the game is to gradually build muscle memory through rapid repetition, not necessarily to "win."

32. Infield Footwork Progression (Beginner)

Purpose: Progressive drill designed to help young players catch on the run while stepping on the bag with either foot	**Number of repetitions:** 15 reps for 2 sets
	Allocated time: 5 to 7 minutes per player
Equipment: Supply of softballs, masking tape or chalk	**Parent-friendly drill:** ✔
Number of players: 1	**Cardio index:** ♥ ♥

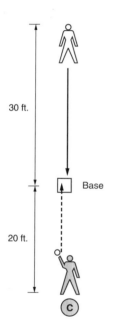

30 ft.

Base

20 ft.

C

1. A player stands 30 feet away from the bag. This drill also can be done on a driveway or in a gymnasium. Mark the "bag" by using masking tape or chalk to draw a standard 15-inch square bag. (Wear sneakers, not cleats, when executing this drill on asphalt or indoors.)
2. A coach stands on the opposite side of the bag about 20 feet away.
3. On the coach's cue, the player should do the following:

   - **Beginner (glove-side foot).** A beginner walks or jogs "through" the bag, making sure to land her glove-side foot on the bag and then make her next stride with her throwing-side foot off the bag (proper footwork). The player holds her glove out ready to receive the ball as she approaches the bag. She keeps running for a few steps and returns to the starting position for the next repetition. Once she can do this comfortably without the ball, toss her a ball (adjust speed per player's ability) so that she receives the ball just as she steps on the bag with her glove-side foot.
   - **Beginner (throwing-side foot).** Repeat above step, but have the player land with her throwing-side foot on the bag.
   - **Beginner/intermediate player.** The intermediate player runs at game speed through the bag using the proper footwork. Once she can do this comfortably without the ball and starting from any distance or angle from the bag, throw her a ball from directly in front of her line of sight so that she receives the ball just as she arrives at the bag.
   - **Intermediate/advanced player.** The more advanced player runs at game speed through the bag using the proper footwork. Throw her the ball at game speed from 10 to 20 feet and from different angles and throwing heights to simulate game-situation throws.

4. The player catches the ball, keeps running for a few steps, and throws it back to the coach for the next repetition.

Advanced Variations

- **Throw to the Bag, Not the Player.** Have another player take the place of the coach and toss or throw the ball to the player running through the bag. This will reinforce the concept that more advanced players should throw to the bag in advance of the covering player arriving at the bag. Of course, in a game situation, this only works if everybody knows who should cover what base in any situation. Otherwise, the ball sails into the outfield. For the youngest players, the coach should reverse roles with the player and have the player throw to the coach running through the bag. Young players are not as shy to throw harder to coaches than to fellow players, which will help build the young player's confidence to make a straight, hard throw to the bag.

- **Watch the Incoming Ball.** Execute any variation of the drill and have another coach walk, jog, or run to the bag simulating a base runner. Make sure the covering player focuses on the incoming throw rather than fixating on the runner. Assure your players that the risk of collision is low if the offensive and defensive players follow league rules.

Hints

Often in junior softball, the player who fields the ball does not throw to the player covering second base until after the covering player arrives and sets up in a straddle ready to receive the ball. This happens in all likelihood because base coverage is not automatic in junior softball, and the fielder will not throw (and in fact is encouraged not to throw) to a bag unless she is confident that someone will be there to receive the ball. Advanced fielders, however, are expected to throw to the bag in advance of the covering player arriving at the bag, and covering players are expected to get to the bag in time for the ball's arrival using advanced and efficient footwork like the crossover pivot or the rocker pivot (covered in Chapter 3).

This is a progressive drill designed to help in the transition between these two styles of play by reinforcing the prerequisite skill of being able to catch the ball while running through the bag. Once she has mastered this technique, she is ready to move on to the footwork for advanced infielders.

Infield and Outfield Defense

Have you ever wondered why so many runners from first base reach second safely on easily fielded ground balls, even at the middle school all-star level? For many junior teams, coverage is not automatic, so the player who fields the ball is not confident that someone will be at the bag if she throws the ball. Nor are many junior players comfortable with doing three things at the same time—catching the ball while on the run and having to time her steps so she steps on the bag with the correct foot and either crosses the bag or pushes off the bag to execute a double play. The player who fields the ball ends up not throwing the ball until the covering player gets to the bag and sets up. Of course, by then it's usually too late to make one out, not to mention the double play.

The drills in this chapter are designed to teach and reinforce the following skill sets for novice to advanced position players (the drills are grouped by position):

- **Defensive play knowledge.** Drills enhance the defensive player's cognitive development and the muscle memory to execute plays against myriad game situations. For example, our Which Way? drills for second- and third-base players and shortstops contain dozens of defensive scenarios that should be memorized like the multiplication tables.
- **Advanced fielding mechanics.** Drills teach infielders and outfielders advanced bag coverage footwork like the crossover and rocker pivots as well as ball tracking skills.
- **On-field communication skills.** Drills reinforce communication among infielders and outfielders.

Double-Play Footwork for Second-Base Players and Shortstops

Second-base footwork is complex and varied. We've included the following suggestions to help you teach the appropriate second-base footwork to second-base players and shortstops, reinforced by the drills in this chapter. There's more than one way to skin a cat, so your players will need to test which footwork works best for them in various situations. In fact, players at the very upper echelons of elite play sometimes use abbreviated versions of the advanced footwork to shave milliseconds on the play, and some of these are described in the drills.

For a lot of junior players, the advanced footwork will be like chewing gum and walking at the same time. These players should master the Infield Footwork Progression drill (drill 32) in Chapter 2 before trying the advanced footwork.

For double-play coverage for right-handed second-base players (it's very difficult for left-handed players to play second base), use the following drills to practice footwork to catch throws from the left side of the field:

- **Second-base player crossover pivot (drill 40).** Step on the bag with the left foot, step off the bag with the right foot, and finally step toward the target with the left foot.
- **Second-base player rocker pivot (drill 41).** Step on the bag with the left foot, push back simultaneously with the left foot, land off the bag with the right foot, and finally step toward the target with the left foot.
- **Straddle and standard pivot (drills 38 and 39).** Used if the second-base player arrives very early (this only happens in youth softball because fielders usually wait for the second-base player to arrive and set up before throwing), as well as for non-force plays at second.

It's very difficult for left-handed players to play second base. Most second-base players are right-handed and step forward with their left foot.

For double-play coverage for shortstops, use the following drills to practice footwork to catch throws from the right side of the field:

- **Right-handed shortstop crossover pivot (drill 45).** Step on the bag with the left foot, step off the bag with the right foot, and finally step toward the target with the left foot (feet pointing to first base).
- **Left-handed shortstop crossover pivot (drill 45).** Step on the bag with the right foot, step off the bag with the left foot, and finally step toward the target with the right foot (feet pointing to first base).
- **Standard pivot (drill 44).** If a right-handed shortstop arrives early, she can catch with the right foot on the bag, pivot on this foot, and step with the left toward first and throw all in one motion. The left-handed shortstop can catch with her left foot on the bag and already be in the correct position to throw to first, so for the lefty shortstop this is an easy turn.

We've not included a rocker variation for shortstops because it's more advantageous for them to cross over or pivot; pushing back, while physically possible, takes too long, especially considering that the shortstop already has the momentum toward first base.

Keep the following in mind when teaching and practicing the drills in this chapter.

- **Get busy.** Instill in your players that each of the nine players has a role in every play of the game, whether it's to field a ball hit to her, to cover the correct bag, or to back up her teammates. For example, junior players often complain that nothing ever happens in the outfield. (This is only true at the most junior levels.) As a consequence, junior outfielders are often lax to back up. And nine times out of ten, whether an outfielder moves has no practical impact on the play. But guess what . . . on the tenth play, the catcher overthrows third base during a rundown, and the left fielder is nowhere to be found, allowing the runner to advance home.

- **Know what to do.** Train each player to think before each at bat about what she is going to do if the ball is hit to her, and what she is going to do if the ball isn't hit to her. Kick it up a notch for advanced players—they should be thinking before each pitch what might happen next and what they should be doing to react.

- **It's not over until . . . the play is over.** Train your players to look for the second option or a secondary play and at least to get the ball back to the pitcher to stop the play. Then, by all means, celebrate a good play!

- **Ninety-nine percent of the game is mental.** Athleticism is a huge factor in elite-level play, but knowledge, poise, and sound mechanics can go a long way to turn a below-average athlete into a credible candidate to play high school varsity ball.

- **Keep your eye on the ball.** This adage applies to defense as well. Teach your defensive players to concentrate on the ball because "the ball controls the game"; players have to know where the ball is at all times. Junior defenders sometimes have the tendency to watch only the runner. While you don't want players running into each other, help your players realize that if the covering player is only watching the runner, she can't sprint to the bag, she won't be on the lookout for the incoming ball, and the fielder won't throw it to her until it's too late.

- **Who's the boss?** It's amusing to watch some of the "cat and mouse" games that junior fielders and runners play against each other. Some fielders spend so much time trying to figure out what the runner is going to do that they miss everything else that's going on. While we never want to squelch a young person's decision-making inclinations, teach your young players that if they are supposed to cover or back up, then they should just do it. In softball and in life, you want to be prepared, and a big part of being prepared is putting yourself in the right position so you can do something about the situation.

- **Set the bar high.** Great footwork will elevate your players into the advanced echelons. Some of the drills in this chapter reinforce skills that are quite advanced, and it's best to introduce your players to the advanced concepts gradually, but there's no reason to wait until eighth grade to start learning the prerequisite skills.

- **Push the envelope.** Make each practice session a valuable experience for the players. For example, encourage your fielders to throw to the bag *as* the covering player arrives and not to delay throwing until she arrives and sets up. By the same token, encourage your covering fielders to sprint to the bag and anticipate the arrival of the ball even before arriving at the bag.

Chapter 3 Skills Matrix

Drill Number	Drill Title (Indented drills are "named" Advanced Variations)	Infielders Footwork	Infielders Situation	First-Base Footwork	First-Base Situation	Second-Base Footwork	Second-Base Situation	Shortstop Footwork	Shortstop Situation	Catcher Situation	Third-Base Footwork	Third-Base Situation
First-Base Drills												
33.	First-Base Player Footwork	●		●								
	First-Base Throw to Home Plate	●	●	●	●					●		
34.	First-Base Player Tag the Runner	●	●	●	●							
35.	First-Base Overthrow	●	●	●	●	●	●					
36.	First- and Second-Base Player Bunt	●	●	●	●	●	●			●		
	Catcher—First Base Bunt Communication	●	●	●	●	●	●			●		
	Catcher-Infield Bunt Communication	●	●	●	●	●	●			●		
Second-Base Drills												
37.	Second-Base Player Which Way?		●				●					
	Second-Base Which Way? Live Action	●	●			●	●					
	Second-Base Player Response to Hit-and-Run	●	●			●	●			●		
38.	Second-Base Player Footwork—Straddle	●				●						
	Shortstop Footwork—Straddle	●				●		●				
39.	Second-Base Player Footwork—Standard Pivot	●				●						
40.	Second-Base Player Footwork—Crossover Pivot	●				●						
	Glove-to-Glove Second-Base Player Timing	●	●	●		●						
41.	Second-Base Player Footwork—Rocker Pivot	●				●						
	Second-Base Player Combination Footwork	●		●		●						
42.	Second-Base Player Double Play	●		●		●	●	●	●		●	●

Fielding	Throwing	Catching	Tag Out	Bunt Situation	Decision Making	Crossover Step	Drop Step	Crow Hop	Simultaneous Arrive and Catch	Throw to Bag	Runners— Baserunning	Pop-Ups	Communication	Outfielders Situation
		●												
	●	●								●				
●			●		●						●			
●	●	●			●			●		●			●	
●	●	●		●										
●	●	●		●	●								●	
●	●	●		●	●								●	
●	●	●		●	●					●	●		●	
●	●	●	●							●	●		●	
		●												
		●												
		●												
		●							●					
	●	●			●				●					
		●							●					
	●	●							●					
●	●	●			●				●					

(continued)

Chapter 3 Skills Matrix *(continued)*

Drill Number	Drill Title (Indented drills are "named" Advanced Variations)	Infielders Footwork	Infielders Situation	First-Base Footwork	First-Base Situation	Second-Base Footwork	Second-Base Situation	Shortstop Footwork	Shortstop Situation	Catcher Situation	Third-Base Footwork	Third-Base Situation
Shortstop Drills												
43.	Shortstop Which Way?		●						●			
	Work Outs to Third Base	●	●					●	●		●	
	Shortstop Which Way? Live Action	●							●			
44.	Shortstop Footwork — Standard Pivot	●						●				
45.	Shortstop Footwork — Crossover Pivot	●						●				
	Shortstop 180 Degrees to Third Base	●						●	●			
46.	Shortstop Bunt	●	●	●	●	●	●	●	●	●	●	●
47.	Double Play Second Base—Shortstop Interaction	●	●	●	●	●	●	●	●	●	●	●
	Unassisted Double Play	●	●	●	●	●	●	●	●			
48.	Who's the Cutoff?	●	●	●	●	●	●	●	●			
	Bases Loaded — Who's the Cutoff?	●	●	●	●	●	●	●	●	●	●	●
	Specific Cutoff Situations	●	●	●	●	●	●	●	●	●	●	●
Third-Base Drills												
49.	Third-Base Player Which Way?		●									●
	Third-Base Which Way? Live Action	●									●	●
50.	Third-Base Player Bunt	●	●	●	●	●	●	●	●	●	●	●
	Force at Third Bunt	●	●	●	●	●	●	●	●	●	●	●
51.	Third-Base Player Throw to First	●		●	●						●	●
52.	Third-Base Player Double Play	●	●	●	●	●	●				●	●
	Third-Base Lead Runner Double Play	●	●	●	●	●	●	●	●		●	●

Fielding	Throwing	Catching	Tag Out	Bunt Situation	Decision Making	Crossover Step	Drop Step	Crow Hop	Simultaneous Arrive and Catch	Throw to Bag	Runners— Baserunning	Pop-Ups	Communication	Outfielders Situation
⚾	⚾	⚾			⚾									
⚾														
		⚾												
		⚾							⚾					
⚾	⚾	⚾												
⚾				⚾						⚾			⚾	
⚾	⚾	⚾			⚾									
⚾	⚾	⚾			⚾									
⚾	⚾	⚾			⚾	⚾	⚾			⚾		⚾	⚾	⚾
⚾	⚾	⚾	⚾		⚾	⚾	⚾	⚾		⚾		⚾	⚾	⚾
⚾	⚾	⚾			⚾	⚾	⚾	⚾		⚾		⚾	⚾	⚾
⚾														
⚾	⚾	⚾		⚾							⚾		⚾	
⚾	⚾	⚾		⚾							⚾		⚾	
⚾	⚾	⚾											⚾	
⚾	⚾	⚾			⚾						⚾		⚾	
⚾	⚾	⚾			⚾						⚾		⚾	

(continued)

Chapter 3 Skills Matrix *(continued)*

Drill Number	Drill Title (Indented drills are "named" Advanced Variations)	Infielders Footwork	Infielders Situation	First-Base Footwork	First-Base Situation	Second-Base Footwork	Second-Base Situation	Shortstop Footwork	Shortstop Situation	Catcher Situation	Third-Base Footwork	Third-Base Situation
53.	Rundown	⚾	⚾									
	Multiple Runner Rundown	⚾	⚾									
	Multiple Runner Rundown, Play at Home	⚾	⚾									
	Outfield Rundown Backup	⚾	⚾									
54.	Infield Communication	⚾	⚾									
Outfield Drills												
55.	Outfield One-Knee Blocking	⚾										
	Outfield Mix-It-Up	⚾										
	Outfield Recovery	⚾										
56.	Outfield Line-Drive Interceptor	⚾										
	Two Interceptors	⚾										
57.	Outfield Tracker	⚾										
	Outfield Fence	⚾										
58.	Outfield Communication	⚾	⚾				⚾		⚾			
	Outfield Communication Short Bloopers	⚾	⚾				⚾		⚾			
59.	Infield-Outfield Communication	⚾	⚾									
60.	Outfield Do or Die	⚾										

Fielding	Throwing	Catching	Tag Out	Bunt Situation	Decision Making	Crossover Step	Drop Step	Crow Hop	Simultaneous Arrive and Catch	Throw to Bag	Runners— Baserunning	Pop-Ups	Communication	Outfielders Situation
	⚾	⚾	⚾		⚾						⚾		⚾	
	⚾	⚾	⚾		⚾						⚾		⚾	
	⚾	⚾	⚾		⚾						⚾		⚾	
	⚾	⚾	⚾		⚾						⚾		⚾	⚾
	⚾	⚾										⚾	⚾	
⚾	⚾					⚾	⚾	⚾						⚾
⚾	⚾	⚾			⚾	⚾	⚾	⚾						⚾
⚾	⚾					⚾	⚾	⚾						⚾
⚾	⚾	⚾				⚾	⚾	⚾					⚾	⚾
⚾	⚾	⚾				⚾	⚾	⚾					⚾	⚾
⚾	⚾	⚾				⚾	⚾	⚾					⚾	⚾
⚾	⚾	⚾												
⚾		⚾			⚾	⚾	⚾	⚾	⚾	⚾		⚾	⚾	⚾
⚾		⚾			⚾	⚾	⚾	⚾	⚾	⚾		⚾	⚾	⚾
⚾					⚾								⚾	⚾
⚾	⚾	⚾			⚾									⚾

Infield and Outfield Defense Drills

33. First-Base Player Footwork (Intermediate)

Purpose: To practice first-base player's footwork for catching balls thrown by teammates
Equipment: Softball
Number of players: 1
Number of repetitions: 10 reps for 2 sets

Allocated time: 5 to 7 minutes per player
Parent-friendly drill: ✔
Cardio index: ♥

1. A player assumes her on-field position as first-base player.
2. A coach with a ball stands at various positions in the infield, starting between first and second base, and begins the drill by signaling a fielded ball.
3. The player runs to first base by pivoting on her right leg and then crossing over with her left leg. This will turn her face into the field so she can track the play.

Although known as an Olympic double-threat (pitching and offense), Michele has also played first base at the national level. She straddles the bag (first frame) until she determines the path of the ball. If it's a straight throw, she touches the edge of the bag with her throwing-side foot and extends her glove-side foot into the field for maximum coverage. If the throw is off-target, Michele may have to put her glove-side foot on the bag to catch the ball. Either way, she's able to concentrate on the ball because she knows that her foot placement allows the runner to run through the bag without interference.

4. As she approaches first base, she will do the following:

- **Beginner.** A beginner will step on the bag with the heel of her throwing-side foot, with her glove-side foot extended toward the incoming ball.
- **Advanced player.** An advanced player will straddle the corner of the bag using only her heels to make contact with the bag. If the ball is thrown to the home-plate side of her body, she will keep her right heel on the bag and step forward with her left foot. If the ball is thrown to the outfield side of her body, she will keep her left heel on the bag and step forward with her right foot.

5. The coach throws the ball to first base.

6. The player moves her glove toward the incoming ball without stabbing at it and catches the ball.

Advanced Variations

- The coach should move around the infield to simulate throws from different directions.
- Vary the strength and trajectory of the throw, including balls thrown high, low, to either side of the bag, and bouncing (short hops) in front.
- The coach can throw the ball before the player arrives at first base.
- **First-Base Throw to Home Plate.** Place a runner at third base, and after the first-base player makes the catch, have the runner from third attempt to score so that the first-base player has to perform proper footwork on the catch and then get into proper position to make a strong throw to the catcher. The catcher should try to block home plate.

Hints

Some young players have a tendency to be too polite—to defer to the base runner when running to the base (some base runners also have this tendency). Encourage your first-base players to peripherally look where the ball is coming from when running to the bag, not at the base runner. If the first-base player uses proper footwork and the runner runs straight through the bag, there is little risk of a collision. So sprint to the bag, don't jog. It's a race!

The first-base player should make herself a big target and not stretch forward until the ball is arriving. If she stretches too early, then she can't adjust in time if the throw to first is not made exactly to her stretched-out position.

Softball Versus Baseball

First-base baseball players often move to first base using a J-move, which assumes the player is starting from the outfield side of the bag. The J-move is not used in softball; first-base softball players start from in front of the base and have to turn and run back to the bag.

34. First-Base Player Tag the Runner (Beginner)

Purpose: To help the first-base player overcome her instinct to run back to the bag with the ball when the runner is near her (first-base player is allowed to tag the runner)
Equipment: Softball

Number of players: 2
Number of repetitions: 10 reps
Allocated time: 3 to 5 minutes per player
Parent-friendly drill: ✔
Cardio index: ♥ ♥

1. A player assumes her on-field position as first-base player.
2. A base runner stands at home plate.
3. A coach on the third-base line about 10 feet from home plate simulates a ground ball by rolling or hitting a ball into the first-base player's area of responsibility.
4. The runner takes off for first base.
5. The first-base player fields the ball, and if she is between the runner and the bag, attempts to tag the runner out.

Hints

Even though the first-base player may have time to run to the bag, she should tag the runner out if she is between the runner and the bag. With the additional time gained from making the tag out, encourage your first-base player to then quickly scan the field for other opportunities before throwing the ball back to the pitcher. Also, if there are other runners on base, a quick look by the first-base player at the lead runner could keep the runners at their current base; the first-base player can then make the tag out of the batter.

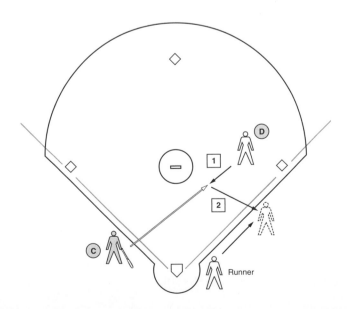

35. First-Base Overthrow (Beginner)

Purpose: To practice recovering from first-base overthrow and throwing to second base to tag out the advancing runner
Equipment: Softball
Number of players: 2
Number of repetitions: 10 reps

Allocated time: 3 to 5 minutes per player
Parent-friendly drill: ✔ Execute drill with parent taking dual role— making errant throw and covering second base.
Cardio index: ♥ ♥

1. Players assume their on-field positions as first-base and second-base players.
2. A coach simulates a shortstop making an errant throw to first base (but not out of play).
3. The second-base player covers second base.
4. In the meantime, the first-base player gets off the bag to catch the ball if possible, but if the ball sails into foul territory, she turns to find the ball and executes a crow-hop throw to second base.
5. Repeat drill for allocated time, but the coach can reverse the drill by simulating an errant throw from the second-base player. In this case, the shortstop covers second base.

Advanced Variation

Add a base runner stationed halfway from home plate to first base and have her run to second on the overthrow. The runner will have a head start to lend urgency to the drill.

Hints

Make sure all the players are using proper footwork on their throws; this will give them more of an opportunity to get the runner attempting to take the extra base out. Many fielders who rush their throws have a tendency to cut short their footwork and therefore make bad throws. Good footwork equals good throws!

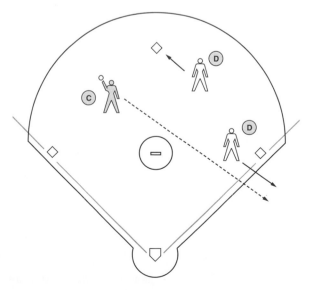

36. First- and Second-Base Player Bunt (Beginner)

Purpose: To practice first-base player's reaction to bunts
Equipment: Softball
Number of players: 2
Number of repetitions: 10 reps
Allocated time: 3 to 5 minutes per player

Parent-friendly drill: ✔ The parent assumes the role of the second-base player. Rather than rolling the ball to start the drill, place multiple balls for the first-base player to execute the drill with.
Cardio index: ♥ ♥

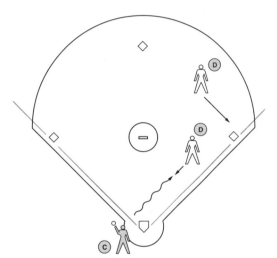

1. Players assume their on-field positions as first-base and second-base players.
2. A coach standing at home plate simulates a bunt by rolling a ball (or placing several balls) in the first-base player's area of responsibility.
3. The second-base player covers first base.
4. In the meantime, the first-base player charges the ball and plants her throwing-side foot next to the ball while bending down and picking up the ball with her bare hand (if the ball is stationary) or with her glove hand (if the ball is still moving).
5. In one smooth motion, she pushes off her throwing-side foot, steps forward with her opposite foot, and throws the ball to first base.

Advanced Variations

- Add a base runner at home plate, who will run to first base.
- **Catcher–First Base Bunt Communication.** Coach-pitch balls for a player to bunt with proper bunt mechanics (Chapter 4) and run to first base to make the drill more gamelike. In this case, add a catcher in full gear. The catcher and first-base player must coordinate depending on whose area of responsibility the ball is bunted to. (See Chapter 7 for catcher's area of responsibility.)
- **Catcher-Infield Bunt Communication.** Same as above, but place a runner at first base and have the catcher yell out to the fielders which runner to go after, the lead runner or the bunter.

Hints

For more advanced players, in a bunt situation with a runner on first, the second-base player will shade toward first base. This will enable her to cover first because the first-base player is way up the line, about 5 feet beyond the halfway point between first base and home plate. The third-base player is similarly situated way up the line on the left side. The shortstop shades over toward second base.

37. Second-Base Player Which Way? (Intermediate)

Purpose: To develop second-base player's reaction to various game situations
Equipment: Softball, cones or markers
Number of players: 1

Number of repetitions: 10 reps for 2 sets
Allocated time: 5 to 7 minutes per player
Parent-friendly drill: ✔
Cardio index: ⓥ ⓥ

1. A player assumes her on-field position as second-base player. This drill can be used as a station drill—set up first- and second-base markers in the outfield.
2. A coach standing 15 feet away in the infield calls out various common situations for the second-base player to react to.
3. The player responds to the coach's calls as follows:

   • A ground ball hit to the shortstop or third base, runner at first: the second-base player covers second base, catches the ball (thrown by coach acting as left infielder), and makes a phantom throw to first for the double play.
   • A bunt to first base, runner at first: the second-base player covers first base and catches the ball (thrown by coach acting as first-base player) for the force-out.
   • A ground ball hit to the second-base player with nobody on base: the second-base player catches the ball (rolled/tossed by coach simulating hit) and makes a phantom throw to first.
   • A ground ball hit to the second-base player's right side with a runner at first: the second-base player catches the ball (rolled/tossed by coach simulating hit to her right side) and makes a phantom throw to second (covered by an imaginary shortstop).
   • A fly ball hit to the second-base player with a runner at first: the second-base player catches the ball (tossed by coach simulating hit) and checks the runner at first.
   • A fly ball hit to the second-base player with runners at first and second: the second-base player catches the ball (tossed by coach simulating hit) and checks the runners at second base and then first base.
   • A ground ball hit to second base, bases loaded, fewer than two outs (in this situation the second-base player should be playing up or inside the line): the second-base player fields the ball (rolled/tossed by coach simulating hit) and makes a phantom throw to home plate. She also looks to make the easiest out.
   • A ground ball hit to second base, bases loaded, two outs (in this situation the second-base player is in the normal position): the second-base

player fields the ball (rolled/tossed by coach simulating hit) and makes a phantom throw to the easiest base (tags second base if hit to her right side close to second base).

- Work any other situations that appear often in your games.

Advanced Variations

- **Second-Base Which Way? Live Action.** Do this drill by actually hitting to the second-base player. Include other infielders and base runners, and have the athletes play out the situations, making real throws and communicating as they would in a game.
- **Second-Base Player Response to Hit-and-Run.** A ground ball hit to second base, real runners at second and third, fewer than two outs—the second-base player fields the ball (rolled/tossed by coach simulating hit) and makes a throw to home plate. Have the runners break as in a hit-and-run so that the throw to home plate needs to be low for the blocking catcher to make the tag.
- Have the real runner at third stay, and after the second-base player fields the ball and throws to first base, have her break for home. This will work both the first- and second-base players.

Hints

This is a mental drill. That's why, for example, the coach can either toss or roll grounders in this drill; tossing speeds up the drill and allows more repetitions, even though rolling the ball is not the most realistic way to simulate a grounder. Of course, as a coach, you will want to correct mechanical problems, but the focus of this drill is to ingrain all the permutations until they become second nature. Players should memorize these plays like the multiplication tables.

38. Second-Base Player Footwork—Straddle (Intermediate)

Purpose: To practice second-base player's footwork for catching balls thrown from the left side of the field (when the second-base player arrives at the bag well in advance of the ball and runner, for example, a double hit to the left side or a force play at second in junior softball—in junior play, the fielder often does not throw until the second-base player arrives at the bag)

Equipment: Softball
Number of players: 1 (second base is typically a right-handed player position)
Number of repetitions: 10 reps for 2 sets
Allocated time: 5 to 7 minutes per player
Parent-friendly drill: ✔
Cardio index: 💙 💙

1. A player assumes her on-field position as second-base player.
2. A coach with a ball stands in the area the shortstop normally occupies and begins the drill by signaling a hit ball that the coach will field.
3. The second-base player covers second base.
4. The second-base player arrives at second base and straddles the bag with both feet square to the coach (the plane of her body perpendicular to the direction of the incoming ball). If possible, she should straddle the bag on the left side of the field to avoid collision should the runner arrive quickly. Remember, this positioning is mostly used in plays where the fielder is arriving well before the runner.
5. The coach throws the ball to second base.
6. In one smooth motion, the second-base player catches the ball, lifts her right foot and touches the bag, and then steps toward first base with her left foot, all the while keeping her right foot planted (pivoting where necessary) behind the second-base bag.
7. The second-base player makes a phantom throw to first base for the double play.
8. Alternative: there is no one on base, and the imaginary batter hits a double to the left side. The second-base player arrives at and straddles the bag. The coach simulates a shortstop cutoff who throws to second base for the tag out.

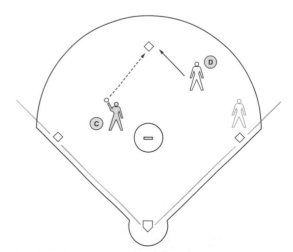

By touching the bag with her throwing-side foot, Morgan puts herself in a good position to make the double play because she is able to immediately step with her glove-side foot and make the throw.

Advanced Variations

- Have runners sliding into the bag to try to disrupt the play.
- Have some of the throws be off-line so the focus becomes to make the catch and get one out.
- **Shortstop Footwork—Straddle.** The shortstop executes the straddle if the ball is hit to the right side of the field. The shortstop receives the ball from the coach simulating a throw from the second-base player who may be acting as cutoff. The shortstop catches and makes a phantom throw to first if a double play situation, or she attempts the tag out if the play is not a force play.

Hints

Again, encourage your players to sprint to the bag, not jog so that they arrive "just in time." They should use their feet first so that they arrive comfortably ahead of the ball and have plenty of time to execute their glove work.

It is very difficult for left-handed players to play second base. Most second-base players are right-handed and step forward with their left feet. Thus, this drill is designed for right-handed players only, and it reflects proper footwork using the left foot.

39. Second-Base Player Footwork — Standard Pivot (Intermediate)

Purpose: To practice second-base player's footwork for catching balls thrown from the left side of the field (when the second-base player arrives at the bag well in advance of the ball—used in junior softball, and to stretch to catch throws that fall short of the bag)

Equipment: Softball

Number of players: 1 (second base is typically a right-handed player position)

Number of repetitions: 10 reps for 2 sets

Allocated time: 5 to 7 minutes per player

Parent-friendly drill: ✔

Cardio index: ♥ ♥

1. A player assumes her on-field position as second-base player. (See the diagram for drill 38.)
2. A coach with a ball stands in the area the shortstop normally occupies and begins the drill by signaling a hit ball that the coach will field.
3. The second-base player covers second base.
4. The second-base player arrives at second base and puts her right foot on the bag with her body square to the coach (the plane of her body perpendicular to the direction of the incoming ball). Her left foot is off the bag and can be stretched toward and as far as necessary to reach the incoming ball.
5. The coach throws the ball to second base.
6. In one smooth motion, the second-base player catches the ball, rotates her body counterclockwise toward first base (pivoting on her right foot), and brings her glove and throwing hand together toward her throwing-side ear.
7. The second-base player pushes off her throwing-side leg and steps off the bag toward first base with her glove-side foot as she makes a phantom throw to first base for the double play.

Hints

Again, encourage your players to sprint to the bag, not jog so that they arrive just in time. They should use their feet first so that they arrive comfortably ahead of the ball and have plenty of time to execute their glove work.

Second-base players (mostly right-handed) should keep their right (throwing-side) foot on the bag and use their left (glove-side) foot to step forward. This will allow them to stretch farther to reach a weakly thrown ball.

40. Second-Base Player Footwork—Crossover Pivot (Intermediate)

Purpose: To practice second-base player's footwork in double-play situation with a fast runner advancing to second (player uses the crossover pivot to quickly catch the ball as it arrives on the left-field side of the bag to enable her to be in position to throw to first)

Equipment: Softball

Number of players: 1 (second base is typically a right-handed player position)

Number of repetitions: 10 reps for 2 sets

Allocated time: 5 to 7 minutes per player

Parent-friendly drill: ✔

Cardio index: ♥ ♥

1. A player assumes her on-field position as second-base player.
2. A coach with a ball stands in the area the shortstop normally occupies and begins the drill by signaling a hit ball that the coach will field.
3. The second-base player covers second base.
4. The coach throws the ball to second base, timing it so the ball arrives as the player arrives at the bag.
5. The second-base player arrives at second base, stepping on the bag with her left foot as she catches the ball (preferably on the left-field side of the bag). Her left foot should point somewhat toward first base.
6. She continues across the bag and lands off the left-field side of the bag with her right foot somewhat pointing toward first base, and, using the landed right foot as a pivot, steps toward first base with her left foot while making a phantom throw to first base.

Advanced Variations

- **Glove-to-Glove Second-Base Player Timing.** Use a stopwatch to time how long the second-base players are taking to catch and throw to first base. For elite players the "glove-to-glove" time (for everything—catch, footwork, transfer, release, throw, to when the ball hits the first-base player's glove) should be under 1.90 seconds.
- Have a player replace the coach and challenge her to throw to the bag as the second-base player arrives, rather than wait for the second-base player to arrive and set up before throwing the ball to her.
- Change the timing of the throws to second, or throw some balls high and some as one bouncers or short hops.

Hints

The crossover pivot is a useful maneuver that can be summarized as follows: step on the bag with the left foot, step off the bag with the right foot, and finally step toward the target with the left foot.

41. Second-Base Player Footwork — Rocker Pivot (Intermediate)

Purpose: To practice second-base player's footwork in double-play situation with a fast runner advancing to second (player uses the rocker pivot to catch the ball "late," after it travels through the bag, on the right-field side of the bag before throwing to first)
Equipment: Softball

Number of players: 1 (second base is typically a right-handed player position)
Number of repetitions: 10 reps for 2 sets
Allocated time: 5 to 7 minutes per player
Parent-friendly drill: ✔
Cardio index: ♥ ♥

The first frame shows Morgan stepping on the back of the bag with her glove-side foot as she catches the ball (one out!). She immediately pushes back and sets up the throw to first base. Note in the second frame that Morgan doesn't have to push back very far to set up for her throw to first.

1. A player assumes her on-field position as second-base player.
2. A coach with a ball stands in the area the shortstop normally occupies and begins the drill by signaling a hit ball that the coach will field.
3. The second-base player covers second base.
4. The coach throws the ball to second base, timing it so the ball arrives on the right-field side of the bag just as the player arrives at the bag.

5. The second-base player arrives at second base, stepping on the bag with her left foot as she catches the ball (preferably on the right-field side of the bag), while simultaneously pushing backward off the bag with her left foot.

6. She lands off the bag on the right-field side of the bag with her right foot and, using the landed right foot as a pivot, steps toward first base with her left foot while making a phantom throw to first base.

Advanced Variations

- **Second-Base Player Combination Footwork.** Unless the coach can time the throws precisely, the coach may have no choice but to combine all the second-base footwork drills together. Unpredictability will help the players develop good judgment on which footwork to use. If the player arrives at the bag very early, she should use the straddle or standard pivot. If the ball arrives on the left-field side of the bag as the player arrives, she should execute the crossover pivot. If the ball sails through the bag and arrives on the right-field side of the bag, she should use the rocker pivot. Time your athletes glove to glove to see which footwork is best suited for your players.

- Have a player replace the coach and challenge her to throw to the bag as the second-base player arrives, rather than wait for the second-base player to arrive and set up before throwing the ball to her.

Abbreviated Version

An elite player sometimes catches the ball while stepping on the bag with her right foot, immediately pushing off the bag with her right foot and—voilà!—landing off the bag with her left foot while throwing in one smooth motion. Two steps and the ball is gone, instead of the three steps of the conventional rocker pivot. Why is the abbreviated version more difficult? It's a bit more awkward because the player has to push off the bag just that much more aggressively to build the momentum to make the throw on the next step. In the conventional version, the second-base player has two steps before the third throwing step, which allows her to moderate her first step in case the runner is really barreling in.

Hints

The rocker pivot is a useful maneuver that can be summarized as follows: step on the bag with the left foot, push back simultaneously with the left foot, land off the bag with the right foot, and finally step toward the target with the left foot.

42. Second-Base Player Double Play (Intermediate)

Purpose: To develop second-base player's execution of a double play (used when base runner is at first base)

Equipment: Supply of softballs

Number of players: 4

Number of repetitions: 10 reps for 2 sets

Allocated time: 5 to 7 minutes per player

Cardio index: ♥ ♥

1. Players assume their on-field positions as first-, second-, and third-base players and shortstop.
2. A coach at home plate hits a ground ball to the third-base player or shortstop.
3. The third-base player or shortstop fields the ball and throws the ball to second base.
4. The second-base player covers second base and executes proper footwork utilizing the straddle, standard pivot, crossover pivot, or rocker pivot.
5. The second-base player completes the double play by throwing the ball to first.

Advanced Variation

Execute the drill with a base runner stationed one-third of the way off first base. This head start lends a sense of urgency to the drill. Depending on the speed of the runner and trajectory of the ball thrown to second, the second-base player will need to vary her footwork to make the out and get out of the path of the runner while still being able to make the throw to first.

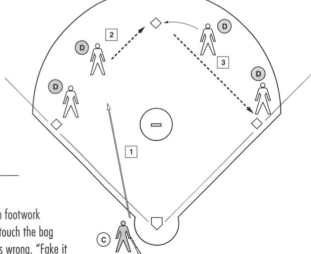

Hints

Footwork is very important to selling the play to the umpire; smooth footwork will often get the close call. Your players should never go back to retouch the bag after missing it. Sell the play as if the bag was touched and nothing is wrong. "Fake it 'til you make it!"

43. Shortstop Which Way? (Intermediate)

Purpose: To develop shortstop's reaction to various game situations
Equipment: Softball, cones or markers
Number of players: 1
Number of repetitions: 10 reps for 2 sets

Allocated time: 5 to 7 minutes per player
Parent-friendly drill: ✔
Cardio index: ♥ ♥

1. A player assumes her on-field position as shortstop. This drill can be used as a station drill—set up first- and second-base markers in the outfield.
2. A coach standing 15 feet away in the infield calls out various common situations for the shortstop to react to.
3. The player responds to the coach's calls as follows:

   - A ground ball hit to second base, runner at first: the shortstop covers second base, catches the ball (thrown by coach acting as second-base player), and makes a phantom throw to first for the double play.
   - A bunt to first base, runner at first: the shortstop covers second base and catches the ball (thrown by coach acting as first-base player) for the force-out. She looks to make double play at first.
   - A ground ball hit to the shortstop with nobody on base: the shortstop catches the ball (rolled/tossed by coach simulating hit) and makes a phantom throw to first.
   - A ground ball hit to the shortstop's right side with a runner at first: the shortstop catches the ball (rolled/tossed by coach simulating hit to her right side), pivots, and makes a phantom throw to second (covered by an imaginary second-base player).
   - A fly ball hit to shortstop with a runner at first: the shortstop catches the ball (tossed by coach simulating hit) and checks the runner at first.
   - A fly ball hit to the shortstop with runners at first and second: the shortstop catches the ball (tossed by coach simulating hit) and checks the runners at first and second.
   - A ground ball hit to shortstop, bases loaded, fewer than two outs (in this situation, the shortstop should be starting in front of the line in order to make the play at home): the shortstop fields the ball (rolled/tossed by coach simulating hit) and makes a phantom throw to home plate. She also looks to make the easiest out if the play at home is not possible.
   - A ground ball hit to shortstop, bases loaded, two outs: the shortstop fields the ball (rolled/tossed by coach simulating hit) and makes a phantom throw to the easiest base (or tags second base if the ball is hit

to her left side close to second base). Most of the time, to make sure of the inning's final out, the play is made at first base.

- Work any other situations that appear often in your games.

Advanced Variations

- **Work Outs to Third Base.** Have the third-base player work on getting back to the bag in time for a good throw from the shortstop.
- **Shortstop Which Way? Live Action.** Do this drill by actually hitting to the shortstop, including high hoppers. The shortstop needs to work on charging the ball back up the middle and throwing off the throwing-side foot. Off-balance throws are common in elite-level play.

Hints

This is a mental drill. That's why the coach can either toss or roll grounders in this drill—tossing speeds up the drill and allows more repetitions, even though rolling the ball is not the most realistic way to simulate a grounder. Of course, as a coach, you will want to correct mechanical problems, but the focus of this drill is to ingrain all the permutations until they become second nature. Players should memorize these plays like the multiplication tables.

44. Shortstop Footwork—Standard Pivot (Intermediate)

Purpose: To practice shortstop's footwork for catching balls thrown from the right side of the field (when the shortstop arrives at the bag well in advance of the ball—used in junior softball and to stretch to catch weakly thrown balls)
Equipment: Softball

Number of players: 1
Number of repetitions: 10 reps for 2 sets
Allocated time: 5 to 7 minutes per player
Parent-friendly drill: ✔
Cardio index: ♥ ♥

1. A player assumes her on-field position as shortstop.
2. A coach with a ball stands in the area the second-base player normally occupies, and begins the drill by signaling a hit ball that the coach will field.
3. The shortstop covers second base; the coach throws the ball to second base.
4. **Right-handed shortstop.** The right-handed shortstop arrives at second base and puts her right foot on the edge of the bag with her body square to the coach (i.e., plane of body perpendicular to the direction of the incoming ball). Her left foot is off the bag and can be stretched toward and as far as necessary to reach the incoming ball.
5. The right-handed shortstop then pushes off her right foot and steps toward first base with her left or glove-side foot as she makes a phantom throw to first base for the double play.
6. **Left-handed shortstop.** The left-handed shortstop arrives at second base and puts her left foot on the edge of the bag with her body square to the coach (i.e., plane of body perpendicular to the direction of the incoming ball). Her right foot is off the bag and can be stretched toward and as far as necessary to reach the incoming ball.
7. The left-handed shortstop then pushes off her left foot and steps toward first base with her right or glove-side foot as she makes a phantom throw to first base for the double play.

Advanced Variations

- Have runners sliding into the bag to try to disrupt the play.
- Have some of the throws be off-line so the focus then becomes to make the catch and get one out.
- Vary the speed of the throws to the player.

45. Shortstop Footwork—Crossover Pivot (Intermediate)

Purpose: To practice shortstop's footwork in double-play situation with a fast runner advancing to second (shortstop uses the crossover pivot to quickly catch the ball as it arrives on the right-field side of the bag to enable her to be in position to throw to first)

Equipment: Softball
Number of players: 1
Number of repetitions: 10 reps for 2 sets
Allocated time: 5 to 7 minutes per player
Parent-friendly drill: ✔
Cardio index: ♥ ♥

1. A player assumes her on-field position as shortstop.
2. A coach with a ball stands in the area the second-base player normally occupies and begins the drill by signaling a hit ball that the coach will field.
3. The shortstop covers second base.
4. The coach throws the ball to second base, varying the timing and speed of the throws.
5. The shortstop arrives at second base, stepping on the bag with her glove-side foot as she catches the ball (preferably on the right-field side of the bag). Her glove-side foot should point somewhat toward first base.
6. **Right-handed shortstop.** The right-handed shortstop continues across the bag, lands off the right-field side of the bag with her throwing-side foot somewhat pointing toward first base, and, using the landed right foot as a pivot, steps toward first base with her left or glove-side foot while making a phantom throw to first base.
7. **Left-handed shortstop.** The left-handed shortstop continues across the bag and is already in position to make the throw to first.

Advanced Variations

- Have runners sliding into the bag to try to disrupt the play.
- Have some of the throws be off-line so the focus then becomes to make the catch and get one out.
- Vary the speed of the throws to the player.
- Have a player replace the coach and challenge her to throw to the bag as the shortstop arrives, rather than wait for the shortstop to arrive and set up before throwing the ball to her.
- **Shortstop 180 Degrees to Third Base.** This drill practices the situation when a right-handed shortstop fields a hard-hit ball to her glove side and has to quickly throw to third base (the shortstop is going one way, but then has to throw the other). Position a right-handed shortstop in the infield. Stand at home plate and throw (or hit if you can do it accurately) "line drives" to the shortstop's glove side. The shortstop

must jump pivot (her whole body jumps up and rotates in the air), lands and throws, or, pivoting with her glove-side foot, executes a drop step with her throwing-side leg and steps back, and then throws back to third. Shortstops coming across the infield to get a short hop will have to dig the ball out of the ground and then half step and throw to get rid of the ball quickly. A softball field is smaller than a baseball field, so the softball shortstop has much less time to get the ball and get rid of it.

Hints

The shortstop has the advantage of usually being able to move across the bag and toward first base on double plays, and should therefore use this advantage. Thus we have not included the Rocker Pivot variation for shortstops because using it will take her away from first and slow down the double play.

Use a stopwatch to time your shortstops from glove to glove to find out which footwork is best for their abilities. This will also show the right-side fielders where the ball needs to be thrown at the shortstop to make the best play possible for her most natural footwork.

An Abbreviated Double Play

Right-hander Emi Naito, Michele's teammate on the Toyota Shokki in the Japan Pro Softball League, is one of the finest shortstops in the world and a member of the Japanese National Team—Japan's Olympic softball team. Emi likes to turn double plays by stepping on the back of the bag with her right foot and then crossing over the bag and throwing to first on her next step. When Emi arrives early to second base on bunts hit to the front (with a runner on first), she has her right foot on the bag, catches the fielded ball, and throws to first without stepping! Emi can get away with it because of her adult arm strength and her perfect throwing mechanics. But we don't recommend encouraging junior players to throw without stepping. We don't want kids to go down that slippery slope of finding ways to "cut corners." That's why we call these "abbreviated versions," and not "shortcuts."

46. Shortstop Bunt (Beginner)

Purpose: To practice shortstop's reaction to bunts
Equipment: Softball
Number of players: All infielders
Number of repetitions: 10 reps for 2 sets

Allocated time: 5 to 7 minutes per player
Cardio index: ♥ ♥

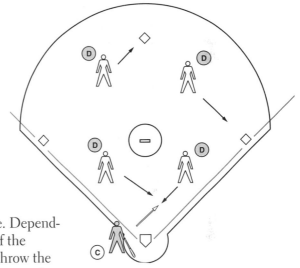

1. All infielders assume their on-field positions, with imaginary runners at first and home plate.
2. A coach at home plate simulates a bunt by lightly hitting or rolling a ball in front of the pitcher or first- and third-base players.
3. The appropriate player fields the ball, while the other players cover correctly.
4. The fielder throws to second base or first base, depending on which base the coach calls out.

Advanced Variation

Station base runners at first base and home plate. Depending on where the bunt is placed and the speed of the runners, the catcher will decide where she will throw the ball. If the ball is bunted outside of the catcher's area of responsibility, have the catcher call out which base the fielder should throw to. Give the bunter a head start by placing her 10 feet off home plate; this will give the drill some urgency.

Hints

If at all possible, encourage your infielders to throw out the runner advancing to second. Given the placement of the ball on a bunt, a double play is very possible for elite players and should be practiced. The footwork and strength of the shortstop arm is very important while trying to turn a double play in a bunt situation. For advanced teams, if the third-base player fields the bunt and throws to first base to go after the batter, the pitcher should cover third base to prevent the lead runner from attempting to advance yet another bag.

47. Double Play Second Base–Shortstop Interaction (Intermediate)

Purpose: To develop second-base player's and shortstop's execution of double-play feeds (used when base runner is at first base)

Equipment: Supply of softballs

Number of players: 3

Number of repetitions: 10 reps for 2 sets

Allocated time: 5 to 7 minutes

Cardio index: ♥ ♥

1. Players assume their on-field positions as first- and second-base players and shortstop.
2. A coach at home plate hits a ground ball to the second-base player or shortstop.
3. If the ball is hit to the shortstop, she fields the ball and throws to the second-base player covering second base. If the ball is hit close to second base, she can use the momentum of fielding the ball in that direction to underhand-flip the ball to second. For longer throws the shortstop will need to pivot and make the throw.
4. If the ball is hit to the second-base player, she fields the ball and throws to the shortstop covering second base. If the ball is hit close to second base, she can use the momentum of fielding the ball in that direction to underhand-flip the ball to second. Otherwise the second-base player will need to pivot and make the throw.

Advanced Variation

Unassisted Double Play. Hit the ball close to the base and have the short-stop and second-base player decide if they should make the double play unassisted or make the throw to the teammate. Add runners to make the plays more difficult.

48. Who's the Cutoff? (Intermediate)

Purpose: To develop second-base player's and shortstop's execution of cutoff plays
Equipment: Supply of softballs
Number of players: 9

Number of repetitions: 10 reps for 2 sets
Allocated time: 5 to 7 minutes
Cardio index: ♥ ♥

1. All defensive players assume their on-field positions.
2. A coach hits a fly ball or line drive to any outfielder.
3. If the ball is hit to the left side of the field, the shortstop runs to her position as cutoff and catches the ball thrown by the outfielder. She pivots and throws the ball to the second-base player covering second base.
4. If the ball is hit to the right side of the field, the second-base player runs to her position as cutoff and catches the ball thrown by the outfielder. She pivots and throws the ball to the shortstop covering second base.
5. The player covering second base pivots and promptly throws the ball to the pitcher to stop the action.
6. If the player runs the ball to the pitcher, she checks the runner to let her know "I'm watching you."

The diagram shows only players involved in a hit to left field.

Advanced Variation

Bases Loaded—Who's the Cutoff? Call out different situations. For example, if calling "Bases loaded less one out," then the sequence would be outfield to cutoff to the bag the catcher calls out. Get your catchers involved as much as possible. The first option is a throw to home plate. If the play at the plate is too late, have the catcher yell "Cut" and then the bag she wants the infielder to throw to.

Hints

Remind your outfielders to throw immediately to the cutoff, and your cutoffs to call out "Cutoff" and throw immediately to the appropriate infielder. Correct the tendency of outfielders and cutoffs to eviscerate an otherwise great fielding play by freezing (holding onto the ball for too long) while they decide what to do with it.

Try standing near the pitcher and throwing the ball to the outfielders. While throwing the ball is not as game-like as hitting the ball, it speeds up the drill (adds repetitions) and distills the drill to its essential core—prompt execution of the cutoff sequence.

Outfield to cutoff to second base to pitcher is the default sequence for up to U12 or U14 play when the force is at first and all you want to do is to get the ball back to the pitcher to stop the play and prevent an extra base. But know your team and their level of play. Go to second base only if opposing players are advancing on your defense. For advanced players the default sequence is outfield to cutoff to the pitcher.

Specific Cutoff Situations

Execute these other cutoff situations if the ball is hit to:

- **Center field with a runner on first base.** The shortstop becomes the cutoff. The center fielder throws the ball to the shortstop. The third-base player will tell the shortstop either to cut the ball to another base or throw it to third base for a play on the runner. The pitcher backs up third base. If the ball gets into the gap and there is a chance the runner on first will try for home, the shortstop should go out for the cut (in left-center gap—the second-base player in the right-center gap) with the first-base player being lined up as the secondary cut for the middle infielders to throw through should the catcher yell for the throw to come home. If the runner is not coming home, then the catcher will yell for the middle infielder to cut the ball and throw to third base. Elite teams should be able to judge this accordingly and have the middle infielders line up for a throw to either home or third base—this takes good judgment by the catcher to determine early if the play will be at third or home. Remember that you never want your players to throw "behind" the runner; this will allow the runner to advance another bag in many cases.

- **Center field with a runner on second base (scoring position).** The first-base player lines up in the middle of the infield between the center fielder and the catcher and becomes the cutoff. The center fielder throws the ball to the first-base player who cuts the ball and throws home if this is what the catcher tells her to do (catcher yells "Cut home" or "Cut four"). The catcher should yell "No" if no cut is needed, or "Cut" and a base to throw to in order to get a trailing runner. The pitcher backs up home plate.

- **Left-center gap with a runner on first base.** The shortstop becomes the cutoff. The center fielder throws the ball to the shortstop, who throws the ball to third base. The pitcher backs up third base.

- **Left-center gap with a runner on second base (scoring position).** The shortstop becomes the cutoff going out to help make the long throw into home, and the first-base player is the secondary cut at about the pitching circle area. The left fielder throws the ball to the shortstop, who throws the ball to home plate, through the first-base player who is the second cut. The pitcher backs up home.

- **Left-field line with a runner on second base (scoring position).** Some coaches will wish for the third-base player to be the cut in this situation. The shortstop will cover third base and the catcher will tell the third-base player either to cut the ball or let it continue to home for a play at the plate.

- **Right-center-field gap with a runner on first base.** The second-base player becomes the cutoff. The right fielder throws the ball to the second-base player, who throws the ball to third base. The pitcher backs up third base. In some cases the shortstop will be the cut and the second-base player will circle back and cover second base.

- **Right field with a runner on second base (scoring position).** The first-base player becomes the cutoff. The right fielder throws the ball to the first-base player, who cuts the ball and throws home if this is what the catcher tells her to do (catcher yells "Cut home" or "Cut four"). The catcher should yell "No" if no cut is needed, or "Cut" and a base to throw to in order to get a trailing runner. If no cut is called, the first-base player lets the ball pass her and continue to the catcher for a play at the plate. The pitcher backs up home plate.

49. Third-Base Player Which Way? (Intermediate)

Purpose: To develop third-base player's reaction to various game situations

Equipment: Softball, cones or markers

Number of players: 1

Number of repetitions: 10 reps for 2 sets

Allocated time: 5 to 7 minutes per player

Parent-friendly drill: ✔

Cardio index: ⓥ ⓥ

1. A player assumes her on-field position as third-base player. This drill can be used as a station drill—set up second- and third-base markers in the outfield.
2. A coach standing 15 feet away in the infield calls out various common situations for the third-base player to react to.
3. The player responds to the coach's calls as follows:

   - A ground ball hit to third base, nobody on base: the third-base player fields the ball (rolled/tossed by coach simulating hit) and makes a phantom throw to first.
   - A bunt to third base, nobody on base: the third-base player charges the ball, fields it, and makes a phantom throw to first.
   - A ground ball hit to the third-base player's right side, runners on first and second: the third-base player fields the ball (rolled/tossed by coach simulating hit to her right side) and steps on third, if possible, but more likely she should throw to the shortstop covering third since the third-base player is "up the line." If the batter is slow, she also looks to make the play at second for a possible double play to first.
   - A ground ball hit to the third-base player's left side, runners on first and second: the third-base player fields the ball (rolled/tossed by coach simulating hit to her left side) and makes a phantom throw to third (covered by imaginary shortstop). If the batter is slow, the shortstop can then attempt a double play to first, or the third-base player that originally fielded the ball can make the play at second for a possible double play to first.
   - A fly ball hit to the third-base player with a runner at first: the third-base player catches the ball (tossed by coach simulating hit) and checks the runner at first.
   - A fly ball hit to the third-base player with runners at first and second: the third-base player catches the ball (tossed by coach simulating hit) and checks the runners at first and second.
   - A ground ball hit to third base, bases loaded, fewer than two outs: the third-base player fields the ball (rolled/tossed by coach simulating hit) and makes a phantom throw to home plate.

- A ground ball hit to third base, bases loaded, two outs: the third-base player fields the ball (rolled/tossed by coach simulating hit) and makes a phantom throw to the "easiest base" (tags third base if hit to her right side close to third base).

Advanced Variation

Third Base Which Way? Live Action. Do this drill by actually hitting balls to the third-base player, including line drives to develop quick reaction skills. Work one hoppers, and high hoppers with runners at third.

Hints

This is a mental drill. That's why, for example, the coach can either toss or roll grounders in this drill—tossing speeds up the drill and allows more repetitions, even though rolling the ball is not the most realistic way to simulate a grounder. Of course, as a coach, you will want to correct mechanical problems, but the focus of this drill is to ingrain all the permutations until they become second nature. Players should memorize these plays like the multiplication tables.

50. Third-Base Player Bunt (Beginner)

Purpose: To practice third-base player's reaction to bunts.
Equipment: Softball
Number of players: 4
Number of repetitions: 10 reps for 2 sets

Allocated time: 5 to 7 minutes per player
Cardio index: ♥ ♥

1. Players assume their on-field positions as first-, second-, and third-base players and shortstop, with imaginary runners at first and home plate.
2. A coach at home plate simulates a bunt by lightly hitting a ball that travels outside the catcher's area of responsibility and into the third-base player's area.
3. The third- and first-base players charge. The player who reaches the ball first plants her throwing-side foot next to the ball and picks it up.
4. The fielding player steps with her glove-side foot toward her target and throws to second base (covered by shortstop) or first base (covered by the second-base player), depending on which base the coach calls out.

Advanced Variation

Force at Third Bunt. Hit a few bunts to the left side of the infield with actual runners on first and second. In this case the shortstop should cover third base. Once in a while have the runners steal as the coach "misses" the bunt so the shortstop has to cover the steal at third base. The catcher should make a good throw to third base.

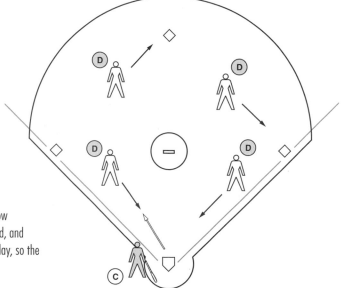

Hints

Correct any tendency of your third-base player to sidearm-throw the ball. Make sure all throws are overhead, have good speed, and are on-line toward the target. The play at second is a force play, so the throw should be chest high to the shortstop.

51. Third-Base Player Throw to First (Beginner)

Purpose: To practice third-base player's technique for fielding the ball and throwing to first base (used when the only force-out is at first)

Equipment: Softball

Number of players: 2

Number of repetitions: 15 reps for 1 set

Allocated time: 5 to 7 minutes per player

Parent-friendly drill: ✔ The parent throws the ball from the halfway point between home plate and first base and then goes to first base to receive the ball.

Cardio index: ♥ ♥

1. Players assume their on-field positions as first- and third-base players.
2. A coach at home plate simulates a ground ball by rolling or hitting a ball into the third-base player's area of responsibility.
3. The third-base player fields the ball and throws the ball to first base.

Hints

Third-base players should use the infield variation crow hop if they are unable to get the ball across the infield on a regular throw. Elite players will not need the crow hop to make the throw.

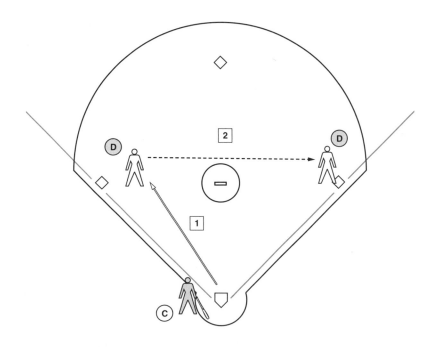

52. Third-Base Player Double Play (Intermediate)

Purpose: To develop third-base player's decision making and execution of double play (used when base runners are at first and second base)

Equipment: Softball

Number of players: 3

Number of repetitions: 15 reps for 1 set

Allocated time: 5 to 7 minutes per player

Cardio index: ♥ ♥

1. Players assume their on-field positions as first-, second-, and third-base players, with imaginary runners at home plate, first, and second base.
2. A coach at home plate simulates a ground ball by rolling or hitting a ball into the third-base player's area of responsibility.
3. The third-base player fields the ball and must decide her next step.
4. If the ball was hit to her left side, then the third-base player uses her momentum in that direction and throws the ball to second base to initiate a double play, using the infield variation crow hop (see Chapter 2) if necessary. The player at second base completes the double play by throwing the ball to first.
5. If the ball was hit to her right side, then the third-base player might be in a good position to tag third base and then throw the ball to first base, using the infield variation crow hop.

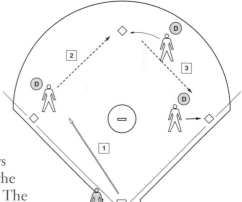

The diagram shows a situation where the ball is hit to the third-base player's left side.

Advanced Variation

Third-Base Lead Runner Double Play. This drill reinforces decision making on double plays. However, in almost all situations we want to get the lead runner out. If there is time, no matter where the ball is hit, the third-base player should try to get the ball to the shortstop who is covering third. The shortstop can then throw across the infield to first for the double play. The throw across the field is a tricky one; that's why this is an advanced variation.

Hints

Footwork and good snap throws are very important for making double plays. Whenever possible, the third-base player should cut off slowly hit ground balls by angling toward the pitching mound. Any balls she can cut off from the shortstop by taking this angle will give her the opportunity to make a good play at any bag depending on where the runners are. Keep in mind that if slowly hit balls are getting past the third-base player, there is a good chance the shortstop will not be able to make a play due to further deceleration of the ball.

53. Rundown (Intermediate)

Purpose: To develop infielder's decision making and execution of rundown

Equipment: Softball

Number of players: 3 (2 defensive players and a base runner)

Number of repetitions: 10 reps for 2 sets

Allocated time: 7 to 10 minutes per player

Cardio index: ♥ ♥ ♥

Morgan makes a dartlike throw to Katelyn playing third base. Jenn tries to run toward Katelyn's glove to make the throw more difficult.

1. Position a base runner on one of the baselines between two defensive players.
2. The defensive player with the ball begins the rundown by running toward the runner, holding the ball high in her throwing hand.
3. The runner runs to avoid the tag out.
4. The receiving defensive player calls "Now!" telling her teammate to toss her the ball, but only if the runner is at full speed toward the receiving player (that is, committed).
5. The player with the ball makes a quick dartlike throw to the receiving player.
6. The receiving player catches the ball, steps forward, and makes the tag on the runner, or if the runner has changed directions, the defensive players switch roles and continue the rundown.
7. After making a throw, the defensive player either follows the throw or circles back to the bag she came from.

Advanced Variations

- **Multiple Runner Rundown.** Have a secondary runner advancing to the next bag. As soon as the first rundown is over, defensive players should look for a secondary play. You'll need to station all infield positions on this and the next variation.
- **Multiple Runner Rundown, Play at Home.** Have a rundown take place between first and second base, with a runner on third. When the

runner on third attempts to go home, the defensive players in the rundown should attempt to get the runner going home out.

- **Outfield Rundown Backup.** Add outfielders to the drill, and start the drill by having the coach temporarily step in and intentionally overthrow third base into the outfield. The left fielder should back up the rundown.

Hints

Good rundowns require as few throws as possible. The defensive players working the rundown should keep moving closer to each other during the rundown; this will give the runner less room to work with and keep her away from the base so she can't dive back in and be safe. Fielders without the ball need to take care not to obstruct the runner; if a collision occurs with a runner and a defensive player without the ball, the runner will be called safe by the umpire.

The defensive player with the ball should not pump fake her throwing arm because it doesn't accomplish anything except maybe to confuse the receiving player. The receiving player should position herself slightly to either side of the baseline to accommodate a quick throw that will not hit the runner.

Don't forget to use this drill to teach *runners* how to outsmart the defenders. Runners should always run toward the receiving player's *glove*; the ball might hit the runner in the back and draw a "safe" call, or at least the runner may block the thrower's line of sight. Very advanced runners can at the last second drop and roll back toward the fielder coming at them. What this does is trip up the fielder; she can't get down to tag the runner. The runner then gets up and runs to the nearest base. This is a very dangerous move and can injure either player. It's also difficult to pull off if the other fielders are backing up at the bags.

54. Infield Communication (Intermediate)

Purpose: To develop infield communication skills	**Number of repetitions:** 10 reps for 2 sets
Equipment: Supply of softballs	**Allocated time:** 5 to 7 minutes
Number of players: All infielders	**Cardio index:** ♥ ♥

1. Infielders assume their on-field positions.
2. A coach standing at home plate throws or hits fly balls to various locations in the infield.
3. The appropriate player calls for the ball ("OK, OK!" or "Ball, ball!") if the ball is hit to her area of responsibility.
4. The appropriate fielder makes the catch and throws to the base the coach calls out.

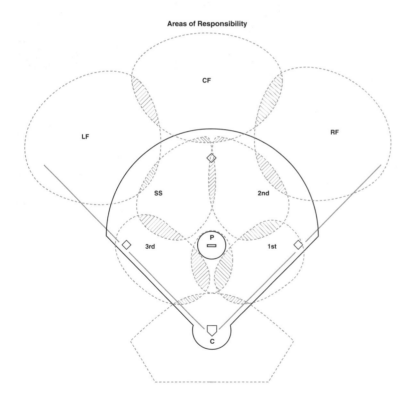

Areas of Responsibility

Hints

The infielder should point to the pop-up and wave her arms to help let her teammates know she is calling for the ball. When other teammates are close by, the fielder should keep calling the ball to help avoid collisions.

In most cases, the middle infielders have priority for fielding infield pop-ups. Encourage your shortstop and second-base players not to cross the imaginary line running from home plate to second base into the other player's area of responsibility just to make the play. Ball hogging dampens team spirit. It also sends the message that the player does not trust her teammates.

However, for close calls the shortstop has final say over all infield positions, and the center fielder has final say over all outfield positions. All outfielders have final say over the infielders because it's easier to catch a ball coming in than going out.

55. Outfield One-Knee Blocking (Beginner)

Purpose: To practice outfielder's technique to field medium-strength ground balls

Equipment: Supply of softballs

Number of players: 1

Number of repetitions: 10 reps for 2 sets

Allocated time: 5 to 7 minutes per player

Parent-friendly drill: ✔

Cardio index: ♥ ♥

1. A player stands facing a coach 40 feet away. This drill should be executed in the grassy part of the field.
2. A coach hits a medium-strength ground ball in front or to the left or right of the fielder.
3. The fielder uses the appropriate footwork (cross-over step or slide step) to move to the ball.
4. The fielder drops to one knee—preferably her throwing-side knee—extending it out horizontally to the ball.
5. The fielder puts her glove on the ground in the space between her legs and fields the ball.
6. In one smooth motion, the fielder brings the ball in to her stomach area, stands up, and makes a crow-hop throw back to the coach for the next repetition.

Katelyn (left) demonstrates one-knee fielding. Morgan (right) is being a good sport in demonstrating the incorrect way to field a ball. Morgan is trying to field the ball in front of her and has her glove down, which is good. But she's bending at the waist, not her knees, which leaves a big gap for the ball to go through and impairs her vision.

Advanced Variations

- **Outfield Mix-It-Up.** Add some "do or die" situations so the fielder has to come in hard on the ball, pick it up off the ground, and make a strong throw to home as if a runner from second is trying to score.
- **Outfield Recovery.** Have her get down on her knee and let a couple of balls get past her. She then has to get up, run after the ball, pick it up, and find the appropriate teammate for the cut.

Hints

Work footwork and body position to make sure the fielders are on balance at all times. Use this drill in pregame warm-ups to test the outfield conditions. On bad outfields, the ball will jump all over the place and be difficult to field.

56. Outfield Line-Drive Interceptor (Intermediate)

Purpose: To practice using the cross-over step and drop step to field line drives and to develop outfield communication and backup skills
Equipment: Supply of softballs

Number of players: 2
Number of repetitions: 10 reps for 2 sets
Allocated time: 5 minutes per player
Cardio index: ♥ ♥ ♥

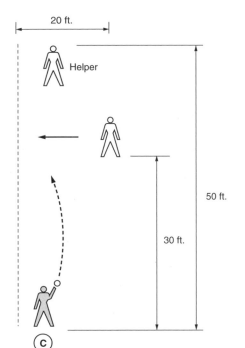

1. The first player (helper) stands facing a coach standing 50 feet away.
2. The second player (interceptor) stands facing the coach 30 feet away and 20 feet off the midline.
3. The coach throws a line drive/low fly ball toward the helper. The helper moves left or right and/or forward or back by a few feet on each repetition to vary the direction of the throw.
4. The interceptor calls out for the ball.
5. The interceptor uses a crossover step or drop step to move toward the ball, crosses the flight path, and catches the ball before it reaches the helper.
6. The interceptor crow-hop throws the ball to the coach for the next repetition; the interceptor starts from the opposite side for the next repetition since she's already there.
7. The helper catches the ball if the interceptor misses and throws the ball to the coach for the next repetition.

Advanced Variations

- Increase the distance (width or length) the interceptors have to run to intercept the ball.
- Throw or hit fly balls behind or bloopers in front of the interceptors. In this case, execute the drill without the helper to avoid collisions.
- **Two Interceptors.** Execute the drill with two interceptors starting about 20 feet on opposite sides of the midline. Communication will be key to avoiding collisions. The appropriate player calls out for the ball and intercepts it. The other player backs up by using appropriate footwork to move toward the ball, but behind the primary interceptor. Throw fly balls or soft line drives for this variation. Hard line drives may lead to collisions as the players may not have enough time to decide who the primary interceptor will be.

Hints

Sometimes when a coach throws to either side of a player in crossover or drop step practice, she's not quite certain how hard or how far to the side to throw it. Often the ball just sails away to be collected later. This drill is good because the coach throws it to a target (the helper player)—just like in a game of catch. The coach can throw it as hard as the backup can handle.

In the Two Interceptors drill, encourage both players to go for the ball with proper communication. Young players have a tendency to stop moving as soon as another player calls for the ball. Outfielders do not act as cutoffs, so the second player should make herself useful by backing up the player who calls for the ball. Building muscle memory to move no matter what will help avoid the common situation where both players freeze and do nothing.

57. Outfield Tracker (Advanced)

Purpose: To practice tracking skills and changing directions in the outfield
Equipment: Supply of softballs
Number of players: 1

Number of repetitions: 15 reps for 2 sets
Allocated time: 7 to 10 minutes per player
Cardio index: ♥ ♥ ♥

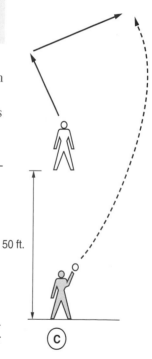

1. A player stands facing a coach 50 feet away. This drill may be executed in the grassy part of the field.
2. The coach indicates which direction the player will run and then throws or machine throws a fly ball at about a 45-degree angle in the *other* direction.
3. The player, keeping her eyes on the ball, runs but needs to change directions as follows:

   - Plants her outside foot and rotates her shoulders to go in the opposite direction,
     or
   - Drop steps around to head in the other direction
4. The player runs at about a 45-degree angle at full speed to run down the ball.
5. As she approaches the ball, she turns toward the ball and makes the catch.
6. The player catches the ball and makes a crow-hop throw to the coach for the next repetition.

Advanced Variations

- Increase the distance (width or depth) the player has to run to catch the ball.
- Throw the ball over the player's opposite shoulder so she has to adjust her footwork to make the catch.

- Have the player start running early and then underthrow her so she has to change direction and come back in hard for the ball.
- **Outfield Fence.** Have a coach stand 50 feet from a fence and a player facing the coach about 30 feet from the fence. The coach throws a fly ball over the player's head toward the fence, and the player uses the appropriate footwork to field the ball. This drill will address a situation that comes up often during advanced play—fly balls or line drives hit to the deep outfield very close to the fence. Use a fence where there is convenient and safe access to retrieve balls thrown over the fence.

In cases where the ball is hit in the air and the outfielder is approaching the outfield fence, she should start to reach out with her throwing-side hand to feel for the wall or fence. This will help the outfielder be able to keep her eye on the ball and still be aware of the distance and location of the fence. Many softball fields do not have warning tracks so it is important to practice these situations with your outfielders. Many outfielders miss easily caught balls because they are afraid of running into the fence.

If the ball bounces off the fence and hopefully back toward her, she will field the ball and then pivot and go into a crow hop and throw the ball to her cut. If the ball is lying at the base of the fence, she should run up to the ball, put her throwing-side foot next to the ball, and in one motion bend down and grab the ball in her throwing hand. She should be driving with her glove-side leg down against the ground, bring her hand from the ground up, and make a throw in one smooth motion to her cut. She should resist the habit of picking up the ball and bringing her glove and throwing hands together and pumping the ball in her glove, which wastes time. As she is bending down to pick up the ball with her bare hand she should be listening for her cut, who is behind her, so she knows exactly where the cut is, prior to even seeing her. It is important for cutoff players to be very vocal in these situations.

Hints

Changing directions is quite an advanced maneuver. The player will need to take her eyes off the ball for a split second when changing directions.

Watch for players not running at a 45-degree angle. This will slow them down if they are running incorrectly. Watch the player's glove arm. Her glove arm should be pumping just like her throwing arm as she runs. Make sure her glove arm is not just hanging down at her side. She should also avoid running with her glove arm up in the air as if making the catch well before getting to the spot where the ball will be. She must pump the glove arm, otherwise she will be late to the ball!

58. Outfield Communication (Intermediate)

Purpose: To develop outfield communication skills
Equipment: Supply of softballs
Number of players: 5 (3 outfielders, second-base player, and shortstop)

Number of repetitions: 10 reps for 3 sets
Allocated time: 10 minutes
Cardio index: ♥ ♥

See the diagram for drill 54 showing areas of responsibility.

1. Players assume their on-field positions as outfielders, second-base player, and shortstop.
2. A coach standing in the infield hits fly balls to the gaps between the outfielders.
3. The appropriate outfielder calls for the ball ("OK, OK!" or "Ball, ball!"), makes the catch, and throws to the appropriate middle infielder (second-base player or shortstop) covering second base. Depending on the depth of the pop fly, the outfielder can throw to the cutoff or directly to second base, or in case of a very shallow pop fly, run directly to the bag. However, this is a decision for the outfielder, not the middle infielders—the cutoff and player covering second base should always hustle into position.

Advanced Variations

- Hit balls into the gap to make sure the outfielders are backing up and the middle infielders are going to the correct cut positions.
- **Outfield Communication Short Bloopers.** Have the middle infielders start in a pulled-in position as when the bases are loaded. This will make short-hit "bloopers" harder to field for both the infielders and outfielders.

Hints

While the center fielder is in charge, she should not run into another outfielder's territory just to make the play. If the center fielder legitimately calls for the ball, the other outfielder should yield but not stop running. The other outfielder backs up the play by running at a deeper angle so she is in good position to back up the center fielder in case she misjudges the flight path or miffs the catch.

Oftentimes, the ball will be hit into the gap. The following lists will help explain which outfielder is in a better position to field balls hit into the gap. As a general rule, the outfielder going away from the bag to be thrown to will have the hardest throw. Every play is different, of course, and the outfielders' relative distance to the ball may be the determining factor.

For plays to second base, if the ball is hit to the

- Left field–center field gap (LF–CF gap), the left fielder (LF) will have the easiest throw to second
- Right field–center field gap (RF–CF gap), the right fielder (RF) will have the easiest throw to second

For plays to third base, if the ball is hit to the

- LF–CF gap, the center fielder (CF) will have the easiest throw to third
- RF–CF gap, the RF will have the easiest throw to third

For plays to home plate, the fielder whose throwing side is toward the middle of the gap is in a better position. For example, if the ball is hit to the

- LF–CF gap, a left-handed LF will have the easier throw to the plate versus a left-handed CF
- LF–CF gap, a left-handed LF and a right-handed CF are in equal position to make the play
- RF–CF gap, a right-handed RF will have the easier throw to the plate versus a right-handed CF
- RF–CF gap, a right-handed RF and a left-handed CF are in equal position to make the play

59. Infield-Outfield Communication (Intermediate)

Purpose: To develop infield-outfield communication skills
Equipment: Supply of softballs
Number of players: 7 (3 outfielders; first-, second-, and third-base players; and shortstop)

Number of repetitions: 10 reps for 2 sets
Allocated time: 5 to 7 minutes
Cardio index: ♥ ♥

See the diagram for drill 54 showing areas of responsibility.

1. Players assume their on-field positions as outfielders, first-, second-, and third-base players, and shortstop.
2. A coach standing in the infield hits fly balls to the gap between the outfielders and infielders.
3. The appropriate fielder calls for the ball ("OK, OK!" or "Ball, ball!") based on the following order of priority:
   Center fielder calls off the other outfielders.
   The outfielders call off the infielders.
   The middle infielders call off the corners.
4. The fielder makes the catch and throws to base the coach calls out.

Advanced Variations

- Hit ground balls and fly balls to keep all players on their toes.
- Put runners on base to make the defensive players have to get the runners who try to tag up on the play.
- Hit balls into the sun to make them more difficult to catch.

60. Outfield Do or Die (Intermediate)

Purpose: To develop quick fielding skills to defend against an important base runner (used in situations where there are runners in scoring position with fewer than two outs and the batter hits a ground ball, line drive, or fly ball in front of the outfielder)

Equipment: Supply of softballs

Number of players: 3 to 5 (1 to 3 outfielders, third-base player, and catcher)

Number of repetitions: 10 reps for 2 sets

Allocated time: 5 to 7 minutes

Parent-friendly drill: ✔ Parent throws to one player who executes do-or-die fielding technique to field and throws the ball back to the parent.

Cardio index: ♥ ♥ ♥

Katelyn shows how to field the ball "do or die" with either foot forward. She'll immediately be able to make a crow-hop throw to home plate without stopping and bracing or pushing backward. Think, "Keep moving forward!"

1. Players assume their on-field positions as outfielders, third-base player, and catcher, with an imaginary runner at second base.
2. A coach standing at home plate throws or hits ground balls or fly balls to the outfielder(s).
3. The outfielder fields the ball on the glove side of her body as follows:

If a ground ball, the outfielder

- Sprints toward the ball
- Approaches the ball with the glove side of her body so that she will field the ball with her glove-side leg closest to the ball

- As she approaches the ball, drops her throwing-side knee toward the ground, but not all the way down (her glove-side leg is in front)
- Fields the ball in front of the glove-side foot
- Brings her glove and throwing hand together in to her body and transfers the ball to her throwing hand
- Makes a crow-hop throw to the catcher

If a line drive or fly ball, the outfielder

- Sprints toward the ball
- Catches the ball shoulder high on the throwing-side of her body, if possible
- Brings her glove and throwing hand together in to her body and transfers the ball to her throwing hand
- Makes a crow-hop throw to the catcher

Advanced Variation

Send runners home, but then have them stop halfway and return to third base. The catcher should call "Cut," and the defensive cut players should cut and hold or throw where the catcher tells them. It is important that the outfielder "throws through the cut." If she does not—meaning the throw is an uncatchable throw for the cut person—the ball will continue home when not needed, or worse yet there will be a missed opportunity to get an advancing runner out at second or third.

Hints

Remind your players to avoid catching the ball and then stopping, slowing down, or even bracing and pushing backward, which defeats the purpose of charging to the ball in the first place—to build the forward momentum necessary to make a quick and powerful throw. The slightest hesitation may give the runner just enough time to reach home plate.

Hitting

Softball and baseball are unique among team sports because it's difficult to play under the radar. When a batter steps into the box, she will engage the pitcher in a high-pressure duel for the whole world to see. Add poor mechanics and a pinch of self-doubt, and it becomes a self-fulfilling prophecy for the batter to jog back to the dugout.

Have you ever watched an outstanding pure shooter during a basketball shootaround? The player will make almost all of her 18-footers, using a stroke developed over many years and committed to muscle memory. Hitting a fast-moving target like a softball is arguably more difficult, yet young players spend less time honing their batting mechanics. In addition to taking her thirty swings at batting practice, a player must work in the backyard, at the batting cage, and at every opportunity she can to perfect her mechanics. And she'll need a knowledgeable and committed parent to toss to her, retrieve balls, correct mistakes, and provide support. There's no reason why a player who works hard shouldn't be able to hit almost every machine-pitched fastball by the time she reaches high school. Armed with confidence, she'll do well against live pitching, just like a pure shooter with the confidence to execute in traffic.

The drills in this chapter are designed to get your players to that level by reinforcing the following skill sets for youth, middle school, and high school players:

- **Mechanics of hitting.** Drills reinforce hand-eye coordination, proper stride, rotation, balance, and swing.
- **Specialty skills/tactical hitting.** Drills on bunting, slap hitting, hit placement, and pitch recognition cover these advanced skills.

Mechanics of Hitting

Make sure the hitter *sets up* in the batter's box in the proper *batting stance* and *ready position*, with the proper *grip*, and prepares for the swing as described in the following sections.

Stance

The batter should do the following in her stance:

- Keep her feet shoulder-width apart
- Keep her weight balanced on the inside of the balls of her feet
- Keep her feet straight (not ducked out) (In fact, many elite hitters are pigeon-toed.)
- Slightly bend her knees
- Slightly bend forward at the hips, but not so much that her head enters the strike zone
- Bend her elbows at about a 90-degree angle so that her forearms form an inverted V shape
- Keep her eyes on the ball; concentrate!

Grip

For a proper grip, the batter should do the following:

- Hold the bat in her fingers (more fingers than palm), with the right hand on top for right-handed players and left hand on top for left-handed players
- Avoid squeezing the bat too tightly; grip with the bottom hand slightly more tightly and deeply than with the top hand
- Keep her hands together, choking up on the bat as appropriate for control
- Align the second knuckles of both hands ("knocking knuckles")
- Draw the bat back and rest it on her shoulder

Ready Position

To prepare for the pitch, the batter should do the following:

- As the pitcher sets up in her pre-motion, lift the bat a couple of inches up from her shoulder.
- Avoid the temptation to get a head start on the swing by overtwisting and bringing the bat too far behind her head or rear shoulder; maintain the position where the bat points directly behind her. The bat is now in the *launch mode*.

- Transfer her weight slightly to her back foot by twisting her body slightly away from the pitcher.
- *Trigger* or *load* by bending her front knee slightly in before taking her stride. She is now ready to explode into her stride.
- Keep her hands close to her body. The best swings are compact and "inside out." Starting with her hands close to her body will help her *swing* with her hands inside of the ball (between her body and the path of the ball). If her hands start away from her body, her swing will be outside in or long. A long swing resembles a kind of sweeping or casting action, making it difficult to make contact because the bat head takes longer to reach the ball.

The ready stance. Note how the knuckles of both hands are aligned.

Michele makes a short, compact, and level swing into the strike zone. There's very little head movement as she "smashes the bug" with her back foot. In the last frame, note how Michele still has her head down as she begins her follow-through. Only as she finishes her follow-through will Michele look up.

The Swing

The batter, fully loaded, is now ready to transfer potential energy into kinetic energy and swing for the fence! Often in fast-pitch young athletes are afraid to strike out and become defensive hitters. Don't let this happen; teach your kids a good technical and explosive swing. Let them swing free. The batter should do the following:

- Take a short *stride* with her front leg slightly into the strike zone (slightly into the path of the ball and not directly toward the pitcher). Striding outside or "in the bucket" will cause pop-ups and missed outside pitches.
- Execute a *backside rotation*—rotate her hips (counterclockwise from the right-handed batter's perspective, clockwise from the left-handed batter's), driving and pivoting her rear foot into the ground to smash the bug. Today, many good hitters move the back foot around quite a bit, which is fine as long as there is leg drive and energy coming from the back leg.
- Avoid overrotating her hips; her belly button should be pointed at the ball at contact. This is called "taking a picture of the ball with the belly button." It's hard enough to make contact; don't make it more difficult by overrotating, which allows the hitter to use only a small percentage of the field. Think linear—moving the body in a line toward the pitcher.
- Throw her hands or the knob of the bat at the ball across her chest toward the contact zone. This will keep the swing compact and hands inside of the ball.
- Hit the ball while it is in front of the plate with a level swing.
- Keep her hips and shoulders level and chin down throughout the swing. During the swing her chin will go from her front shoulder to

her back shoulder. After contact her head and chin should be looking down over her back shoulder.

- Keep her eyes on the ball; she shouldn't look up until the ball is hit.
- Follow through with both hands on the bat for as long as possible until the bat reaches around to her shoulders. Stopping the swing immediately after contact without follow-through means significantly less power. Remember "short to, long through"—a short swing to the ball and a nice long follow-through of the hands into the field of play.
- Release the bat and run like the wind.

The Level Swing (Softball Versus Baseball)

Youth softball coaches often admonish their players to make a level swing when hitting the ball. A level swing starts with the bat in the proper launch mode (above the strike zone) and is executed by swinging the bat down so that the bat is parallel to the ground and on the same plane as the ball. However, to compensate for the upward trajectory of most underhand pitches, the plane of the swing as the bat hits the ball is slightly downward. Keeping the bat in this *power plane* will help generate line drives. The downward power plane for fast-pitch softball contrasts with the slight upward motion for baseball; baseball's slightly upward power plane compensates for the generally downward trajectory of a hard ball dealt from a raised pitching mound.

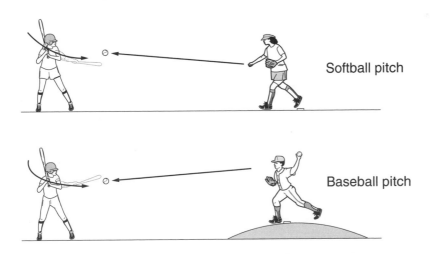

Softball pitch

Baseball pitch

Chapter 4 Skills Matrix

Drill Number	Drill Title (Indented drills are "named" Advanced Variations)	Full Mechanics	Level Swing	Compact Swing	Hitting Stride	Separation (Stride with Hands Back)	Rotation	Rear Foot Action— "Smash the Bug"	Hitting Follow-Through	Bat Speed	Bottom Hand Extension, Top Hand Drive	Endurance	Balance
Hitting Mechanics													
61.	No Uppercut Tee	◉	◉										
	Changeup Tee	◉	◉		◉	◉							
62.	Double Tee Level Swing	◉	◉										
	Advanced Double Tee One Ball	◉	◉										
	One-Hand Double Tee	◉	◉								◉		
63.	Double Tee No Sweep	◉	◉	◉									
	One-Hand No Sweep Tee		◉	◉							◉		
	One-Knee No Sweep Tee		◉	◉									
64.	Double Tee Inside/Outside	◉											
	Competitive Double Tee	◉											
65.	Tee Stacker	◉	◉	◉									
	Stacker Snapbacks	◉		◉						◉		◉	
66.	Stride/No Stride Tee				◉	◉	◉	◉					
	Changeup Stride Tee				◉	◉	◉						
	Foot Pickup Tee				◉								
	No Stride Tee						◉						
67.	Volleyball Stride Pinch Tee	◉			◉								
68.	Power Ball Tee	◉							◉				
	Rapid-Fire Power Ball Tee	◉							◉	◉		◉	
69.	Back Foot Pivot Tee	◉					◉	◉					
70.	One- and Two-Hand Extension Tee										◉		
71.	Rotation—Backside Isolation						◉						
72.	Rotation—Balance				◉		◉						◉

Concentration	Hand-Eye Coordination	Power	Inside and/or Outside Pitches	Different Height Pitches	Decision Making	Hitting Changeups	Pitch Reading	Relax Before Trigger	Bunt Mechanics	Bunt Situations	Defense— Bunt/Slap Hitting	Slap Hit Mechanics	Upper-Body Mechanics	Reaction Time
						⚾								
			⚾											
													⚾	
			⚾											
			⚾											
			⚾	⚾										
				⚾										
						⚾								
													⚾	
		⚾												
		⚾												

(continued)

Chapter 4 Skills Matrix *(continued)*

Drill Number Drill Title **Skills Reinforced** ———————➤

Drill Number	Drill Title (Indented drills are "named" Advanced Variations)	Full Mechanics	Level Swing	Compact Swing	Hitting Stride	Separation (Stride with Hands Back)	Rotation	Rear Foot Action— "Smash the Bug"	Hitting Follow-Through	Bat Speed	Bottom Hand Extension, Top Hand Drive	Endurance	Balance
73.	Rotation — Balance Check												⬤
	Balance Weight Training												⬤
	One-Leg Balance												⬤
	Uphill Dry Swing												⬤
74.	Extension — No Sweep			⬤									
	Snapbacks			⬤						⬤		⬤	
75.	Coach Pitch — Drop Zone	⬤								⬤			
	Command	⬤											
	Decision Making	⬤											
76.	Coach Pitch — Soft Toss	⬤											
	Changeup Soft Toss	⬤				⬤							
	Breakdown Soft Toss										⬤		
	Front-Knee Soft Toss												
	Speed Stick									⬤			
	Bat Behind Back Soft Toss						⬤	⬤					
	Bat off Shoulder Soft Toss			⬤									
	Soft Toss Machine	⬤											
77.	Coach Pitch — Soft Toss Two Ball	⬤											
	Spinning Soft Toss	⬤											
78.	Coach Pitch — High Toss	⬤				⬤							
79.	Coach Pitch — Hit-N-Stik	⬤	⬤	⬤									
80.	Coach Pitch — Front Toss	⬤											
	Front Toss Numbered Balls	⬤											
	Varying Speed Pitch Simulation	⬤											
81.	Coach Pitch — Bounce Toss	⬤											

Concentration	Hand-Eye Coordination	Power	Inside and/or Outside Pitches	Different Height Pitches	Decision Making	Hitting Changeups	Pitch Reading	Relax Before Trigger	Bunt Mechanics	Bunt Situations	Defense— Bunt/Slap Hitting	Slap Hit Mechanics	Upper-Body Mechanics	Reaction Time
		●												
		●												
	●													
	●			●										
	●				●									
	●													
	●					●								
		●												
													●	
	●													●
	●							●						
						●								
	●													
					●									●
●														●
				●				●						

(continued)

Chapter 4 Skills Matrix *(continued)*

Drill Number **Drill Title** **Skills Reinforced** ⟶

Drill Number	Drill Title (Indented drills are "named" Advanced Variations)	Full Mechanics	Level Swing	Compact Swing	Hitting Stride	Separation (Stride with Hands Back)	Rotation	Rear Foot Action—"Smash the Bug"	Hitting Follow-Through	Bat Speed	Bottom Hand Extension, Top Hand Drive	Endurance	Balance
82.	Coach Pitch — Call'm Toss	●											
83.	Coach Pitch — Blind Toss	●			●					●			
84.	Coach Pitch — Machine Gun Toss	●											
	Ten Toss											●	
85.	Coach Pitch — Changeup Simulation	●				●							
86.	Coach Pitch — Changeup Hesitation	●				●							
87.	Live Pitch — Dry Swing												
88.	Live Pitch — Call Location												
	Call the Pitch Grid												
Specialty Hitting													
89.	Bunt — Basic												
90.	Bunt — Barehand Catch												
91.	Bunt — Low Pitch												
	"And Run"												
92.	Bunt — Outside Pitch												
93.	Bunt — Push Bunt												
94.	Bunt — Bunt for Base Hit												
	Right-Handed Sneak Bunt												
	Left-Handed Pivot Sneak Bunt												
95.	Bunt — Third-Base Squeeze Play												
96.	Bunt — Fake-Out												
97.	Slap Hitting — Basic												
	Outside Pitch Slap Hit												
98.	Slap Hitting — Power Slap												

Concentration	Hand-Eye Coordination	Power	Inside and/or Outside Pitches	Different Height Pitches	Decision Making	Hitting Changeups	Pitch Reading	Relax Before Trigger	Bunt Mechanics	Bunt Situations	Defense— Bunt/Slap Hitting	Slap Hit Mechanics	Upper-Body Mechanics	Reaction Time
●	●			●										
	●													●
●	●													
●	●													
						●								
						●								
●							●							
●							●							
●							●							
									●					
									●					
				●					●	●				
									●	●				
				●					●					
									●	●				
									●	●				
									●	●				
									●	●				
									●	●	●			
										●	●			
												●		
												●		
												●		

Hitting Mechanics

61. No Uppercut Tee (Beginner)

Purpose: To practice proper batting mechanics and to correct common hitch and uppercut swing problems
Equipment: Batting tee(s), bat(s), supply of balls (softballs or Wiffle balls)
Number of players: 1

Number of repetitions: 10 reps
Allocated time: 5 minutes per batter if only 1 tee (multiple tees will speed up this drill)
Parent-friendly drill: ✔
Cardio index: ♥

1. A batter wearing a batting helmet sets up in her *batting position* next to a batting tee (around waist-high) facing the backstop or screen (it's best to execute tee drills into some kind of screen or the backstop; hitting into the field takes way too long). A coach places a ball on the tee and steps a safe distance away.
2. The batter checks her position relative to the plate by taking a slow practice swing and making sure the "sweet spot" of the bat touches the ball on top of the tee.
3. On the coach's cue, the batter strides with proper backside rotation, executes a proper swing, and hits the ball off the tee into the screen or backstop.
4. The batter keeps her chin down, focused on the contact point, until follow-through.

Advanced Variations

- Adjust the level of the tee to simulate pitches low and high in the strike zone. On low pitches the batter should concentrate on hitting the bottom of the ball. This will reverse the spin on the ball at contact and may result in a line drive. On a high pitch, the batter should concentrate on hitting the top of the ball; this will help her hit line drives and not pop-ups.
- **Changeup Tee.** Have the batter "stride" and "swing" on your separate commands. This will reinforce the separate stride and swing components. Make sure she swings promptly on the swing cue; this will minimize the opportunity to hitch or sweep. Try to delay the swing command by a tad to simulate the response to a changeup. On this simulation, the front foot is down before the hands move (the batter should keep her hands back). Make sure of this; if the hands move forward while the feet are still moving the batter will lose the ability to hit the pitch with power if her timing is off.

Hints

This is a mechanics (not power) drill. Consider using Wiffle balls to reduce hit distance. To make this drill game-like add your defense in the field, use real softballs, and have the defense play each hit ball as a live game situation.

Correct the tendency of some players to drop (hitch) their hands to around waist level or to drop their rear shoulder during the swing. Either can result in an uppercut swing. Remember that T-ball players instinctively use the uppercut to get impressive distance off the tee. But an uppercut in coach pitch or player pitch will more likely yield a swing and a miss or an easily negotiable pop fly. Make sure your players swing with their hands inside of the ball, rather than fully extend and sweep their arms. Sweeping or casting results in slow bat speed and, if the player manages to make contact with the ball, a discernable lack of power.

Make sure your players are using bats that aren't too heavy. The barrel of a too-heavy bat will sag below the ball's flight path and force the batter to uppercut to compensate. Heavy bats also diminish bat speed. If a lighter bat is not available, it sometimes helps if the batter chokes up on the handle.

Another diagnostic tool is to tape around the bat's sweet spot. This will give you a point of reference in observing the mechanics and help novice players gauge where to stand.

Finally a word about the level swing. The most successful hitters have a flat and level bat in the strike zone for the longest time possible. By keeping the bat in the zone for as long as possible, the batter will increase her chances of making solid contact and getting a base hit.

In this photo, Julia (left) and Jennifer (middle) are good sports and demonstrate the wrong way to hit the ball. Julia is fully extended and is "sweeping" or "casting." Jenn shows bat position during an uppercut swing, which can be caused by dropping the hands instead of going from the launch position straight into the zone. In either case, the bat head takes too long to reach the strike zone. Michele shows the correct body and bat position at contact for a short, compact swing.

62. Double Tee Level Swing (Intermediate)

Purpose: To practice hitting the ball with a level swing
Equipment: Two batting tees, bat, supply of balls (softballs or Wiffle balls)
Number of players: 1

Number of repetitions: 15 reps
Allocated time: 3 to 5 minutes per player
Parent-friendly drill: ✔
Cardio index: ♥

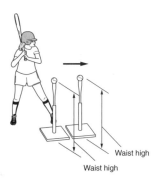

Waist high
Waist high

1. A batter wearing a batting helmet sets up in her batting position facing the backstop or screen, next to two batting tees as shown, set up at the same height (around waist-high). A coach places balls on each tee and steps a safe distance away.
2. The batter checks her position relative to the plate by taking a slow practice swing and making sure the sweet spot of the bat touches the ball on the back tee.
3. On the coach's cue, the batter strides with proper backside rotation, executes a proper swing, and hits the ball off the back tee into the backstop or screen.
4. A level swing will make the first ball hit the second ball off the front tee into the backstop or screen. Reaching for the ball or uppercutting will result in the first ball not hitting the second.

Advanced Variations

Advanced Double Tee One Ball.

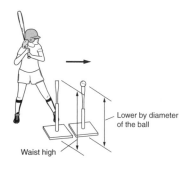

Lower by diameter of the ball

Waist high

1. A batter wearing a batting helmet sets up in her batting position facing the backstop or screen, next to two batting tees as shown. A coach adjusts the height of the front tee so that it is shorter than the back tee by about the diameter of the ball and places a softball on the front tee.
2. On the coach's cue, the batter strides with proper backside rotation, executes a proper swing, and hits the ball off the front tee into the backstop or screen.
3. Improper mechanics such as an uppercut will cause the bat to strike the back tee. Remember that the power plane of the bat swing is slightly down to compensate for the upward trajectory of the underhand pitch.

One-Hand Double Tee. Have the batter execute this drill with only the top hand, and then only the bottom hand. Have the batter shorten up on the bat or use commercially available club bats that are made extra short for one-handed drills. The bottom, or extension, hand and wrist should be somewhat loose at the start and will naturally tighten as the swing starts. This will help build a swing with greater extension through contact, which helps drive the ball.

Hints

Make sure the batter keeps her head down and sees the empty tee after contact. This will make sure she is not pulling her head out of the contact zone early.

63. Double Tee No Sweep (Intermediate)

Purpose: To practice hitting an inside pitch with the sweet spot of the bat using a level swing and to practice hitting with hands inside of the ball
Equipment: 2 batting tees, bat, supply of balls

Number of players: 1
Number of repetitions: 10 reps for 2 sets
Allocated time: 5 minutes per batter
Parent-friendly drill: ✔
Cardio index: ♥

Hit this one

1. A batter wearing a batting helmet sets up in her batting position facing the backstop or screen, next to two batting tees, set up at the same height (around waist-high). A coach places softballs on the tees and steps a safe distance away.

2. The batter checks her position relative to the plate by taking a slow practice swing and making sure the sweet spot of the bat touches the ball on the inside tee.

3. On the coach's cue, the batter strides with proper backside rotation, executes a proper swing, and hits the ball off the inside tee into the backstop or screen, without touching the second ball on the outside tee.

4. If the batter accidentally hits the second ball, she may be sweeping or casting "long to the ball."

Advanced Variations

- **One-Hand No Sweep Tee.** Have the batter use her top or bottom hand only.
- **One-Knee No Sweep Tee.** Have the batter use her top or bottom hand only while down on one knee (always the front knee).

Hints

Set the inside tee closer to the front of the plate to train your players to hit the ball in front of the plate.

64. Double Tee Inside/Outside (Intermediate)

Purpose: To practice hitting inside and outside pitches
Equipment: 2 batting tees, bat, supply of balls
Number of players: 1

Number of repetitions: 20 reps
Allocated time: 5 minutes per player
Parent-friendly drill: ✔
Cardio index: ♥

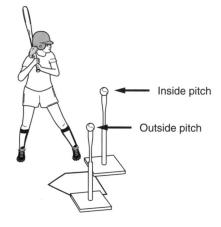

Inside pitch

Outside pitch

1. A batter wearing a batting helmet sets up in her batting position facing the backstop or screen, next to two batting tees as shown, set up at the same height (around waist-high). A coach places softballs on each tee and steps a safe distance away.
2. The batter checks her position relative to the plate by taking a slow practice swing and making sure the sweet spot of the bat touches the ball on each tee.
3. The coach will command "In" or "Out," and the batter will promptly stride with proper backside rotation, execute a proper swing, and hit the ball off the appropriate tee into the backstop or screen.

Advanced Variations

- Have the batters execute the drill off coach pitch, player pitch, or machine pitch.
- **Competitive Double Tee.** Do this drill from home plate and put cones or buckets in left field and right field for the batters to aim at. Give them points for hitting near the cones or buckets.

Hints

Set the inside tee closer to the front of the plate to train your players to hit the ball in front of the plate. The outside tee should be farther back over the plate; this will allow contact back over the plate and allow the batter to hit the ball the opposite way.

She should be able to hit either ball without hitting the other ball. There is no difference in the stride for inside versus outside pitches. The only the differences are the contact point location and bat angle at contact.

65. Tee Stacker (Beginner)

Purpose: To practice hitting different height pitches with proper contact through the ball using correct batting mechanics and to correct common hitch and uppercut swing problems

Equipment: Batting tee, bat, supply of softballs, and Tee Stacker

Number of players: 1
Number of repetitions: 10 reps
Allocated time: 5 minutes per batter if only 1 tee
Parent-friendly drill: ✔
Cardio index: ♥

1. A batter wearing a batting helmet sets up in her batting position next to a batting tee (around waist-high), facing the backstop or screen. A coach places a ball on the tee, and then a Tee Stacker on top of the ball, with another ball on top of the Tee Stacker, and steps a safe distance away.
2. The batter checks her position relative to the plate by taking a slow practice swing and making sure the sweet spot of the bat touches the ball on top.

Standard stack

Beginner stack—two stackers used together—gives more distance between balls for younger athletes

Double stack for inside and outside pitches—advanced

Triple stack—very advanced

3. On the coach's cue, the batter strides with proper backside rotation, executes a proper swing, and hits the top ball off the Tee Stacker into the screen or backstop. Although the batter should hit the ball on top, and not the Tee Stacker, the force of the hit will knock the Tee Stacker off and allow the batter to hit the next ball.

4. Repeat for the second ball.

Advanced Variations

- Multiple Tee Stackers can be used to either increase or decrease the distance between the balls, as well as the number of balls hit off the tee in one sequence.

- **Stacker Snapbacks.** Have the batter do *snapbacks* of up to three stacked balls off the tee, more if you set up inside/outside tees. Snapbacks are swings executed in rapid succession without sacrificing proper mechanics. Many hitters get a little long in their swings when they get tired; this will help build endurance and give immediate feedback if their swing is getting long. Practicing snapbacks will help improve hand and bat head speed.

Hints

The Tee Stacker is a neat little device Michele uses that allows batters to practice hitting softballs off the tee in rapid succession. A Tee Stacker allows up to three softballs to be stacked onto one tee without the balls touching each other. You can use the Tee Stacker to run any of the tee drills in this book more efficiently and make them more fun to do! The stackers are connected by string to one another, and a stacker can be temporarily fastened to the tee so it won't fly away even if a batter strikes it.

Coaches can also use the Tee Stacker to run fielding practices more efficiently. Using the Tee Stacker will allow the coach to hit grounders to fielders more quickly and accurately. Make sure the fielder is ready before hitting the next ball.

66. Stride/No Stride Tee (Beginner)

Purpose: To practice making the proper stride with backside rotation
Equipment: Batting tee, bat, supply of balls (softballs or Wiffle balls), masking tape or chalk to draw lines
Number of players: 1

Number of repetitions: 5 reps for 4 sets
Allocated time: 5 minutes per player
Parent-friendly drill: ✔
Cardio index: ❤

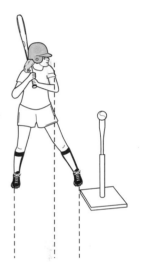

1. A batter wearing a batting helmet sets up in her batting position facing the backstop or screen, next to a batting tee as shown, set up around waist-high. A coach places a ball on the tee and steps a safe distance away.
2. The batter checks her position relative to the plate by taking a slow practice swing and making sure the sweet spot of the bat touches the ball on the tee.
3. The coach draws lines (line in dirt, chalk or paint in grass, masking tape) or places markers shoulder-width apart to help the player position her feet, and a third line or marker indicating about where the player should stride out during her swing. The coach steps a safe distance away.
4. On the coach's cue, the batter rotates on her back foot, strides forward (and slightly into the strike zone) with proper backside rotation, and lands on the stride line as she swings the bat with proper swing mechanics, hitting the ball into the backstop or screen.

Advanced Variations

- **Changeup Stride Tee.** Make sure the stride leg is down, then have the batter swing. This simulates a response to a changeup.
- **Foot Pickup Tee.** Have batters who constantly overstride try to pick their foot up and bring it straight down in the same spot instead of striding out.
- **No Stride Tee.** Have the batter execute her backside rotation correctly without taking a stride. This is also called a squat hitting drill and helps the batter use the upper body correctly (helps prevent overrotation of the hips).

Hints

The term *stride* in softball parlance is somewhat of a misnomer. Encourage your players to take a *small, soft step* during their strides (no stomping; leave the "bug smashing" to the back leg). Some young players overstride in an anxious attempt to reach out to hit a slow pitch. The purpose of the stride is to enable the batter to shift her weight; the batter is not striding to go get the ball. For these players, or more advanced players who have difficulty hitting changeups or off-speed pitches, go to the drills in this chapter that teach them how to separate their stride (with hands back) from their swing. Even when not going after off-speed pitches, many junior players often take strides that are longer than necessary, and sometimes longer than those of their much taller college counterparts! A stride that is too long will cause a batter's weight to be on her front leg, and she will lose power. For some hitters, an overstride will actually cause their weight to be too far back, but this is not as common. Most young players who overstride develop the bad habit of hitting off their front leg.

Also watch out for the tendency of some novice players to take a three-step stride (front foot, back foot, and front foot). Draw a line and correct if the batter moves her back foot off the line.

Another culprit in a "swing and a miss" is a stride too far away from the side of the plate where the pitch is thrown, or "stepping in the bucket." In fast-pitch, batters have no time to do this. For batters who make this mistake, draw a perpendicular line to help the batter make her stride. Remember that striding slightly into the path of the ball is allowable.

67. Volleyball Stride Pinch Tee (Intermediate)

Purpose: To practice taking a small stride with proper backside rotation
Equipment: Batting tee, bat; deflated volleyball or soccer ball, squish bean bag, or batting helmet; supply of balls (softballs or Wiffle balls)
Number of players: 1

Number of repetitions: 5 reps for 4 sets
Allocated time: 3 to 5 minutes per player
Parent-friendly drill: ✔
Cardio index: ♥

1. A batter wearing a batting helmet sets up in her batting position facing the backstop or screen, next to a batting tee. A coach places a ball on the tee and steps a safe distance away.
2. The batter places a deflated volleyball (or soccer ball, squish bean bag, or batting helmet) between her thighs.
3. The batter checks her position relative to the plate by taking a slow practice swing and making sure the sweet spot of the bat touches the ball.
4. On a coach's cue, the batter strides with proper backside rotation, executes a proper swing, and hits the ball off the tee into the backstop or screen. The deflated ball should stay in position between her thighs.
5. The deflated ball will fall to the ground if the player lunges or overstrides.

Advanced Variation

Have the batter execute the drill off soft toss (coach or machine toss), and then once proficient, off coach pitch, player pitch, or machine pitch.

Hints

Have your batters think of being relaxed with the lower body. They should keep the legs relaxed and take short strides with good backside rotation of the hips. Even in linear hitting, the backside hip rotates, adding power to the swing. But remind players not to overrotate.

Jenn is checking her distance to the plate before doing the drill. If her stride is too long, the large ball held between her legs will drop to the ground.

68. Power Ball Tee (Beginner)

Purpose: To practice hitting through the ball with power

Equipment: Batting tee, bat, slightly deflated volleyball or soccer ball

Number of players: 1

Number of repetitions: 5 reps for 5 sets

Allocated time: 3 to 5 minutes per player

Parent-friendly drill: ✔

Cardio index: ♥

1. A batter wearing a batting helmet sets up in her batting position next to a batting tee.
2. A coach puts a slightly deflated volleyball or soccer ball on the tee and steps a safe distance away.
3. The batter checks her position relative to the plate by taking a slow practice swing and making sure the sweet spot of the bat touches the ball.
4. On the coach's cue, the batter strides with proper backside rotation, executes a proper swing, and hits the ball off the tee.
5. For players who hit weakly, have the player repeat the drill with more power until she gets some distance on the ball.

Advanced Variations

- Soft toss the balls to the batter.
- **Rapid-Fire Power Ball Tee.** Once proficient, toss five balls in quick succession to help build quick and explosive swings.

Hints

This is a power drill, but mechanics should not be sacrificed to gain power. The bottom, or extension, hand and wrist should be loose compared to the top hand, which drives through the ball. Make sure your players follow through on the swing with two hands. If your batter has problems with her extension, execute drill 70 (One- and Two-Hand Extension Tee).

69. Back Foot Pivot Tee (Beginner)

Purpose: To develop strong backside rotation, including a speedy rear foot pivot during the swing
Equipment: Bat, supply of balls (softballs or Wiffle balls)

Number of players: 1
Number of repetitions: 10 reps
Allocated time: 3 minutes per batter
Parent-friendly drill: ✔
Cardio index: ♥

1. A batter wearing a batting helmet sets up in her batting position next to a batting tee facing the backstop or screen.
2. A coach places a ball on the tee, and a softball next to the heel of the batter's rear foot, and steps a safe distance away.
3. On the coach's cue, the batter strides with proper backside rotation (pivoting and driving the back foot into the ground), executes a proper swing, and hits the ball off the tee into the backstop or screen.
4. Speedy rear-foot pivot action will cause the ball next to the batter's heel to roll with conviction. An improperly pivoted back foot (heel lifted too high) will not.

Advanced Variation

Have the batter execute the drill off soft toss, and once proficient, off coach pitch, player pitch, or machine pitch.

Hints

This drill helps a batter be aware of her back leg. Many hitters today will unlock the back leg and there will be some movement forward or off the ground at contact with the ball. This is fine. Not all players will "smash the bug" with the back leg. The main flaw the drill is designed to correct is a back leg that does not rotate at all because the hips do not engage in the swing.

70. One- and Two-Hand Extension Tee (Intermediate)

Purpose: To develop good bat extension technique—bottom "extension" hand (and wrists) looser than top hand, which drives through the ball

Equipment: Batting tee, Wiffle bat, regulation bat, supply of Wiffle balls and softballs

Number of players: 1

Number of repetitions: 10 with bottom hand, 10 with top hand, 10 with both hands

Allocated time: 5 minutes per batter

Parent-friendly drill: ✔

Cardio index: ♥

1. A batter wearing a batting helmet sets up in her batting position facing the backstop or screen, next to a batting tee, set up around waist-high.
2. A coach places a ball on the tee and steps a safe distance away.
3. The batter executes the drill with the bottom hand only and then top hand only using a Wiffle bat and ball, and finally with both hands using a regulation bat and softball.
4. On the coach's cue, the batter strides with proper backside rotation, executes a proper swing, and hits the Wiffle ball (if one hand) or softball (if two hands) off the tee into the backstop or screen.
5. When executing the drill with the bottom hand only, her hand and wrist are relaxed at the start to facilitate clean contact with the ball; as the swing starts, the grip on the bat will naturally tighten as the bat travels into the contact zone.
6. When executing the drill with the top hand only, make sure the palm of her hand is facing the ball on the tee (not facing up).
7. After the one-hand repetitions, repeat the drill with both hands using regulation equipment, combining the bottom and top hand techniques.

Advanced Variations

- Use special short bats made for one-handed drills.
- Use real balls for one-handed as well as the two-handed reps.
- Have the batter execute the drill off soft toss.
- Have the batter go down on one knee to direct all efforts only to the upper body. When doing this, the front knee should be on the ground to prevent hitting the front leg with the follow-through part of the swing.

Hints

Watch the batter's elbows during her swing. If she keeps them bent all the way through the swing, she may be pushing the barrel into the contact zone instead of executing a full extension. Pushing results in weak hits.

71. Rotation—Backside Isolation (Intermediate)

Purpose: To develop good backside rotation in isolation
Equipment: Tambourine or bell and string, or bat, and supply of balls
Number of players: 1
Number of repetitions: 10 reps for 2 sets

Allocated time: 5 minutes for whole team together
Parent-friendly drill: ✔
Cardio index: ⓥ

1. A batter wearing a batting helmet sets up in her batting position.
2. A coach secures a tambourine or bell to a piece of string about 1 foot long.
3. The batter holds the string with her bottom hand. Some coaches prefer that their batters hold a bat (hanging down) somewhat loosely between their thumbs and index fingers.
4. On the coach's cue, the batter strides with proper backside rotation while holding the string (or bat) as still as possible.
5. This drill isolates the lower-body movements of hitting mechanics. If the tambourine or bell rings (or the bat swivels), the batter may be lunging at the ball. Her stride is too long, and she has too much movement in her lower body.

Advanced Variation

Have your batter hold the bat barrel up between her thumb and index finger.

72. Rotation—Balance (Intermediate)

Purpose: To develop good backside rotation and balance in isolation
Equipment: Bat, wooden board as described in step 1
Number of players: 1

Number of repetitions: 10 reps for 3 sets
Allocated time: 5 minutes
Parent-friendly drill: ✔
Cardio index: ♥

1. A batter wearing a batting helmet sets up in her batting position standing on the balls of her feet on a wooden 2-by-6-inch board about 4 feet long (long enough to accommodate a shoulder-width stance and a small stride).
2. On a coach's cue, the batter strides with proper backside rotation and pivots her rear foot.
3. The batter executes this drill with her heels hanging over the edge of the board, but with good mechanics, she should be able to do the drill without losing her balance, falling off or striding off the board.

Advanced Variation

Have your players execute the drill by hitting a softball off the tee or off soft toss.

Hints

Make sure the batter is balanced before starting her swing. If she starts off balance, she will finish off balance.

4 ft.

73. Rotation—Balance Check (Intermediate)

Purpose: Self-diagnostic to check balance

Equipment: Bat

Number of players: 1

Number of repetitions: 25 reps for 2 sets; 1 minute rest between sets

Allocated time: 5 minutes for whole team doing it together

Cardio index: ♥ ♥

1. A batter wearing a batting helmet sets up in her batting position.
2. The batter strides with proper backside rotation and executes a proper swing.
3. The batter finishes her swing and immediately jumps straight up into the air with both feet.

Advanced Variations

- **Balance Weight Training.** Batters execute the drill wearing ankle weights for a good training and conditioning exercise.
- **One-Leg Balance.** The batter keeps all her weight on her back leg, with the front leg up, and takes a full cut off the tee while maintaining her balance. This drill helps batters learn what it feels like to keep their weight back and hit for power. Experienced players can do this drill off soft toss, front toss, or machine toss.
- **Uphill Dry Swing.** The batter gets into her batting position while standing on a shallow hill, with her front foot up the hill, and takes a dry swing (no bat). This drill reinforces the concept of keeping a batter's weight back and preventing a premature weight shift—that is, drifting forward too early before the swing. After swinging, the weight is evenly distributed in both feet. For this variation, the athlete should not jump after swinging. This drill can also be executed by having the batter get into her stance with her front foot on a two-by-four-inch piece of wood and taking either a dry swing or a swing of a real bat off the tee, again without jumping after her swing.

Hints

Proper mechanics result in the weight being evenly distributed in both feet after a normal swing. The batter should be able to quickly leap with both feet at the same time after the swing.

74. Extension—No Sweep (Intermediate)

Purpose: Self-diagnostic to check extension mechanics—helps to maintain compact, inside out swing

Equipment: Bat

Number of players: 1
Number of repetitions: 25 reps
Allocated time: 3 minutes
Cardio index: 🔻

1. A batter wearing a batting helmet sets up in her batting position facing a fence. The batter stands about one bat length away from the fence (measured abdomen to fence). Use an older bat if possible.
2. The batter strides with proper backside rotation and executes a proper swing without the bat touching the fence.

Advanced Variation

Snapbacks. Execute 5 reps of 5 sets of snapbacks without touching the fence. Snapbacks are swings executed in rapid succession without sacrificing proper mechanics. Many hitters get a little long in their swings when they get tired; this will help build endurance and give immediate feedback if their swing is getting long. Practicing snapbacks will help improve hand and bat head speed.

Hints

Make sure the batter's front arm forms a 90-degree angle at the elbow. This will help keep the swing short and compact. This is what keeps the bat from hitting the screen or fence.

75. Coach Pitch—Drop Zone (Beginner)

Purpose: To develop quick bat speed and hand-eye coordination
Equipment: Stepladder, bat, supply of balls
Number of players: 1
Number of repetitions: 10 reps for 2 sets

Allocated time: 3 to 5 minutes per batter
Parent-friendly drill: ✔
Cardio index: ♥

1. A batter wearing a batting helmet sets up in her batting position facing the backstop or screen.
2. A coach stands on a stepladder or on top of a sturdy bucket in the batting box opposite the batter and holds a ball over the strike zone.
3. The coach drops the ball.
4. The batter strides with proper backside rotation, executes a proper swing, and hits the ball into the backstop or screen.

Advanced Variations

- **Command.** Have your batter swing the bat high or low in the strike zone. Watch her mechanics.
- **Decision Making.** Add colored balls and tell the batter which ball color to hit. She should let the wrong colored balls go. This develops quick reaction decision-making skills.

Hints

Decision-making time will decrease and hand-eye coordination will increase with more reps. Even so, this might not translate into line-drive hits. Make sure your batters make contact with the middle of the ball. Most hitters will instinctively hit either the top of the ball (resulting in dribblers) or the bottom of the ball (resulting in pop-ups). Batters that naturally hit the bottom of the ball need to aim for the top of the ball, and batters that naturally hit the top of the ball need to aim for the bottom of the ball.

76. Coach Pitch—Soft Toss (Beginner)

Purpose: To work on a proper swing while hitting a moving ball
Equipment: Bat, supply of balls (softballs or Wiffle balls)
Number of players: 1

Number of repetitions: 20 reps for 3 sets
Allocated time: 5 to 7 minutes
Parent-friendly drill: ✔
Cardio index: ♥

1. A batter wearing a batting helmet sets up in her batting position facing the backstop or screen.
2. A coach kneeling (or sitting on a bucket) several feet to the side tosses a ball in the strike zone in front of the batter. The toss should be straight up and down, so that the ball "stops" at the apex before falling (simulates a ball on a tee).
3. The batter strides with proper backside rotation, executes a proper swing, and hits the ball into the backstop or screen.
4. The coach corrects any mechanical errors.

Advanced Variations

- **Changeup Soft Toss.** Have the batter stride on your command just prior to releasing the toss. This will force her to separate her stride from her backside rotation. Make sure she keeps her hands back during her stride. If her hands move forward during her stride, she will have to reload—and be late every time. Another changeup variation is to simply use two quick flicks of the wrist—the first, no-release (her cue to stride) and the second, release the ball (her cue to rotate and swing).
- **Breakdown Soft Toss.** Execute the drill using the top hand only and the bottom hand only. The bottom hand is used to explosively pull the bat to the ball for power. The top hand is used to drive through the ball. This drill will develop proper mechanics for each arm, as well as build forearm strength.
- **Front-Knee Soft Toss.** Execute the drill with the batter kneeling on the front knee to isolate upper-body mechanics. Have the batter choke up on the bat. Make sure her head moves from her front shoulder to her back shoulder during the swing; this keeps her head down.
- **Speed Stick.** Execute this drill using a lightweight speed stick (made by a variety of manufacturers). These are designed to develop bat speed.
- **Bat Behind Back Soft Toss.** A batter places a bat behind her back secured by her elbows and executes the drill by using proper backside rotation and driving her back leg into the ground.

Michele waits for the ball to pop up into the strike zone from the JUGS soft toss machine and uses good rotation to hit the ball into the screen. In the second frame, note how Michele drives her back leg into the ground. This is a great drill to reinforce the concept that hitting is about using your entire body, not just the arms.

- **Bat off Shoulder Soft Toss.** A batter does the drill by swinging the bat off her shoulder and immediately into the strike zone to make contact. She keeps her hands close to her body. This drill encourages compact, inside out swings by taking away the opportunity to drop the hands.
- **Soft Toss Machine.** An advanced player can execute this drill and any of these advanced variations by herself using a soft toss machine (made by a variety of manufacturers, including JUGS).

Hints

Proper tossing takes some practice, but try to make short tosses that travel straight up and down in front of the batter simulating where the ball should be when the batter hits it. When the ball reaches its peak, it should be as though it is sitting on a tee. This is the point at which the batter should hit the ball. Not on the way up or, as in the Coach Pitch—Drop Zone drill (drill 75), on the way down. Take care because incorrect tosses will actually hurt a batter's swing. Many young players and inexperienced coaches will incorrectly toss the ball *at* the batter from the side. The ball should never be tossed from the side toward the batter or at her hips.

77. Coach Pitch—Soft Toss Two Ball (Intermediate)

Purpose: Develops reaction time and hand-eye coordination
Equipment: Bat, supply of softballs or Wiffle balls
Number of players: 1

Number of repetitions: 10 reps for 2 sets
Allocated time: 3 to 4 minutes
Parent-friendly drill: ✔
Cardio index: ♥

Julia waits for Michele to toss both balls. She'll hit the one called by Michele. It's important to toss the ball up, not at the player. Julia should hit the ball at the apex, as if the ball were resting on top of a tee.

Julia waits for Michele to toss one of the spinning balls. This drill teaches batters to relax before swinging the bat.

1. A batter wearing a batting helmet sets up in her batting position facing the backstop or screen.
2. A coach kneeling (or sitting on a bucket) several feet to the side holds two balls of different colors and tosses them simultaneously in the strike zone in front of the batter. The toss should be straight up and down—one ball will be above the other when airborne.
3. The batter strides with proper backside rotation, executes a proper swing, and hits the color ball called by the coach into the backstop or screen.
4. The coach corrects any mechanical errors.

Advanced Variations

- Vary the space between the tossed balls; for this variation, use two hands to toss the balls. Try some far apart and some that are close together. Hitting the balls tossed closer together will be more challenging for the batter.
- **Spinning Soft Toss.** This variation teaches hitters to relax prior to the trigger. Execute the drill the same way, but rather than toss two balls, the coach spins two balls (medium speed spin in toward the coach) and tosses just one ball up and into the strike zone for the batter to hit. Remind your batters to focus on staying relaxed prior to the trigger; this will help them explode to the ball.

Hints

Good tosses take some practice; try to toss the balls in front of the batter vertically. If you're standing on the side and toss the ball horizontally from a direction that would be from foul territory, you are simulating a situation that the batter will never face in a game. A proper toss is one that is straight up and down so when it reaches its peak it looks as though it is sitting on a tee.

Resist the temptation to call out "High" or "Low." Rather call out the color of the ball to be hit. The batter can then focus on hitting the designated ball, rather than on your interpretation of high versus low.

78. Coach Pitch—High Toss (Beginner)

Purpose: To encourage patience on changeups and other slower pitches
Equipment: Bat, supply of balls
Number of players: 1
Number of repetitions: 10 reps for 3 sets

Allocated time: 5 minutes
Parent-friendly drill: ✔
Cardio index: ♥

1. A batter wearing a batting helmet sets up in her batting position facing the backstop or screen.
2. A coach kneeling (or sitting on a bucket) several feet to the side tosses a ball up to about the batter's head level above the strike zone in front of the batter.
3. The batter waits until the ball drops into the strike zone, strides with proper backside rotation, executes a proper swing, and hits the ball into the backstop or screen.

Hints

Like the regular soft toss, toss the ball vertically. Batters who swing too early hit the ball too far in front, and usually off the front tip of the bat (not the sweet spot). Remind the batter to stride first with hands back, then swing. If she strides and her hands drift forward, she'll have to reload. By then, it's usually too late.

79. Coach Pitch—Hit-N-Stik (Beginner)

Purpose: To develop hand-eye coordination
Equipment: Hit-N-Stik or equivalent, bat
Number of players: 1
Number of repetitions: 10 reps for 2 sets

Allocated time: 3 to 4 minutes per player
Parent-friendly drill: ✔
Cardio index: ♥

1. A batter wearing a batting helmet sets up in her batting position.
2. A coach holds a Hit-N-Stik by the handle so that the target (the ball-like knob) is in the strike zone.
3. On the coach's cue, the batter strides with proper backside rotation, executes a proper swing, and hits the target.
4. The coach corrects any mechanical errors.
5. Repeat, making sure to vary the target's location (inside, outside, high, low, etc.) in the strike zone.

Advanced Variation

Have the batter attempt to hit the target as you move it into the strike zone. Note that the Hit-N-Stik has a flexible shaft, so moving it horizontally may cause unrealistic, erratic up-and-down movements as well.

Hints

Use a Hit-N-Stik or other commercially available equivalent. Avoid using homemade stationary targets. The flexible shaft and handle of the Hit-N-Stik are designed to absorb some of the shock from impact. This protects the batter and the coach/parent holding the stick. The rubber-coated target knob is designed to prevent damage to the bat.

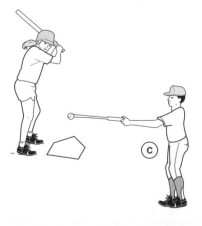

80. Coach Pitch—Front Toss (Beginner)

Purpose: Standard batting practice
Equipment: Bat, supply of balls, screen
Number of players: 4 (batter; outfielders to field the ball)
Number of repetitions: 10 reps for 3 sets

Allocated time: 5 to 7 minutes per player
Parent-friendly drill: ✔
Cardio index: ♥

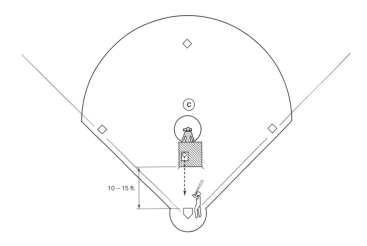

1. A batter wearing a batting helmet sets up in her batting position in the batter's box.
2. A coach standing 10 to 15 feet in front of the batter, and standing behind a screen, tosses a ball underhand for the batter to hit. The trajectory of the ball should be flat, not an arc like in slow-pitch softball.
3. The batter strides with proper backside rotation, executes a proper swing, and hits the ball.
4. The coach corrects any mechanical errors.

Advanced Variations

- **Front Toss Numbered Balls.** Execute the drill using balls with numbers written on them. Have the batter hit only even or odd numbers, and pitch at various speeds. This will make the batter have to think fast and react quickly.
- **Coach Pitch—Varying Speed Pitch Simulation.** Set up three home plates 16, 12, and 8 feet from the pitching circle. Even though a coach might not have the physical ability to simulate a very fast pitcher, she'll be able to work on a batter's timing by pitching to a batter who sets up to hit from these plates—the closer the plate is to the pitching circle,

the less time the batter will have to react, just like against a very fast pitcher. These are close distances, and it is imperative that the coach stand behind a protective screen. The coach should toss three pitches at each distance, for two sets and a total of 18 pitches to each player performing the drill. The player should start at the 16-foot distance, then go to the 12-foot plate, and finally the 8-foot plate. This drill will also help batters learn to stay back, keep their weight balanced, and keep their center of gravity in control.

- Toss changeups and high and low pitches to make the drill more gamelike.
- Throw the pitches on the inside and outside corners of the plate.

Hints

This drill is great for coaches to be able to see what their batters are doing right and wrong. The front view of a swing reveals the most about a batter's mechanics, including flaws. That is why good, aware pitchers can pick up a batter's weaknesses while pitching against her in games. Front toss is Michele's favorite hitting drill other than hitting against live pitching.

Encourage batters that tend to hit the bottom of the ball (pop-ups) to aim for the top of the ball, and batters that tend to hit the top of the ball (dribblers) to aim for the bottom of the ball. Line drives are best. Perhaps this is easier said than done, but practice makes perfect.

81. Coach Pitch—Bounce Toss (Intermediate)

Purpose: To practice hitting low pitches with proper timing; works on "trigger"
Equipment: Bat, supply of tennis or bouncy balls
Number of players: 1

Number of repetitions: 10 reps for 3 sets
Allocated time: 5 minutes per batter
Parent-friendly drill: ✔
Cardio index: ♥

1. A batter wearing a batting helmet sets up in her batting position facing the backstop or screen.
2. A coach standing several feet to the side (in front) and 5 to 6 feet away bounces a ball so that it enters the strike zone in front of the batter.
3. The batter loads or triggers by slightly bending the front knee just prior to striding when the ball bounces on the ground, not before that. She then strides with proper backside rotation, executes a proper swing, and hits the ball as it comes off the bounce and into the strike zone.
4. The coach corrects any mechanical errors.

Advanced Variation

Bounce the ball high and low. Also try bouncing the ball so it goes into the strike zone on the inside and outside corners of the plate.

Hints

This takes some practice, but try to bounce the ball so that the bounce isn't too vertical. The ball should bounce about 3 to 4 feet in front of home plate and bounce into the strike zone. The batter needs time to be able to load and swing. A bounce that is too vertical will not allow for this.

Make sure the batter's timing is correct. The load or trigger should take place when the ball bounces on the ground, not before or after.

The batter should use the same basic mechanics for low pitches as waist-level pitches. She should throw the knob of the bat at the ball toward the contact zone, which for a low pitch is lower than for a waist-level pitch, and make as level a swing as possible through the strike zone. She should resist the temptation to use her legs (bend her front knee) to go down in the zone to get the ball on low pitches. A slight bend of the knees or hips is OK, but you don't want to use your legs to go way down in the zone like you would do to bunt a low pitch. On the other hand, she shouldn't stand high and uppercut; she won't see the ball as well, making it harder to hit. And if she's lucky and hits it, it's likely to be an easily negotiable pop fly. That being said, on an outside pitch—low and out—the batter may at times have to use her legs to go down and stay low through it; otherwise the batter may miss the ball. Also, advanced batters facing known drop ball pitchers sometimes start a little lower, that is, make an adjustment in the stance before the actual swing.

Some coaches teach their players to move their arms down and then back up again as another form of trigger. This might not work so well for younger players because they might develop the habit of not bringing their arms back up, leading to a hitch or an uppercut. It's best to swing the bat directly into the strike zone from the shoulders.

82. Coach Pitch—Call 'm Toss (Advanced)

Purpose: To practice hitting low and high pitches; develops concentration and hand-eye coordination
Equipment: Bat, supply of balls with numbers or letters written on them
Number of players: 1

Number of repetitions: 15 reps for 2 sets
Allocated time: 5 minutes per batter
Parent-friendly drill: ✔
Cardio index: ♥

1. A batter wearing a batting helmet sets up in her batting position facing the backstop or screen.
2. A coach kneeling (or sitting on a bucket) several feet to the side randomly tosses any one of multiple balls numbered or lettered in permanent marker in the strike zone in front of the batter.
3. The batter strides with proper backside rotation, executes a proper swing, and hits the ball, simultaneously calling out the number or letter of the ball hit.
4. The coach corrects any mechanical errors.

Advanced Variations

- As the players become more proficient at the drill, use different colored markers and ask the batters to call out the color as well as the number or letter on the ball.
- Toss "balls" as well. The batter should call out the color and number or letter while not swinging.
- Use smaller balls, smaller numbers or letters, or a combination.

Hints

Hide the ball prior to tossing. Make sure your batters only swing at tossed strikes.

83. Coach Pitch—Blind Toss (Advanced)

Purpose: To develop quick reaction time, hand and bat speed, hand-eye coordination, and a short stride
Equipment: Bat, supply of balls (softballs or Wiffle balls)
Number of players: 1

Number of repetitions: 5 reps for 5 sets
Allocated time: 5 minutes per batter
Parent-friendly drill: ✔
Cardio index: ⊙

1. A batter wearing a batting helmet sets up in her batting position facing the backstop or screen.
2. A coach kneeling (or sitting on a bucket) several feet to the side, but behind the batter tosses a ball in the strike zone in front of the batter. If the batter is standing at the center of a clock, with the imaginary pitcher's mound at 12 o'clock, the coach will be positioned at about 4 o'clock.
3. As the ball comes into view, the batter strides with proper backside rotation, executes a proper swing, and hits the ball.
4. The coach corrects any mechanical errors. Overstriding, for example, will result in a "swing and a miss."

Advanced Variation

Shift from about 4 o'clock to about 5 o'clock relative to the batter to make the drill more difficult.

Hints

Make sure the batter does not cheat and look for the ball behind her. She should have her head forward and eyes looking as if the ball is coming from the pitcher. Make sure she keeps her head down during her swing.

84. Coach Pitch — Machine Gun Toss (Intermediate)

Purpose: To develop concentration and hand-eye coordination
Equipment: Bat, supply of balls
Number of players: 1
Number of repetitions: 5 reps for 5 sets

Allocated time: 5 minutes per batter
Parent-friendly drill: ✔
Cardio index: ♥ ♥

1. A batter wearing a batting helmet sets up in her batting position facing the backstop or screen. The batter will not stride as part of her swing, so the batter steps out to stride distance with the appropriate leg, making sure to pivot the stride foot as and when necessary.
2. A coach kneeling (or sitting on a bucket) several feet to the side tosses five balls in rapid succession in the strike zone in front of the batter.
3. The batter executes proper backside rotation and a proper swing and hits the ball.
4. The batter snaps back her bat into proper position, ready to hit the next tossed ball.
5. The coach corrects any mechanical errors.

Advanced Variations

- Toss balls high and low, inside and outside.
- **Ten Toss.** Toss balls in sets of ten. Be sure the player uses proper mechanics even when tired.

Hints

Your batters should relax and not rush the drill just to hit every ball. They should hit as many as possible quickly but using correct mechanics. Make sure the timing of the tosses is correct. Too slow and the drill is too easy, too fast and the batter will rush the swing and her form will break down. A good rule of thumb is to toss when the batter is midway through her snapback.

85. Coach Pitch—Changeup Simulation (Intermediate)

Purpose: To practice response to changeups	**Number of repetitions:** 20 reps
	Allocated time: 3 to 4 minutes
Equipment: Bat, ball	**Parent-friendly drill:** ✔
Number of players: 1	**Cardio index:** ♥

1. A batter wearing a batting helmet sets up in proper batting position facing a coach standing 20 feet away.
2. The coach, standing behind a screen, simulates a pitch by winding up and presenting one of two colored balls (one representing a fastball and the other representing a changeup).
3. For fastballs, the batter strides with proper backside rotation and immediately executes a proper swing.
4. For changeups, the batter strides and calls out "changeup," and then takes a swing with proper backside rotation. Calling out helps the batter identify the pitch and recognize that she will have to time the start of her swing correctly to make contact. The batter needs to adjust the timing of the swing just enough to negotiate the slightly slower pitch.
5. The coach corrects any mechanical errors.

Advanced Variations

- Mix in three different colored balls for fastball, changeup, and off speed. The off-speed pitch is not as slow as a changeup, but not as fast as a fastball either.
- Mix in different colored balls also for drop balls and rise balls. Then allow the hitter to swing at drop balls only, but not at the rise or any other variation of pitches.

Hints

Remind your batters to keep their hands back while they stride during a changeup.

This is a great drill to use when scouting pitchers your team has not hit off of very often. Simulating the types of pitches your opponent throws will be like getting practice at bats off her and makes you and your team more game ready.

86. Coach Pitch — Changeup Hesitation (Intermediate)

Purpose: To practice changeup hitting mechanics
Equipment: Bat, supply of balls
Number of players: 1
Number of repetitions: 10 reps for 2 sets

Allocated time: 4 to 5 minutes per batter
Parent-friendly drill: ✔
Cardio index: ♥

1. A batter wearing a batting helmet sets up in her batting position facing the backstop or screen.
2. A coach kneeling (or sitting on a bucket) several feet to the side simulates a fastball by winding up and tossing a ball in the strike zone in front of the batter. The toss should be straight up and down so that the ball "stops" at the apex before falling (simulates a ball on a tee).
3. To simulate a changeup, the coach winds up and presents the ball without releasing it. This is the batter's cue to stride (keeping her hands back) and will force the batter to separate her stride from her backside rotation. After presenting the ball, the coach recoils the wrist and quickly tosses the ball in the strike zone in front of the batter.
4. The batter strides with proper backside rotation, executes a proper swing, and hits the ball. The coach corrects any mechanical errors.

Advanced Variations

- Execute this drill by having the coach stand in front of the batter about 15 feet away, as in regular coach front pitch. The coach should stand behind a protective screen in this case. Some batters will be able to adjust to the changeup simply by watching the coach's arm, which is different from identifying a slower pitch in a game using depth perception. Therefore, mix in slower tosses while having the same arm movements as the fastball tosses. (This is hard for most coaches to do since real changeups require the pitcher to use the same arm movements as a fastball but then relies on a deeper grip to slow the ball down.) This requires the batter to use her eyes to judge the pitch speed.
- Have your fast hitters work on reacting to changeups by sneak bunting the pitch. Most defensive corners are set up back and are back on their heels when changeups are thrown.

Hints

Be sure the batter's movements are quiet and not jerky. Jerky swings at changeups will take away power. Also, tell batters to always try to think about hitting changeups to the opposite field. This will keep their hands inside out and allow the pitch to get deeper into the contact zone.

87. Live Pitch—Dry Swing (Intermediate)

Purpose: To develop pitch-reading skills and concentration
Equipment: Softball
Number of players: 3 (batter, pitcher, and catcher in full gear)
Number of repetitions: As many pitches as possible during pitching workouts

Allocated time: Any amount of time during pitching practice
Cardio index: ♥ ♥ ♥ (for the pitcher)

1. A batter with no bat wearing a batting helmet sets up in her batting position in the batter's box.
2. A pitcher throws a fastball pitch from the pitching rubber to a catcher in her ready stance behind the plate, using all steps of the fast-pitch motion—including pre-motion, motion, and follow-through.
3. The batter reads the pitch, and if the pitch is anywhere in the strike zone, the batter takes a *dry swing* at the pitch, incorporating her stride and proper backside rotation. A dry swing is simply swinging at a pitch without a bat in the hitter's hands. This helps the batter see more live pitches.
4. The coach can act as umpire and indicate if the batter's determination is correct.

Advanced Variations

- Have hitters do the drill while advanced pitchers are working on advanced pitches.
- Do "at bats" where the pitcher and catcher are calling balls and strikes against the hitter as in a game situation. This drill is great for both the pitcher and the hitter. The pitcher will be able to see which pitches are effective at fooling hitters and which ones are not. The hitters will get to see live gamelike tactical pitching.

Hints

This is a great drill to use indoors during the off-season and on rainy days. Having the opportunity to see gamelike pitching year round will give your hitters an advantage. This is another one of Michele's favorite drills as a hitter and a pitcher. As a pitcher it tells her what her pitches are doing and which ones are fooling batters.

88. Live Pitch—Call Location (Advanced)

Purpose: To develop pitch-reading skills and concentration
Equipment: Bat (optional), softball
Number of players: 3 (batter, pitcher, and catcher in full gear)

Number of repetitions: 10 pitches for 2 sets
Allocated time: 5 minutes per batter
Cardio index: ♥ ♥ ♥ (pitcher)

1. A batter wearing a batting helmet sets up in her batting position in the batter's box.
2. A pitcher throws a fastball pitch from the pitching rubber to a catcher in her ready stance behind the plate, using all steps of the fast-pitch motion—including pre-motion, motion, and follow-through.
3. The batter reads the pitch and shouts "In" if the pitch is an inside strike and "Out" if the pitch is an outside strike. Simultaneously, the batter takes her stride and executes proper backside rotation, but doesn't swing if she has a bat in her hands. She can do the drill without a bat, and in that case, she can dry swing at the pitch while calling out the pitch location.
4. The coach can act as umpire and indicate if the batter's determination is correct.

Advanced Variations

- Execute the drill using a pitching machine for increased repetitions.
- **Call the Pitch Grid.** Have the batter execute the drill closer to the backstop (no catcher). Secure a tarp behind the batter with a numbered three-foot-by-three-foot grid pattern of the strike zone consisting of inside-low, inside-middle, inside-high, middle-low, middle-middle, middle-high, outside-low, outside-middle, outside-high. The batter calls out the grid coordinate the pitch hits.

Specialty Hitting Drills

89. Bunt — Basic (Beginner)

Purpose: To practice bunt mechanics
Equipment: Bat, supply of balls
Number of players: 1
Number of repetitions: 10 reps for 3 sets

Allocated time: 5 to 7 minutes per player
Parent-friendly drill: ✔
Cardio index: ♥

1. A batter wearing a batting helmet sets up in her batting position in the batter's box. Make sure the batter's initial position in the box is the same as if she were contemplating a regular hit; otherwise she'll telegraph her intentions.
2. The batter gives a signal to acknowledge an imaginary third-base coach's bunt signal and steps back into the box.
3. A coach standing (behind a screen) 15 to 20 feet in front of the batter tosses a ball for the batter to bunt.
4. The batter bunts the ball using the following *bunt mechanics*:

   - She pivots her front foot and takes a full step forward with her back foot and plants it in front of (and shoulder-width apart from) her forward foot. (Right-handed batters step forward with the right foot, and left-handed batters step forward with the left foot.)
   - She keeps her weight forward; both feet are now in front of home plate, but the batter must not step on home plate (this is an automatic out).
   - For right-handed hitters, the right foot should now be slightly in front of the left foot, or more toward the pitcher. For left-handed hitters, the left foot should be more forward. This will keep the bunter's weight forward and make it easier to get bunts down in fair territory.
   - While stepping forward, the batter slides her top hand up the bat (to just before but not on the barrel) for control, keeping her fingers behind the bat to prevent injury. She should angle the bat slightly upward. Her bottom hand stays at the bottom of the bat. The batter is now in her *bunt stance*.
   - She keeps her arms relaxed with her elbows slightly bent and bunts the ball by "catching" it with the bat.
   - She tries to lay the bunt in the *bunt arc* 5 to 8 feet from home plate.

Michele likes to step around rather than pivot on her bunts. Note that her top hand is behind the bat for protection and that the bat is slightly angled up to help bunt the ball down. Angling the bat up slightly also helps to prevent foul pops — remember that most softball pitches rise.

5. The batter sprints toward first base, stopping partway, and returns for her next repetition.

Advanced Variation

Place buckets or hoops on the bunt arc for the players to bunt into. This will force the batters to relax their arms and catch the ball with the bat.

Hints

Most of the time batters take the bunt sign while outside the batter's box. Make sure the batter does not telegraph the bunt as she sets up in the batter's box. Otherwise, this will give the pitcher and infielders more time to react. On the other hand, the batter shouldn't make a sudden jerky move to get from her ready stance into the bunt stance. There is no need to panic, and there's plenty of time. The batter should *step around* into bunt stance early, but only after the pitcher has started her windup.

Remind your batters to keep their weight forward. This will increase their chances of bunting into fair territory, plus get them out of the batter's box toward first base more quickly.

The batter's arms should be relaxed and act as shock absorbers to put down a soft bunt inside the bunt arc. Some coaches encourage their batters to bunt up to 10, even 15 feet away from the plate. While it's true that a bunt hit too close to home plate can be fielded easily by the catcher, experienced defensive corners will usually pick up anything more than 5 feet out, jeopardizing the lead runner at second base.

Many coaches teach their players the *bunt pivot method*—to stand slightly forward in the box when they know they will bunt and to pivot both feet almost as though the player is on a balance beam (rather than bringing the back foot forward). However, standing slightly forward in the box will telegraph the bunt to more experienced defenses. Bunters who employ the bunt pivot sometimes pivot and bring their bats around stiffly and suddenly. This may cause foul bunts, leaving the batter with only two strikes to try to get it down. Or a stiff pivot may cause the batter to hit the ball right to the defensive corners, rather than "catch the ball" and lay down a soft bunt in the bunt arc. It's also harder to bunt outside pitches with the pivot.

A note to all you baseball coaches out there: angling the bat up slightly to bunt a fast-pitch softball is better than keeping the bat level. For example, baseball does not have the rise ball, a pitch that moves up through the zone. The softball batter must angle the bat slightly up to bunt the rise ball down.

Remind your players that the bunt is only as effective as the effort they put into exploding to first base; they should sprint to first base no matter where the bunt lands. Step 5 (explosive sprint partway to first base) will build the muscle memory to explode to first. For example, don't assume that just because it's a pop-up it's going to be caught, or if it rolls toward foul territory, that it won't roll back in.

90. Bunt — Barehand Catch (Beginner)

Purpose: To develop technique for "catching the ball with the bat" to lay down soft bunts
Equipment: Supply of Wiffle balls
Number of players: 1
Number of repetitions: 10 reps for 3 sets

Allocated time: 5 to 7 minutes per player
Parent-friendly drill: ✔
Cardio index: ♥

1. A batter wearing a batting glove and batting helmet sets up in her batting position in the batter's box. Make sure the batter's initial position in the box is the same as if she were contemplating a regular hit; otherwise she'll telegraph her intentions.
2. A coach standing 10 to 15 feet in front of the batter tosses a Wiffle ball to the batter.
3. The batter gets into her bunt stance and catches the ball with her dominant hand.

Advanced Variation

Throw pitches high in the zone to simulate rise balls, and low in the zone to simulate drop balls. Drop balls are difficult to bunt fair, so make sure your advanced players practice this as advanced pitchers will throw drops as well as rise balls in bunt situations.

Hints

The batter should be aware of her footwork during this drill. She should keep her hands up and go down to get low pitches by bending her knees.

91. Bunt—Low Pitch (Intermediate)

Purpose: To practice bunt mechanics against low pitches
Equipment: Bat, supply of balls
Number of players: 1
Number of repetitions: 10 reps for 3 sets

Allocated time: 5 to 7 minutes per player
Parent-friendly drill: ✔
Cardio index: ♥

Here Michele demonstrates the proper way to bunt a low pitch. She brings the bat down by lowering her entire body using her knees. This way she's better able to keep the ball in her line of sight. Jenn demonstrates the improper way to handle a low pitch by lowering only her bat. See how far Jenn's eyes are from the contact point.

1. A batter wearing a batting helmet sets up in her batting position in the batter's box. Make sure the batter's initial position in the box is the same as if she were contemplating a regular hit; otherwise she'll telegraph her intentions.
2. A coach standing (behind a screen) 15 to 20 feet in front of the batter tosses a ball low in the strike zone for the batter to bunt.
3. The batter bunts the ball using basic bunt mechanics.
4. For pitches low in the strike zone, the batter bends her knees and uses her legs to lower herself, rather than lowering only her arms. The bat stays at a slightly upward angle.
5. The batter sprints toward first base, stopping partway, and returns for her next repetition.

Advanced Variations

- Throw some "balls" and also some pitches that bounce in the dirt. The batter should only bunt strikes.
- **"And Run."** Have the batter do squeeze plays, or "and run" plays, for example, bunt and run, hit and run, slap and run, etc. During "and run" plays, the batter must bunt the ball no matter where the pitch is because the runner on base is running like a steal and the batter has to cover the runner.

Hints

Make sure the batter sees the ball make contact with the bat and sees the ball down. It's important to use the legs to lower the body when going after pitches low in the strike zone. Lowering only the arms or angling the bat down takes her eyes farther from the point of contact and makes the ball harder to see.

Remind your batters to stay off high pitches or pitches above their arms and bats. If the batter has already planted or is about to plant her back foot in front of her front foot and the pitch comes in high, she should pull the bat back and not bunt or hit it. The only time she should try to bunt or hit a "ball" is when it is an "and run" where the batter is covering the runner as described in the And Run variation of this drill.

92. Bunt—Outside Pitch (Intermediate)

Purpose: To practice bunt mechanics against outside pitches

Equipment: Bat, supply of balls

Number of players: 1

Number of repetitions: 10 reps for 3 sets

Allocated time: 5 to 7 minutes per player

Parent-friendly drill: ✔

Cardio index: ♥

1. A batter wearing a batting helmet sets up in her batting position in the batter's box. Make sure the batter's initial position in the box is the same as if she were contemplating a regular hit; otherwise she'll telegraph her intentions.
2. A coach standing (behind a screen) 15 to 20 feet in front of the batter tosses a ball outside in the strike zone for the batter to bunt.
3. The batter bunts the ball using basic bunt mechanics.
4. For outside pitches in the strike zone, the batter should be very aware of having most of her weight on her front foot. This will allow her to lean toward the outside corner and have full plate coverage to bunt the ball.
5. Right-handed batters will use this method to get out of the box faster. Left-handed batters must get a good push off the front leg after the ball is bunted down in order to have an explosive first step toward first base.
6. The batter sprints toward first base, stopping partway, and returns for her next repetition.

Advanced Variation

Every once in a while throw a pitch on the opposite corner to keep your players honest. It is easy to play the game when you know what is coming. Keep them guessing and therefore reacting.

Hints

Make sure the batter is bunting only strikes!

93. Bunt — Push Bunt (Intermediate)

Purpose: To practice push bunt mechanics (used against very aggressive defenses that tend to overcharge in bunt situations—a good push bunt will be pushed past the charging defensive corners for a base hit)

Equipment: Bat, supply of balls

Number of players: 1
Number of repetitions: 10 reps for 3 sets
Allocated time: 5 to 7 minutes per player
Parent-friendly drill: ✔
Cardio index: ♥

1. A batter wearing a batting helmet sets up in her batting position in the batter's box. Make sure the batter's initial position in the box is the same as if she were contemplating a regular hit; otherwise she'll telegraph her intentions.
2. A coach standing (behind a screen) 15 to 20 feet in front of the batter tosses a ball for the batter to bunt.
3. The batter bunts the ball using basic bunt mechanics.
4. However, instead of using her arms as shock absorbers to deaden the ball so that it is bunted into the bunt arc, the batter extends her arms forward in a pushing motion. When executed properly, the bunt should be pushed about 20 to 30 feet out from the batter's box. This will push the ball past the charging corners.
5. The batter sprints toward first base, stopping partway, and returns for her next repetition.

Advanced Variation

Put cones up in the shortstop and second-base positions. This is the area the push bunt should be aimed at. Work in defensive corners to see how well your batters are pushing. Keep the ball on the ground. A popped-up push bunt is an easy double play.

Hints

Try to avoid pushing the ball to the pitcher. Good-fielding pitchers will be able to make an easy double play on a push bunt hit directly at them.

94. Bunt—Bunt for Base Hit (Intermediate)

Purpose: To practice bunting for a base hit (sneak bunt is used in situations where the defensive corners are playing too deep, or for very fast runners)
Equipment: Bat, supply of balls
Number of players: 1

Number of repetitions: 10 reps for 3 sets
Allocated time: 5 to 7 minutes per player
Parent-friendly drill: ✔
Cardio index: ⊙

1. A batter wearing a batting helmet sets up in her batting position in the batter's box. Make sure the batter's initial position in the box is the same as if she were contemplating a regular hit; otherwise she'll telegraph her intentions.
2. A coach standing (behind a screen) 15 to 20 feet in front of the batter tosses a ball for the batter to bunt.
3. The batter bunts the ball using basic bunt mechanics.
4. However, the batter brings her back foot forward and slides her hands up the bat as late as possible to hide the bunt from the defense.
5. The batter sprints toward first base, stopping partway, and returns for her next repetition.

Advanced Variations

- **Right-Handed Sneak Bunt.** A right-handed hitter can employ a sneaky bunt from the right side where rather than taking the normal step forward with her back foot, the batter will actually step back with her back (right) foot. (This is not a right-handed hitter turning around to the left side for slap hitting.) Once the back foot is down and planted, she pushes off the ground while striding toward first base. She should bunt the ball down as she comes through the strike zone. This is a timing play; too early and the batter leaves the box before the ball is in the contact zone, too late and she bunts the ball foul or is slow out of the box.
- **Left-Handed Pivot Sneak Bunt.** A left-handed sneak bunter can use a method (from her normal no-telegraph position in the batter's box) where she only squares the upper body (the legs pivot; the back leg does not come forward) and does so very late. This late movement gives the defense little time to charge the ball and make the play.

Hints

Make sure the batter hides the sneak bunt as long as possible. Showing the movement too early will allow the defense to adjust and make the play.

95. Bunt — Third-Base Squeeze Play (Beginner)

Purpose: To practice bunting with a runner on third base

Equipment: Bat, supply of balls

Number of players: 5 (batter, first- and third-base players, runner at third base, catcher in full gear)

Number of repetitions: 10 reps for 3 sets

Allocated time: 5 to 7 minutes per player

Parent-friendly drill: ✔

Cardio index: ♥ ♥

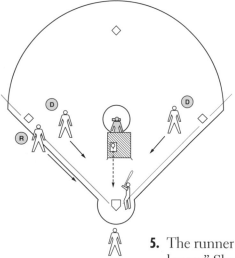

1. A batter wearing a batting helmet sets up in her batting position in the batter's box. Make sure the batter's initial position in the box is the same as if she were contemplating a regular hit; otherwise she'll telegraph her intentions.
2. A coach standing (behind a screen) 15 to 20 feet in front of the batter tosses a ball.
3. The batter bunts the ball using proper bunt mechanics. She should step around as late as possible to keep from telegraphing the play.
4. The batter sprints partway toward first base and returns for her next repetition, taking care not to interfere with the action on the third-base line.
5. The runner at third base is fully committed on a squeeze play to "go for home." She takes her lead and sprints toward home. If the batter misses the ball, the runner tries to get in a "*pickle*" (a rundown—see drill 53) and work toward being safe or eliciting a defensive error.
6. When the batter bunts the ball, the defensive players field the bunt and make the play at home or first base (even as the bunter returns for her next repetition).

Advanced Variation

Use *pitchouts* (a pitch thrown to the batter's box high and opposite the batter's shoulder to enable the catcher to more efficiently throw an advancing runner out) and have the batters still try to make contact. If the batter misses, play it out and let the defense try to get the runner heading toward home out. Most times a pickle play will ensue. A good defense should be able to run down the runner for an out.

Hints

The batter is protecting the runner who is "going" on the pitch. If the batter misses or does not bunt the ball, the runner will surely be out. Therefore, the batter must try to make contact with anything on a squeeze play—a strike, ball, pitchout, anything!

96. Bunt—Fake-Out (Beginner)

Purpose: To practice the fake bunt with base runners on first and second base (fake-outs are meant to confuse the catcher's defensive reaction—also used to see defense positioning for a bunt)
Equipment: Bat, supply of balls
Number of players: 8 (batter; first-, second-, and third-base players; shortshop; runners at first and second base; catcher in full gear)
Number of repetitions: 10 reps for 2 sets
Allocated time: 5 minutes per player
Parent-friendly drill: ✔
Cardio index: 💛 💛 (for runners)

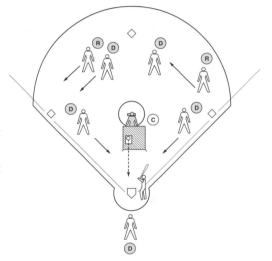

1. A batter wearing a helmet sets up in the batter's box. Make sure the batter's initial position in the box is the same as if she were contemplating a regular hit; otherwise she'll telegraph her intentions.
2. A coach standing (behind a screen) 15 to 20 feet in front of the batter tosses a ball for the batter to bunt.
3. The batter gets into her bunt stance using proper bunt mechanics.
4. Instead of bunting, the batter brings the head of the bat back toward the catcher as the ball passes the plate, making no contact with the ball.
5. The runners at first and second take off once the ball is released by the pitcher. Be sure to understand the rules of the league your team is playing in. For example, some league rules state that the runner cannot leave the base until after the ball crosses home plate.
6. The third-base player is charging, so the shortstop covers third base.
7. The catcher tries to throw out one of the runners, preferably the lead runner going to third.

Advanced Variation

Some coaches like the batter to attempt to bunt and miss intentionally to make the defense think on the run. Have your batter try a fake slap (see drill 97) at the ball as well; the shortstop will have to make sure the play is not a slap-and-run. This slight hesitation might create just enough time for the second-base runner to beat the shortstop to third base for the steal.

Hints

The batter should try to keep the bat head in the line of sight of the catcher. This makes it much harder for the catcher to see the ball into her glove. It also will keep her from seeing that the runners are stealing.

97. Slap Hitting—Basic (Advanced)

Purpose: To practice slap-hitting technique (used to get speedy left-handed hitters—or right-handed hitters who are able to hit from the opposite batter's box—on base by hitting the ball between third base and the shortstop with a running start)

Equipment: Bat, supply of balls

Number of players: 5 (batter; station infielders—to field the ball and work on defending against slappers)

Number of repetitions: 10 reps for 3 sets

Allocated time: 5 to 7 minutes per player

Parent-friendly drill: ✔

Cardio index: ♥ ♥

1. A batter wearing a batting helmet sets up in her batting position in the batter's box (opposite to the normal side for right-handed hitters), slightly toward the back of the box. Some batters like to choke up slightly on the bat. The arms and hands should be kept about shoulder height so a proper short swing can be attempted.

2. A coach standing (behind a screen) 15 to 20 feet in front of the batter tosses a ball for the batter to hit.

3. The batter triggers by lifting and then putting down her front foot (always her right foot) and takes the first step of her sprint by crossing over her back foot (always her left foot) toward the front line of the box, landing it her normal stride length away. This step is explosive. If no swing is attempted, the path of the batter should be toward the pitcher (not first base).

4. Unlike a bunt, only the batter's lower body is open to the pitcher at this point; the upper body is still parallel to the pitcher's power line (see Chapter 6).

5. In one smooth motion, the batter hits the ball by taking a medium-strength swing. At contact, most of her weight should be on her left foot. After contact she takes the second step of her explosive sprint toward first base with her right foot.

6. The batter sprints toward first base, stopping partway, and returns for her next repetition.

Advanced Variation

Outside Pitch Slap Hit. Throw pitches on the outside corner to keep the batter from running out of the box too early. Many young slappers try to get down the line before making contact with the ball. For advanced batters, throw in changeups to keep the batters working on their timing of the pitch.

The second frame shows right-handed Morgan triggering a slap hit from the left side of the plate by lifting and later putting down her front foot. The third through seventh frames show Morgan crossing over her back foot toward the front line of the box and then slapping the ball. Note how she keeps her head down looking at the contact zone throughout the sequence.

Hints

Slap hits work best when the batter hits a medium-strength grounder between third base and the shortstop, so encourage your batters to swing at a slight downward angle and a little bit late (but we're talking milliseconds, when the ball is deeper in the strike zone). Balls hit to the left side of the field give the slapper more time to get down the line to first base due to the longer throw from the left side of the infield. Balls hit to the right side can also be difficult to defend if the slapper deadens the ball. This will make the right-side fielders have to charge the ball away from first base, pick up the ball, stop, and then turn around to make a good throw to first base, which is now behind them.

Another tip is to let your batter release her top hand on the follow-through. Normally, the top hand helps to power the ball, while the bottom hand acts as a guide. Slap hitting is not power hitting, and releasing her top hand on the follow-through will not hurt her swing, but will actually help free up her arms. Instead, she'll use the power of her arms to sprint to first base.

Although the slap hit is executed with a running start, remind your batter not to be overanxious. Her first step is actually toward the pitcher, and she runs in the direction of first base only upon bat-ball contact. If she attempts to break toward first base prematurely, that is, on her first step, she'll miss the ball entirely.

98. Slap Hitting—Power Slap (Advanced)

Purpose: To practice slap-hitting technique executed with power when the defense plays in

Equipment: Bat, supply of balls

Number of players: 2 (batter and catcher in full gear)

Number of repetitions: 10 reps for 3 sets

Allocated time: 5 to 7 minutes per player

Parent-friendly drill: ✔

Cardio index: ♥ ♥

1. A batter wearing a batting helmet sets up in her batting position in the batter's box. Make sure the batter's initial position in the box is the same as if she were contemplating a regular hit.
2. A coach standing (behind a screen) 15 to 20 feet in front of the batter tosses a ball for the batter to hit.
3. The batter rotates her upper body to show she will bunt.
4. As the ball approaches, she rotates her body back to her normal launch position and promptly swings the bat and hits the ball.
5. The batter sprints toward first base, stopping partway, and returns for her next repetition.

Advanced Variation

Have the batter work on bunting some of the balls and then power slapping some of the balls. This will help blend the two forms and make it harder for the defense to read what the batter is actually going to do.

Hints

The batter should make it look like she might attempt to bunt. This will pull the corners in, making it easier to power slap the ball past them. To draw in the defense even more, show bunt with the hands and bat as well.

The batter should fully rotate the upper body back into a good hitting position. If the hands get back too late to the back shoulder, the batter will lose power. Also, once the hands get back, there should be no pause; the hands should promptly start moving forward in the swing toward the ball. If the pitch is a ball, then she should stop the hands at this point. If the hands are moving from forward to back and then forward again with no stop, there is less opportunity for the batter to drop her hands. This is a great drill for hitters who have a tendency to drop their hands because it keeps their hands moving only forward and backward.

Baserunning

Because the act of running around the bases seems so self-evident, baserunning is often given short shrift in the compressed time frames of most practices. Yet aggressive baserunning, including good sliding, often determines the outcome of close games. In U12 ball, sliding is usually the area with the widest disparity in skill levels among players on the same team. Usually players that do it well were taught how to do it early. In a way, sliding is like swimming or skiing, that is, best learned before the player is old enough to be afraid to try it.

The drills in this chapter are designed to reinforce the following baserunning and sliding skills for players of all age groups:

- **Mechanics of baserunning and sliding.** The basic skills for base runners are explained and practiced.
- **Baserunning tactics.** Drills cover running tactics in response to game situations.
- **Advanced sliding techniques.** Drills teach pop-up slides and other advanced slides.

Mechanics of Baserunning

Proper running form is extremely important when running the bases. There are two components of good running form for every softball player to remember:

- **Path around the bases.** The runner should not be too wide on the turns—she should lean and use her arms to make tight turns. She should look for the base coach so there is no hesitation when advancing to the next bag.

Morgan uses her upper body and outside or right arm to keep herself on track as she turns across the bag.

- **Running form.** The athlete should run on the balls of the feet and not her heels. She should lift her knees high so when the balls of her feet hit the ground she can "claw" on the ground to propel herself forward. Her arms should pump from "cheek to cheek"—face cheek to buttock cheek. She should lean slightly forward with her head up at all times so she can see where she is headed.

Bent-Leg Slide

The runner must reach second, third, or home plate as quickly as possible without overshooting. The bent-leg slide is the standard and, if properly executed (together with the detachable bases typically used in junior softball), a safe way to achieve this task. Players should wear sliding pants or sliders and knee pads on the nonthrusting bent leg because that's the leg that touches the ground. In order to execute the bent-leg slide, the player should do the following:

- Sprint toward the bag; momentum is key (run full speed at all times—don't slow down; the sliding action will act as the brakes). Aggressive slides will get more safe calls from umpires than soft slides that look slower.
- Lower herself toward the ground when she is about 5 to 8 feet from the bag while in full stride—she should not jump into a sliding position.
- Thrust out the left leg or the top leg while the right leg is dropping toward the ground. This is the recommended form when the runner is sliding into second or third base and the throw is coming from the infield because it keeps her face pointed toward the outfield and away from the throw for safety. If the throw is coming from the outfield, she should try sliding with the right leg on top and the left leg dropping toward the ground. In this case, the player's face will now be toward the infield and away from the throw for safety.
- Bend the knee of the other leg at about a 90-degree angle so that the foreleg is tucked beneath the thrusted leg.
- While dropping to the ground, distribute her weight more on the bent-leg side of her body, with most of the weight on her buttocks. Players who cut up their knees have too much weight forward on the top of the leg and need to lean back more.
- Keep her back more or less flat against the ground to avoid a high tag.
- Keep her arms extended behind her head and off the ground (to prevent jamming her hands in the ground).
- Glide into the bag, touching it with her thrusted foot.

Here Katelyn is sliding into second base with the throw coming from the outfield. She slides with her right leg on top and the left leg dropping toward the ground. This will help Katelyn keep her face toward the infield and away from the throw.

A low profile will make it harder for the defensive player to make the tag out and will help to evenly distribute her weight to prevent abrasions and knee injuries. Once the runner slides successfully into the base, she should call time out if the bag has moved from its original position before retrieving and standing on the bag.

Most double plays are due to line drives being caught. If the line drive is caught, the runner should dive back to the bag, and if it gets past the fielders, she should advance to the next bag.

Chapter 5 Skills Matrix

Drill Number **Drill Title** — *Skills Reinforced* →

(Indented drills are "named" Advanced Variations)	Batter—Run Through First	Batter—Baserunning Decision Making	Runner—Baserunning Decision Making	Runner—Extra-Base Hit Decision Making	Defense—Against Baserunning	Runner—Tagging Up	Runner—Sliding	Runner—Sliding Situation	Second-Base Player—Short-Hop Fielding	Tag Out	Catcher—Tag Out
99. Run Through First Base	●										
100. Rounding First Base		●									
101. Runner Base Hit/Extra-Base Hit		●			●						
Follow-the-Leader Baserunning		●	●								
102. Runner First to Third				●		●					
Runners at First and Third				●							
103. Runner First to Third Against Defense				●	●						
Runners at First and Third Against Defense		●	●	●	●	●	●	●		●	
104. Runner Response to Fly Ball			●			●					
105. Bent-Leg Slide					●		●			●	
106. Pop-Up Slide							●	●		●	
Pop-Up Slide Against Defense					●		●	●	●	●	
107. Return-to-Bag Slide							●	●		●	
108. Back Door Rollover Slide							●	●		●	●

Baserunning Drills

99. Run Through First Base (Beginner)

Purpose: To practice running through first base

Equipment: Bat

Number of players: Multiple players

Number of repetitions: 5 reps for 2 sets

Allocated time: 5 minutes

Parent-friendly drill: ✔

Cardio index: ♥ ♥ ♥

1. A batter wearing a batting helmet sets up in her batting position at home plate.
2. A coach sets up as first-base coach, slightly off the foul line and about 5 to 8 feet beyond the bag.
3. On the coach's cue, the batter simulates an infield hit, drops her bat, and sprints to first base.
4. The runner looks for the first-base coach's "run through" signal.
5. The runner runs through the bag and slows down only after giving the first-base coach a high-five.

Advanced Variation

Have the runners check with a slight head turn into the field to see what the fielders have done with the ball. The runner will check to see if an error was committed or the ball was fielded cleanly. She can then decide whether to run through the bag or to turn and look for the possibility of advancing to the next bag.

Hints

Continue to have your players work on good running form. Bad form will translate into slow base runners.

100. Rounding First Base (Beginner)

Purpose: To practice rounding first base when the batter hits the ball to the outfield	**Number of repetitions:** 3 to 5 reps for 2 sets
	Allocated time: 5 minutes
Equipment: Bat, cones	**Parent-friendly drill:** ✔
Number of players: Multiple players	**Cardio index:** ♥ ♥ ♥

1. A batter wearing a batting helmet sets up in her batting position at home plate.
2. Position a coach at first base.
3. Position cones along the first-base foul line to help guide the runner around first base.
4. On the coach's cue, the batter simulates an outfield hit, drops her bat, and sprints to first base.
5. The first-base coach gives the signal for a possible extra-base hit, and the runner rounds first base. The runner should be listening for the coach and observing to see what the fielders are doing with the ball—all while running full speed.
6. As the runner approaches the bag, the first-base coach instructs the runner to "go" to second base or to "come back" to first base.

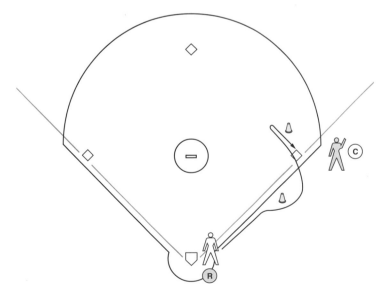

Advanced Variations

- Put a cone 5 feet from first base slightly outside the line from first base to second base so the runner has to turn tightly coming off first base.
- Have outfielders field a ball that a coach hits from the third-base foul line about 15 feet from home plate, and then throw to a shortstop positioned at second base to make the drill gamelike.

Hints

Have the runner use her upper body and outside or right arm to swing herself around as she turns across the bag; this will help keep her momentum from pulling her into right field and rounding the bag too wide.

101. Runner Base Hit/Extra-Base Hit (Beginner)

Purpose: To practice running through first base and to develop extra-base decision-making skills
Equipment: Supply of softballs
Number of players: 5 to 7 (base runner, first- and second-base players, shortstop, and 1 or more outfielders)
Number of repetitions: 3 to 5 reps for 2 sets
Allocated time: 3 to 5 minutes

Parent-friendly drill: ✔ A ball is not hit and there are no fielders in the parent-friendly variation. The parent acts as first-base coach, calls out an imaginary hit (for example, infield hit, outfield hit), and gives the appropriate instruction to the runner to run through the bag or to take a turn toward second base and then to go or come back.
Cardio index: ♥ ♥ ♥

1. The players assume their on-field positions as first- and second-base players, shortstop, and outfielders.
2. A runner wearing a batting helmet stands in the batter's box.
3. Position a coach at first base.
4. Another coach on the third-base line hits ground balls and fly balls of varying strength.
5. As soon as the ball is hit, the runner sprints toward first base.
6. The first-base coach instructs the runner as follows:

   - If a ground ball is hit to an infielder, the runner sprints through the bag, making sure not to slow down until after touching the bag.

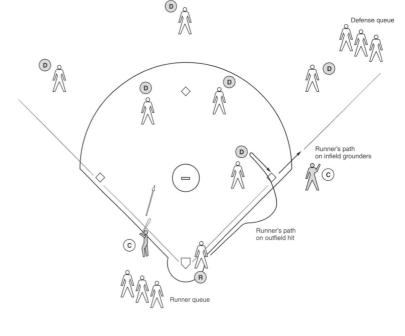

- If the ball is hit to the outfield, the runner sprints and rounds the bag. The first-base coach instructs the runner to go to second base or come back to first base, depending on how the ball is being fielded.

Advanced Variation

Follow-the-Leader Baserunning. Put a runner at first base to start and have the runner starting from home plate watch and follow what the lead runner is doing.

102. Runner First to Third (Intermediate)

Purpose: To practice baserunning from first into scoring position on extra bases hit

Equipment: Cones

Number of players: 1 or more base runners

Number of repetitions: 3 to 5 reps for 2 sets

Allocated time: 5 minutes

Parent-friendly drill: ✔

Cardio index: ♥ ♥ ♥

1. A runner wearing a batting helmet stands on first base. Other runners wait their turn.
2. Position a coach at third base.
3. Position cones along the base paths to help guide the runners.
4. On the coach's cue, the runner takes a two- or three-step lead (adapt this step to league rules).
5. On the next cue, the runner sprints to second base.
6. About two-thirds of the way to second base, the runner looks to the coach for the "hands up" signal to stop at second base or the signal to advance to third base.
7. If the coach signals to advance to third base, the runner rounds second base and slides into third base.

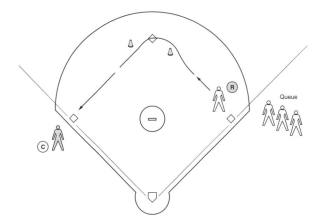

Advanced Variation

Runners at First and Third. Add a runner at third base with a batting helmet. In this drill, a coach near home plate actually hits the ball. As the coach winds up or tosses the ball to hit it, the runner at third takes a two- or three-step lead. The runner tags up as soon as the ball is hit in the air to the outfield. She advances to home plate only after the ball is caught or falls to the ground. Make sure the runner at first base watches what the runner at third is doing before attempting to advance to third.

Hints

Some third-base coaches prefer to get down on one knee when signaling the runner to slide into third base. Fielding ability in advanced play will not allow the runner any time to look over her shoulder to balls hit outside her line of vision (into right field) to decide what to do herself. The runner must learn to trust her third-base coach. Even in youth leagues, it's important to teach your players to trust the coach and only watch for the coach, never to watch or look for a ball behind her. When the ball is in front of her, it's OK to look, but only while running at full speed.

103. Runner First to Third with Defense (Intermediate)

Purpose: To practice baserunning from first into scoring position on extra bases hit and to practice defense against base runners
Equipment: Supply of softballs
Number of players: Multiple players (base runners, outfielders, second- and third-base players, and shortstop)
Number of repetitions: 3 to 5 reps for 2 sets
Allocated time: 5 minutes
Cardio index: ♥ ♥ ♥

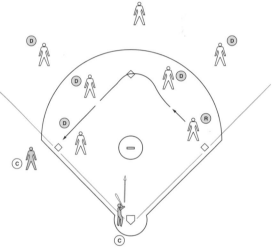

1. A runner wearing a batting helmet stands on first base. Other runners wait their turn.
2. Position a coach at third base.
3. The coach at home plate throws or hits a ball to the outfield to simulate a base hit (hard grounder or one-hop).
4. As the coach winds up or tosses the ball to hit it, the runner takes a two- or three-step lead.
5. As soon as the ball is hit, the runner sprints to second base.
6. The appropriate outfielder fields the ball and throws to the cutoff (see Chapter 3 and drill 48, Who's the Cutoff?), who makes the throw to the appropriate base (second or third).
7. About two-thirds of the way to second base, the runner looks to the coach for the "hands up" signal to stop at second base or the signal to advance to third base.
8. If the coach signals to advance to third base, the runner rounds second base and slides into third base.

Advanced Variation

Runners at First and Third Against Defense. Add a runner at third base with a batting helmet, and execute this drill. Have the defensive players go for outs, and if a rundown situation develops, play out the rundown. This is good practice for both the defenders and the runners.

Hints

To save time, you can instruct your runners to assume that all hit balls (even caught fly balls) are hits. But to maintain realism, it's better to try to throw or hit grounders or one-hops into the outfield.

104. Runner Response to Fly Ball (Intermediate)

Purpose: To practice tagging up on fly balls
Equipment: Supply of softballs
Number of players: Multiple players (base runners, 3 outfielders)
Number of repetitions: 2 to 3 reps for 2 sets
Allocated time: 5 minutes

Parent-friendly drill: ✔ No outfielders and no balls are used. Parent simulates a hit to the appropriate outfield, waits two seconds, and then calls out "Fly ball caught" or "Fly ball dropped."
Cardio index: ♥ ♥ ♥

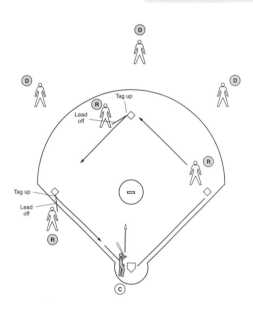

1. Position three players in the outfield.
2. A runner wearing a batting helmet stands on first base. Other runners wait their turn.
3. A coach standing at home plate throws or hits a fly ball to the outfield.
4. As the coach winds up or tosses the ball to hit it, the runner at first base takes a two- or three-step lead.
5. As soon as the fly ball is hit, the runner takes a further lead based on the depth of the hit. She advances if the ball is not caught and returns to first base if the ball is caught.
6. Even if the ball is caught, she then goes to second base for the next part of the drill. A new runner from the queue executes steps 1 to 5 of this drill.
7. As the coach winds up or tosses the ball to hit it, the runner at second takes a two- or three-step lead.

- If the ball is hit to right field, the runner promptly tags up, advancing to third base on a deep fly ball or if the ball is not caught.
- If the ball is hit to shallow center or shallow left field, the runner takes a lead based on the depth of the hit and advances if the ball is not caught.

8. Even if the ball is caught, she goes to third for the next part of the drill.
9. As the coach winds up or tosses the ball to hit it, the runner at third base takes a two- or three-step lead. The runner promptly tags up, advancing to home plate only after the ball is caught or falls to the ground.
10. Each runner executes this drill around the bases two or three times.

Hints

To make the drill useful for the outfielders, they should simulate a proper throw in the direction of the appropriate cutoff. Have the outfielders call out "Cutoff second base" or "Cutoff shortstop." It helps the outfielders learn the game if they know who they should be throwing to, even if in a real game a different infielder (or no infielder) acts as the cutoff.

If some of your outfielders are catching everything, praise them, but you may need to instruct them not to catch a few to make the drill interesting for the runners. Don't forget to rotate your outfielders and runners.

Every once in a while, call out "Bases loaded, two outs." In this case, your runners should sprint whether the ball is hit into the air or on the ground.

105. Bent-Leg Slide (Intermediate)

Purpose: To practice basic sliding technique against defense	**Number of repetitions:** 3 to 5 reps for 2 sets
Equipment: Softball	**Allocated time:** 5 minutes
Number of players: Multiple players (base runners and second-base player)	**Cardio index:** ♥ ♥ ♥

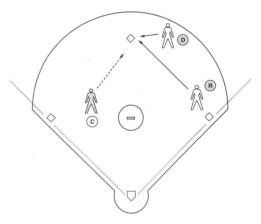

1. A runner wearing a batting helmet stands on first base. Other runners wait their turn.
2. A player takes her on-field position as second-base player.
3. Position a coach with a softball on the left side of the infield.
4. On the coach's cue, the runner sprints to second base.
5. As the coach winds up, the second-base player executes proper footwork (see Chapter 3) to cover second base.
6. The coach throws to second base as the runner executes her slide.
7. The second-base player tags the runner.
8. Optional: keep score between a team of runners and a team of defenders.

Advanced Variation

Station a shortstop and another coach with a softball to throw to her. This coach should be on the right side of the infield.

Hints

This drill also helps infielders learn to catch thrown balls with the gamelike distraction of a live runner barreling toward them. Encourage your infielders to make the tag with both hands and to stay low by bending their knees, rather than just lowering their arms. This will help them see the action as well as put them in a better position to brace for a possible collision. Help develop tagging skills by throwing the ball into tag-ready position, but throw high ones as well to simulate throwing errors.

106. Pop-Up Slide (Intermediate)

Purpose: To practice sliding technique against defensive lapses to advance an extra base

Equipment: Softball

Number of players: Multiple players (base runners, optional second-base player, and helper)

Number of repetitions: 3 to 5 reps for 2 sets

Allocated time: 5 minutes

Parent-friendly drill: ✔ No ball is used. Parent makes phantom overthrow.

Cardio index: 💜 💜 💜

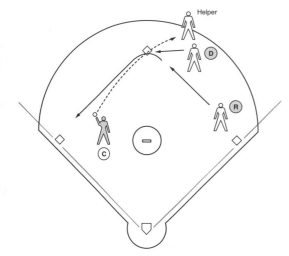

1. A runner wearing a batting helmet stands on first base. Other runners wait their turn.
2. Optional: a player takes her on-field position as second-base player, and a helper goes to the shallow outfield behind second base.
3. Position a coach with a softball on the left side of the infield.
4. On the coach's cue, the runner sprints to second base.
5. Optional: as the coach winds up, the second-base player executes proper footwork to cover second base.
6. The coach simulates a throwing error by throwing substantially over the head of the second-base player to the helper in the outfield as the runner executes her slide.
7. The runner attempts to advance an extra base by recovering from her slide after touching the bag as follows:

In the first frame, Katelyn presses her top leg against the bag and her bent bottom leg against the ground underneath. This enables her to pop up in the second frame. Note how Katelyn scans the outfield to see if she is in position to take an extra base.

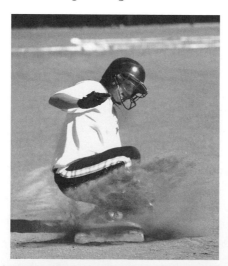

- Presses the top leg (the thrusting leg) against the bag.
- Presses the bent bottom leg against the ground underneath.
- Raise her upper body up from the supine position.
- These three actions will help pop her upright out of her slide and in position to advance to the next bag.

8. The runner advances to third base.
9. The helper throws the ball back to the coach for the next repetition.

Advanced Variation

Pop-Up Slide Against Defense. Throw a variety of balls for the second-base player to catch including short hops. The runner should still do a pop-up slide on a short-hop throw because it is more distracting to the defender.

107. Return-to-Bag Slide (Intermediate)

Purpose: To practice sliding when returning to the bag to prevent being caught in a double play	**Number of repetitions:** 3 to 5 reps for 2 sets
	Allocated time: 3 to 5 minutes
Equipment: Softball	**Parent-friendly drill:** ✔
Number of players: Multiple players (base runners)	**Cardio index:** ♥ ♥

1. A runner wearing a batting helmet stands on first base. Other runners wait their turn.
2. Position a coach with a softball in the infield.
3. As the coach simulates a pop fly by tossing the ball directly above, the runner takes a two- or three-step lead.
4. The coach catches the pop fly and makes a phantom throw to first base.
5. The runner slides back in to the bag to avoid a double play as follows:

- Makes a bent-leg slide with her back and head turned away from the phantom throw
- Makes a *headfirst slide* by lowering her body toward the ground by bending over and in one smooth movement sliding the belly on the ground while making sure her arms and legs are off the ground

6. After reaching the bag, the runner gets off the ground while keeping one hand on the bag (or asks for "time" from the umpire before standing up).

Hints

Runners should not belly flop on the ground for headfirst slides. This will be a hard landing and slam the head down. It's also hard on the neck. Use knee pads to protect the knees from bruising and cuts.

108. Back Door Rollover Slide (Intermediate)

Purpose: To practice specialty sliding technique to home plate (enables the runner to evade the catcher by sliding away from the tag and plate, but still be able to reach back and touch the plate to be safe at home)
Equipment: Softball

Number of players: Multiple players (base runners)
Number of repetitions: 3 to 5 reps for 2 sets
Allocated time: 5 minutes
Parent-friendly drill: ✔
Cardio index: ♥ ♥

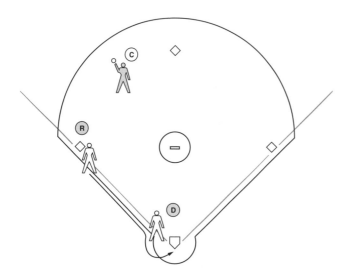

1. A runner wearing a batting helmet stands on third base. Other runners wait their turn.
2. Position a coach with a softball in the outfield.
3. Optional: position a catcher in full gear to block the plate.
4. As the coach simulates a pop fly by tossing the ball directly above, the runner takes a two- or three-step lead, and if the ball is caught returns to tag the bag, and then advances to home plate. If the coach doesn't catch the ball or simulates a ground ball by throwing the ball to the ground, the runner immediately advances to home plate.
5. The coach fields the ball and makes a phantom throw to home plate.
6. The runner slides into home plate using the *back door rollover slide* as follows:

   - Runs past the catcher blocking home plate
   - Slides around the catcher using a traditional slide and then rolls onto her belly as she reaches for home plate
   - In one smooth motion, reaches back and touches the plate

Advanced Variations

   - Have the coach make the throw and challenge the catcher and runner with a close play at home.
   - Have the coach make a throw up the line so the runner can judge this and go straight into the plate.

Pitching

The fast-pitch motion is one of the most complicated and difficult in all of sports. It is also the principal difference between softball and baseball. Youth pitchers start by learning the basic mechanics of pitching. Many high school pitchers deliver heat at up to 55 mph and apply the basic mechanics to an arsenal of pitches like the rise ball designed to confound the batter with sharp ball movement. With the pitching rubber only two-thirds the distance to home plate compared to baseball, this gives batters about the same time to react in the two sports.

A Note from Michele About Pitching

Although I started playing the game at five years old, I only started pitching during my sophomore year in high school. In addition to practice, I learned the science of the motion by studying physics and majoring in biomechanics as a premedical student in college. I constantly apply everything I've learned to my pitching.

The drills in this chapter are designed to reinforce the following skill sets for youth, middle school, and high school pitchers:

- **Mechanics of pitching.** The three phases representing the *basic mechanics* of every pitch: the *setup* or *pre-motion*, the *main motion* (including the *power position* and *release*), and the *follow-through*.
- **Pitch menu.** Describing the grip and delivery of the fastball, changeup, rise ball, drop ball, curveball, and screwball.
- **Pitcher strength and conditioning.** Increases fitness while honing pitcher's skills.
- **Pitcher as fielder.** How to deal with pop-ups, bunts, steals, etc.
- **Pitcher-catcher interaction.** How to make the most of a pitcher's partnership with her catcher.

Basic Mechanics of Pitching

Make sure your pitcher has mastered all phases of the basic mechanics that are used in every variety of pitch as described in this chapter. It's going to be hard for young pitchers to remember all the steps all at once, so the drills are designed to teach individual components of the fast-pitch motion. The basic mechanics are used for standard fastballs and form the foundation for spe-

Some Basic Terminology

The following definitions will help coaches and players visualize the concepts discussed in the drills.

- **Power line.** The straight line perpendicular to the pitching rubber, straight to home plate.
- **Closed position.** Vertical plane of the hips perpendicular to the power line and facing home plate. All pitches start and ultimately end with the closed position.
- **Open position.** Vertical plane of the hips parallel to the power line and facing the direction of the throwing side of the body.
- **Stride leg.** The glove-side leg. For right-handed pitchers, it's the left leg. For left-handed pitchers, it's the right leg.
- **Blocking.** A movement utilized in many sports to use the opposite side of the body to create energy. Think of an imaginary wall on one side of the athlete's body against which she rebounds with explosive force. For example, a high jumper will block using her backside just prior to kick-propelling herself over the bar. Similarly, a softball pitcher uses her stride to build a "hard opposite side" or "hard front side" to generate power.
- **Windmill circle plane.** The plane of a pitcher's windmill action that is parallel to the power line and directly off the body (not too far).
- **Release point.** The point (about 6 o'clock) on the downward swing of a pitcher's windmill circle where the pitcher releases the ball.
- **Half-open position.** The position of the hips at the release point of the ball; the hips are still at a 45- to 52-degree angle to the power line. The hips do not finish rotating to a full closed position until the post-pitch follow-through.
- **Pitcher's area of responsibility.** The pitcher is responsible for fielding balls hit in this area.

cialty pitches like the changeup, rise ball, drop ball, curve-ball, and screwball. Pitchers should master the fastball first, then the changeup, and then proceed to the other pitches in the Pitch Menu. Pitchers will have to make minor adjustments to execute the specialty pitches, for example, striding outside the power line for the curveball, and these adjustments are described in the appropriate Pitch Menu drill.

Setup or Pre-Motion Phase

Every movement in this phase is designed to harness the energy needed to deliver a pitch with blazing speed and/or unpredictable movement. The pitcher's execution of the entire pitch should be quick (almost a blur), smooth, and explosive. She should take her stance and begin with a small arm circle as described in the following sections.

Stance

The pitcher starts in a closed position with both feet on the pitching rubber, shoulder-width apart. The throwing-arm foot should be on the front of the rubber with the glove-arm foot on the back of the rubber. Her arms should be relaxed and hanging down by her sides. Most leagues require a brief pause (of varying length—check your local league rules) before beginning the pre-motion. The pause prevents pitchers from just stepping on the rubber and throwing the ball toward home plate. Sometimes called the *presentation of the pitch*, the pause allows the batter and fielders to get ready for the play to ensue. Encourage your pitchers to get the pause over with early in the pitch. Once the pitcher starts her momentum, she should never want to stop.

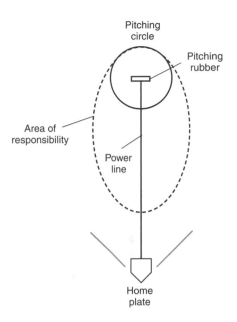

In the first frame, Julia is set up (closed position) and ready to pitch. The second frame shows Julia midpitch in her power position (open position). The third frame shows Julia in a half-open position as she's about to release the ball.

Small Arm Circle

The pitcher begins the pitch by bringing her arms together in front of her stomach area—about 10 inches from her body. Her arms continue around in a small circle, up toward the chest, and then closer to the stomach—about 3 inches now—and down. While the upper body is making the small arm circle, she should rock her body weight from the front leg to the back leg, and then back again to the front leg. At the end of the small arm circle, she will be leaning slightly forward in the *loaded* position. At this point the pitcher is ready to simultaneously stride out with her stride leg and propel her arms into the windmill circle.

Main Motion Phase

The main motion phase of the pitch consists of the stride, windmill circle, prerelease, and release.

Stride

The pitcher explosively strides toward home plate with her stride leg off the pitching rubber along the power line. This will put her hips in an open position. She lands the stride foot a comfortable distance several feet down on the power line at about a 45-degree angle. The pitcher should allow the rear foot to pivot at about a 45-degree angle on the pitching rubber. This will help protect the knee and facilitate proper hip movement. A long stride generates the most power. As the stride lengthens, the pitcher drags the back leg on the ground behind her. This will allow her to drive or *pinch* her back leg into her stride leg in the prerelease phase.

Windmill Circle

In the meantime, during her stride, your pitcher should execute a smooth and explosive windmill circle as follows:

- Point her glove arm at the catcher.
- Rotate (clockwise from the pitcher's perspective) the fully extended throwing arm to the top (around 12 o'clock) and then to around 2 o'clock of the windmill circle. Your pitcher is now in the power position.
- Continue the windmill circle on the windmill circle plane.
- Start to rotate the upper body (hips and shoulders move pretty much in synch) from an open position back to a closed position.
- Shouldn't overrotate or close her hips too early. As discussed below, the hips should only be at a 45- to 52-degree angle to the power line when the ball is released at the release point.

Prerelease

As the stride foot lands on the power line, the pitcher "blocks" or builds an imaginary wall on the stride side of her body, turbo-charging all the energy harnessed during her stride and windmill circle and then driving together all the extended body parts from the power position. She does this smoothly and explosively as follows:

- Brings the glove arm in and down to the body.
- Completes the windmill circle; the downswing will create a slight bend in the otherwise fully extended throwing arm, which is normal.
- Drags her back leg, or throwing-arm leg, on the ground and drives or "pinches" her back leg into her stride leg (still firmly planted on the ground as a result of the stride).
- As the pitcher completes her windmill circle, her upper body (hips and shoulders) rotates from an open position back toward the closed position. The hip pivot point is not stationary; the hips should slide down the power line as they rotate. It's also important to note that at the release point, the hips are still only partially back to the original closed position.

Michele in the classic power position. See how her body makes an X shape. Michele is in full stride, with her glove pointing to her target and her throwing arm in the windmill circle.

Release Point

The pitcher whips the throwing arm to the release point in front of the hips as the hips approach the 45- to 52-degree angle. At the release point, the pitcher "wrist snaps" the ball for the strike! The fast-pitch motion generates a lot of momentum, so the hips will continue to rotate to a closed position after the ball is released—but only after the ball is long gone. Closing the hips early may cause shoulder problems.

Follow-Through Phase

After the release, the pitcher's goal is to get into good fielding position (athletic stance, eyes facing the batter):

- The body will naturally rotate back to the closed position.
- The throwing arm should be relaxed (elbow slightly bent) and continue up along the windmill circle plane toward the center chest as it decelerates.
- Be ready (athletic stance, hands out in front) to field any ball hit in the pitcher's area of responsibility, especially line drives up the middle.

Chapter 6 Skills Matrix

Drill Number	Drill Title (Indented drills are "named" Advanced Variations)	Wrist Snap Mechanics	Elbow Snap Mechanics	Upper-Body Mechanics	Windmill Circle	Pitching Stride	Leg Pinch	Pitching Follow-Through	Balance	Conditioning	Fielding	Throwing
Pitcher Mechanics												
109.	Pitcher Wrist Snaps	●										
110.	Pitcher Elbow Snaps	●	●									
111.	Pitcher One-Knee Windmill Circle			●	●							
112.	Pitcher Stride to Power Position			●	●	●						
	Cardio Stride			●	●	●				●		
	Stride Box			●	●	●						
113.	Pitcher Power Line Windmill Circle	●	●	●	●							
114.	Pitcher Leg Pinch Windmill Circle	●	●	●	●		●	●	●			
115.	Pitcher Balance								●			
	Pitcher Rock the Boat								●			
116.	Pitcher Full Pitch Mechanics—Fastball											
	Inside/Outside Pitch Location Command											
	Pitcher Tee Hurdle											
	Pitcher Big Ball	●	●							●		
Pitch Menu												
117.	Pitcher Changeup—Palm Grip											
	Changeup/Rise Ball Fake-Out											
	Alternating Changeup/Rise Ball											
	Changeup Palm Grip (Solo)											
118.	Pitcher Changeup Flip											
	Changeup Flip (Solo)											
119.	Pitcher Rise Ball											
	Rise Ball (Solo)											
	Rise Ball Football											

Catching	Pitch Location	Pitcher Situation	Pitcher Backup	Bunt Situation	Mechanics—Fastball	Mechanics—Changeup	Mechanics—Rise Ball	Mechanics—Drop Ball	Mechanics—Curveball	Mechanics—Screwball	Catcher Situation	Infield Situation
					⚾							
	⚾											
	⚾				⚾	⚾	⚾	⚾				
					⚾							
						⚾						
						⚾						
						⚾	⚾					
						⚾						
						⚾						
						⚾						
							⚾					
							⚾					
							⚾					

(continued)

Chapter 6 Skills Matrix *(continued)*

Drill Number	Drill Title (Indented drills are "named" Advanced Variations)	Wrist Snap Mechanics	Elbow Snap Mechanics	Upper-Body Mechanics	Windmill Circle	Pitching Stride	Leg Pinch	Pitching Follow-Through	Balance	Conditioning	Fielding	Throwing
120.	Pitcher Drop Ball											
	Drop Ball (Solo)											
	Flip Drop Pitch											
	Drop Ball Football											
121.	Pitcher Curveball											
	Curveball (Solo)											
	Curveball Fielding Response										⚾	
122.	Pitcher Screwball											
	Screwball (Solo)											
Pitcher Strength and Conditioning												
123.	Pitcher Arm and Leg Strength									⚾		
124.	Pitcher Plyometrics									⚾		
Pitcher as Fielder												
125.	Pitcher Follow-Through							⚾				
126.	Pitcher Double Play											⚾
	Pitcher-Catcher Interaction											⚾
	Slap Hit Double Play											⚾
127.	Pitcher Basic Backup											
Pitcher-Catcher Interaction												
128.	Pitcher Bunt											⚾
	Pitcher Blind Bunt											⚾
	Pitcher Bunt and Run											⚾
129.	Pitcher Pitchout											

Catching	Pitch Location	Pitcher Situation	Pitcher Backup	Bunt Situation	Mechanics—Fastball	Mechanics—Changeup	Mechanics—Rise Ball	Mechanics—Drop Ball	Mechanics—Curveball	Mechanics—Screwball	Catcher Situation	Infield Situation
								⚾				
								⚾				
								⚾				
								⚾				
									⚾			
									⚾			
									⚾			
										⚾		
										⚾		
⚾		⚾										⚾
⚾		⚾									⚾	⚾
⚾		⚾										⚾
			⚾									⚾
⚾				⚾							⚾	⚾
⚾				⚾							⚾	⚾
⚾				⚾							⚾	⚾
		⚾									⚾	

Pitching Mechanics Drills

109. Pitcher Wrist Snaps (Beginner)

Purpose: To practice tossing the ball at the release point with a snap of the wrist (solid wrist snap is crucial to pitch speed)
Equipment: Softball
Number of players: 1 or 2 (pitcher and helper; 2 pitchers; or 1 pitcher against a wall or into her glove)

Number of repetitions: 25
Allocated time: 3 minutes
Parent-friendly drill: ✔
Cardio index: ♥

1. Holding the ball, the pitcher assumes a half-open position relative to a coach or helper standing about 5 feet away.
2. The pitcher holds her pitching arm below the elbow with her nonthrowing hand. This will steady the arm and reinforce the wrist-motion-only aspect of the drill.
3. With her pitching arm at 6 o'clock (the release point), the pitcher uses wrist action only to cock the ball back and snap it forward, releasing the ball to the helper.
4. The helper catches the ball and throws it back to the pitcher. If the helper is also a pitcher, the two can alternate wrist snaps.

Advanced Variation

Advanced pitchers can wrist-snap changeups and other pitches with a partner or into their own gloves (solo variation)—refer to the drills in the Pitch Menu section for proper grip and mechanics.

Hints

Having the pitcher stand in a half-open position will reinforce the fact that she will actually be in this position when releasing the ball during a pitch. Thus, make sure she is not closing her hips as she snaps the ball. Closing her hips will occur later during follow-through.

110. Pitcher Elbow Snaps (Beginner)

Purpose: To practice tossing the ball at the release point with a snap of the wrist and follow-through
Equipment: Softball
Number of players: 1 or 2 (pitcher and helper; 2 pitchers; or 1 pitcher against a wall or into her glove)

Number of repetitions: 25
Allocated time: 3 to 5 minutes
Parent-friendly drill: ✔
Cardio index: ⓥ

1. A pitcher starts by setting up with a coach or helper, standing about 5 feet apart as in drill 109.
2. The pitcher holds her pitching arm below the elbow with her nonthrowing hand, but lets go when following through (step 4).
3. With her pitching arm at 6 o'clock (the release point), the pitcher uses only wrist action to cock the ball back and snap it forward, releasing the ball to the helper.
4. She continues by allowing her elbow to flex. She follows through by touching her throwing-hand fingers to either her opposite shoulder or center chest area. After the ball is released, she pivots from the half-open position to the closed position. This simulates the upper-body motion of the follow-through.
5. The helper catches the ball and throws it back to the pitcher. If the helper is also a pitcher, the two can alternate elbow snaps.

Advanced Variation

Advanced pitchers can elbow-snap rise balls and other pitches with a partner or into their own gloves (solo variation)—refer to the drills in the Pitch Menu section for proper grip and mechanics.

Hints

Pitchers should learn to feel the ball roll off the fingertips to make sure they are getting as much snap as possible.

111. Pitcher One-Knee Windmill Circle (Beginner)

Purpose: To practice keeping shoulders back, torso straight, and head up during the delivery
Equipment: Softball
Number of players: 1 or 2 (pitcher and helper; 2 pitchers; or 1 pitcher against a wall or into her glove)

Number of repetitions: 20
Allocated time: 5 minutes
Parent-friendly drill: ✔
Cardio index: ♥

1. Holding the ball, the pitcher kneels on her throwing-side knee and points her glove-side leg toward the target, a coach or helper kneeling about 10 feet away, with her hips at about a 45-degree angle.
2. The pitcher executes a windmill circle, making sure to keep her shoulders back, torso straight, and head up.
3. The pitcher should keep the windmill circle on the windmill circle plane. If your pitcher starts her windmill circle above her head, this will skew the plane of the circle, resulting in a release point that is too far from the body and may cause elbow stress. If she starts too far away from the body, then she'll ram the ball into her hips at the release point. The plane is two-dimensional. Your pitcher should avoid starting on one plane and then adjusting midcircle to the correct plane. This causes undue elbow stress and decelerates the pitch.
4. The pitcher finishes by releasing the ball at the release point (about 6 o'clock) to the helper.
5. She continues by allowing her elbow to flex and follows through by touching her throwing-hand fingers to either her opposite shoulder or center chest area.
6. The helper catches the ball and throws it back to the pitcher. If the helper is also a pitcher, the two can alternate one-knee windmill circles.

Advanced Variation

Advanced pitchers can execute windmill circles and finish with rise balls and other pitches—refer to the drills in the Pitch Menu section for proper grip and mechanics.

Hints

You'll notice that even on one knee, if she wants to throw straight, the pitcher will need to pivot her body from a half-open position to a somewhat open position and back again during her windmill circle. Pivoting helps to keep her windmill circle in the windmill circle plane. While the one-knee position prevents the full range of lower-body movement, this pivot action is essentially what is supposed to happen in an actual pitch. Remember that the pitcher should not start this drill in a closed position. While the front leg is more or less pointing to the target, for this drill, the pitcher can have the side of her front foot toward the target to help her hips start at about a 45-degree angle.

Try to have your pitchers wear knee pads during this drill to avoid injury during any pivoting that might occur.

Don't forget the head. Your pitcher should keep her head over her trunk — the center of gravity. Tipping to any side will cause balance problems.

112. Pitcher Stride to Power Position (Beginner)

Purpose: To practice full extension stride and power position until consistent
Equipment: None
Number of players: 1
Number of repetitions: 2 sets of 25

Allocated time: 5 minutes
Parent-friendly drill: ✔ This drill can be practiced in front of a mirror.
Cardio index: ♥ ♥

1. A pitcher without a ball or glove assumes the proper stance in a closed position on the pitching rubber.
2. The pitcher explosively executes the fast-pitch small arm circle, stride, and windmill circle movements, and stops in the power position.
3. The coach checks for proper body and limb position. Your pitcher should be in an open position, glove arm extended out, throwing arm extended but slightly flexed at between 12 o'clock and 2 o'clock on the windmill circle plane, stride foot on the power line at about a 45-degree angle, and rear foot pivoted at about a 45-degree angle on the pitching rubber. See photo under "Windmill Circle" in skills section of this chapter.
4. Each repetition should yield about the same body and limb position, including stride length. Stride length should increase with age, the athlete's growth, and practice.

Advanced Variations

- **Cardio Stride.** Do the drill with ankle weights for leg and cardio conditioning.
- **Stride Box.** Put a medium-size box to the side of the rubber and have the pitcher pretend the box is on the power line and stride over it.

Hints

To avoid injury, your pitcher must be in an open position during the power position phase. It is physically impossible to be in a closed position and put her throwing arm at 2 o'clock

Draw a line down the power line as a guide to help your pitcher stride correctly.

113. Pitcher Power Line Windmill Circle (Beginner)

Purpose: To practice the windmill circle starting at full stride
Equipment: Softball
Number of players: 1 or 2 (pitcher and helper; 2 pitchers; or 1 pitcher against a wall)

Number of repetitions: 25
Allocated time: 3 to 5 minutes
Parent-friendly drill: ✔
Cardio index: ♥

1. Holding the ball, the pitcher sets up in the power position—open position with glove arm out, throwing arm fully extended between 12 o'clock and 2 o'clock, stride leg in full stride with the stride foot on the power line at about a 45-degree angle. A coach or helper stands about 30 feet away.

2. The pitcher completes the windmill circle and releases the ball in whip-like fashion at the release point (about 6 o'clock) to the helper about 30 feet away. At release, the pitcher is in the half-open position and has brought her glove arm back in toward her body.

3. She continues by allowing her elbow to flex. She follows through by touching her throwing-hand fingers to her opposite shoulder. In the meantime, she pivots to a closed position. For this drill, she keeps the feet planted (no leg pinch) but allows them to pivot as necessary.

4. The helper catches the ball and throws it back to the pitcher. If the helper is also a pitcher, the two can alternate power line windmill circles.

Advanced Variation

Advanced pitchers can execute this drill and finish with changeups and other pitches—refer to the drills in the Pitch Menu section for proper grip and mechanics.

Hints

Make sure your pitcher actually points to the target with her glove arm at the beginning of her windmill circle (no lazy arms!). Explain to your pitcher that the "glove arm out," and then later, in the power position phase executed in this drill, "glove arm in" movement helps to build momentum.

Your pitcher's throwing shoulder acts like a pendulum around which her windmill circle rotates. Trunk rotation from the open power position to the half-open release point position helps to keep the pendulum swinging along the windmill circle plane. The arm works together with the body to keep that pendulum on track. Otherwise, your pitcher risks shoulder injury, not to mention getting tangled up in her own movements or throwing askew. Again, your pitcher should use correct mechanics; concentrating on using correct mechanics will lead to strikes. If she is not throwing strikes, something is wrong with her mechanics. It's not a good idea to tell her to "throw strikes" without fixing the root cause of her inaccuracy.

Remind your pitcher to keep her shoulder back. The proper sequence is elbow snap, followed by wrist snap. Her shoulders will rotate along with her hips from the half-open position to a closed position. If her shoulders close too early and lead her elbow, she will be pushing the ball and lose power.

Finally, stress the importance of the follow-through. The follow-through allows the pitcher to dissipate harmful forces as the arm decelerates. The follow-though also enables the pitcher to seamlessly get into a front-facing athletic position to field hit balls. Some pitchers feel like they have to rush their pitches because they want to quickly get into athletic position. But it's important not to square up until the ball is released. Otherwise, there will be a tendency to close up her hips too early, resulting in errant pitches. Finally, remember that her hips and shoulders are at a 45- to 52-degree angle at release; this is why she touches her opposite shoulder area during her follow-through.

114. Pitcher Leg Pinch Windmill Circle (Beginner)

Purpose: To practice the windmill circle starting at full stride, complete with leg pinch
Equipment: Softball
Number of players: 1 or 2 (pitcher and helper; 2 pitchers; or 1 pitcher against a wall)

Number of repetitions: 25
Allocated time: 3 to 5 minutes
Parent-friendly drill: ✔
Cardio index: ♥ ♥

1. A pitcher executes drill 113, Pitcher Power Line Windmill Circle, to a coach or helper standing about 30 feet away.
2. However, rather than keeping her feet planted (no leg pinch), the pitcher completes the prerelease phase by driving together all the extended body parts of the power position to deliver energy to the pitch. In addition to bringing her glove arm back in toward the body, the pitcher drives or "pinches" the front of her back knee, or throwing-arm knee, into the back of her stride-leg knee.
3. The pitcher releases the ball to the helper and executes the proper follow-through, including continuing from the half-open position at release to a closed position after the follow-through, ready to field any hit ball.
4. The helper catches the ball and throws it back to the pitcher. If the helper is also a pitcher, she can alternate Pitcher Leg Pinch Windmill Circles with the first pitcher.

Advanced Variation

Advanced pitchers can execute this drill and finish with changeups, rise balls, and drop balls using the proper grips as described in the Pitch Menu section of this chapter.

Michele starts the drill with all her weight on her back leg, while her front leg is up in the air, her throwing arm is relaxed at her side, and her glove arm is pointed to the target. The first movements bring her into the power position (second frame). From the power position, Michele drives together all the extended body parts in the release (third frame) to deliver maximum energy for the pitch. She brings her glove arm back in toward her body and drives or "pinches" the front of her back knee into the back of her stride-leg knee.

Hints

The pitcher should pinch by dragging the back leg into the stride leg, not by lifting the back leg. This is also known as driving the back leg into the "hard opposite side"—remember the imaginary stride-side "wall" discussed earlier in the chapter. After each repetition of this drill (as well as after each pitch during practice), inspect the dragline formed in the dirt by your pitcher's back leg. If it looks like a stretched-out letter *S* (inverted for right-handed pitchers), then your pitcher is on the right track.

Don't leave the back leg short. You obviously don't want the pitcher to smash the back knee into the front knee, but the knees should be pretty close at the end of the movement. If they're far apart, that's wasted energy. On the other hand, the feet are apart to help maintain balance. So remember—"knees together, feet apart."

Finally, make sure the pitcher drags the back leg on the inside corner of her big toe. This will help prevent her hips from closing too much. If she instead drags on the front of the toe, she'll overrotate her hips.

115. Pitcher Balance (Beginner)

Purpose: Work on balance by isolating movements
Equipment: None
Number of players: 1
Number of repetitions: 2 sets of 15

Allocated time: 5 minutes
Parent-friendly drill: ✔ This drill can be practiced anywhere with a pivot-friendly surface.
Cardio index: ♥ ♥

1. A pitcher without a ball or glove assumes the proper stance in a closed position on the pitching rubber.
2. The pitcher stands on her throwing-arm leg, lifts up her stride leg, and executes the entire fast-pitch motion including the follow-through keeping her stride leg off the ground.
3. The pitcher should pivot the throwing-arm leg as necessary to execute the closed to open to half-open to closed position sequence of the pitch motion to prevent knee injury.

Advanced Variations

- Have your pitchers execute the drill holding a ball and pitching to a wall or the backstop. A well-balanced pitcher should be able to throw straight even on one leg.
- **Pitcher Rock the Boat.** The pitcher stands on her throwing-side leg and rocks her throwing arm and stride leg back and forth three times. On the third rock, she explodes into a pitch to a catcher or a pitcher partner. She needs to keep good balance through the three rocking movements back and forth. If she is off balance, she should stop and start over.

116. Pitcher Full Pitch Mechanics—Fastball (Intermediate)

Purpose: To practice throwing fastball pitches with proper mechanics (focus on speed and mechanics; good mechanics will take care of control)

Equipment: Softball

Number of players: 1 or 2 (pitcher and catcher in full gear or 1 pitcher against a wall)

Number of repetitions: 25
Allocated time: 5 minutes
Parent-friendly drill: ✔
Cardio index: ♥ ♥ ♥

1. The pitcher throws a pitch from the pitching rubber to a catcher in her ready stance behind the plate (consult local league rules for age-appropriate distance), using all steps of the fast-pitch motion—including setup or pre-motion, the motion, and follow-through. Keep in mind the following as your pitcher executes this drill.

   - **Stride.** Michele is 5 feet 11 inches and has a stride length of about 7 to 7.5 feet. But whatever your pitcher's stride length, her stride should be aggressive and explosive. When the pitcher plants her stride foot on the power line, she should do so heel first. If she lands on the balls of her feet first, she might lurch forward and compromise the pitch.
   - **Windmill circle.** A pitch that veers (to the right for right-handed pitchers, to the left for left-handed pitchers) may mean an off-kilter plane, or the hips being prematurely closed at release and therefore in the way of the throwing arm.
   - **Hip rotation.** Reinforce the closed, open, half-open sequence of hip rotation. The hips should be at only a 45- to 52-degree angle to the power line when the ball is released at the release point. Your pitcher should not overmuscle the pitch by overrotating (past the half-open position) or snapping her hips forward. Overrotation will result in the hips getting in the way of the release and put unnecessary stress on the shoulder. A pitcher has overrotated if her belly button is facing the catcher and home plate at the release point.
   - **Release.** On the other hand, the pitcher also should resist the temptation to "control" the pitch by slowing down at the release point. Teach your novice pitcher that there is a reason for the explosive stride and windmill circle—to build momentum for a speedy pitch. Intentionally slowing down will defeat this purpose.
   - **Leg pinch.** The dragline formed in the dirt by your pitcher's back leg should look like a stretched-out letter S (the S will be inverted for right-handed pitchers).

- **Follow-through.** After the ball is released, proper mechanics will get your pitcher in good fielding position, facing the batter in an athletic stance. Her hips will naturally rotate back to a closed position from the half-open position. She will decelerate her throwing arm and bring it back to touch her shoulder or ear (this will help keep her arm from being stuck down by her hips) and not allow the elbow to rise above the shoulder (that throws her head back).

2. The catcher uses proper mechanics to catch the ball and throw it back to the pitcher.

Advanced Variations

- **Inside/Outside Pitch Location Command.** Have the pitcher place the ball on the inside or outside of the plate. To pitch an inside pitch, she should grip the ball so that her index finger points at the inside part of the plate. To pitch an outside pitch, she should rotate her wrist one-quarter to one-half inch toward the outside of the plate. Pitch location is controlled by the wrist and not by stepping on or striding to a different spot with the lead leg.

Shown is the grip for an inside pitch (left-handed pitcher) dealt to a right-handed batter.

- **Pitcher Tee Hurdle.** Set up two tees about 6 or 7 feet apart from each other and straddling home plate about one foot in front. Attach rope (or caution tape) to each tee about knee high (bottom of the strike zone), and a second rope to each tee about chest high (top of the strike zone). You may need to elevate the tees using boxes or buckets. Don't use a stick as the hurdle; it could fling off the tee and hurt the catcher. Have the pitcher throw fastballs or changeups at game speed between the ropes using proper mechanics to a catcher behind the plate wearing full gear. Or the pitcher can use this drill as a self-diagnostic tool by executing this drill with no catcher and throwing to the backstop.

    You can also use the Tee Hurdle to practice drop balls and rise balls (very advanced). For drop balls, use only the bottom rope and have the rope at the bottom of the strike zone and about 2 to 3 feet in front of home plate. The pitcher should try to throw her drop so the ball goes over the rope but the catcher catches it below the rope, so the ball is dropping as it moves through the strike zone. For the rise, use one rope at about midleg level in the strike zone and in front of the plate by about 2 to 3 feet. Then have the pitcher throw rise balls that go under the rope, but the catcher catches above the rope so the ball is rising through the strike zone.

Shown is the grip for an outside pitch (left-handed pitcher) dealt to a right-handed batter.

- **Pitcher Big Ball.** Have the pitcher throw fastballs (or any variety of pitch) using a 16-inch softball to help build finger and wrist strength. The pitcher will really have to snap it in order to keep the ball from slipping out of her hand, as well as just to get that big ball to home

Kids' Corner

Throwing underhand fast is deceptively difficult. Lots of walks and wild pitches are par for the course in youth softball. Coaches understandably feel pressure to stifle the cringes and complaining in the stands. However, it's not a good idea to encourage a young pitcher to pitch for control, i.e., strikes, at the expense of speed. The best high school pitchers are the ones who were first taught in youth softball to pitch with as much speed as they could muster using good mechanics. The focus should always be on good mechanics; good mechanics will yield both speed and control. By all means temporarily pull a pitcher who is hitting (and possibly hurting) batters, but do so in a manner that does not embarrass or discourage her from pitching in the future. Explain to her that control will come with time, but not all by itself. She must practice the drills in this chapter.

plate. For the advanced pitches, using a big ball also helps reinforce the concept that the pitcher has to use proper mechanics to get the ball to spin properly. A 16-inch softball is very large and is used in Chicagoland slow-pitch. There are 14-inch balls on the market as well.

Hints

Remind your pitcher that her legs are the most powerful part of her body; the more explosive the stride, the faster her pitch.

Pitch Menu Drills

117. Pitcher Changeup — Palm Grip (Advanced)

Purpose: To practice throwing changeup pitches with proper mechanics (an off-speed pitch used to baffle the batter)
Equipment: Softball
Number of players: 1 or 2 (pitcher and catcher in full gear or 1 pitcher against a wall)

Number of repetitions: 25
Allocated time: 5 minutes
Parent-friendly drill: ✔
Cardio index: ♥ ♥ ♥

1. A pitcher from the pitching rubber throws a live changeup to a catcher in full gear behind the plate. Consult local league rules for age-appropriate distance.

2. **Grip.** The pitcher holds the ball deep in her palm. Her index finger and thumb should make a circle on the ball. This will help keep the ball deep in her palm.
3. The mechanics of the changeup and fastball are the same, and these pitches are executed with equal explosiveness. Holding the ball deep in the palm slows the pitch for the changeup.
4. The catcher uses proper mechanics to catch the ball and throw it back to the pitcher.

Advanced Variations

- **Changeup/Rise Ball Fake-Out.** Have your pitcher throw changeups using a simulated rise ball grip. Advanced batters will sometimes try to predict the pitch by "picking" the grip. The pitcher should hold the ball deeper in her palm, but tuck one finger to make the pitch look like a rise ball. The goal is to make the batter think "rise ball" but deliver a changeup.
- **Alternating Changeup/Rise Ball.** Have your pitcher throw changeups and rise balls in quick succession: 10 reps, rest, 10 reps.
- **Changeup Palm Grip (Solo).** The pitcher simply positions her body in release mode, grips the ball properly, and does wrist or elbow snaps into her own glove.

Hints

Remind your pitcher to keep the ball low in the strike zone; it is harder to hit a low changeup. A changeup high in the strike zone is easier for the batter to see and hit.

Remind your novice pitchers not to intentionally dampen the explosiveness of their movements; this will telegraph a slow pitch. The reduced velocity of a changeup is a function of how the pitcher grips the ball. Her stride and windmill circle should be explosive, and if she hides her grip, your pitcher will have a good chance to fool the batter into thinking "fastball." It's all about mechanics—the changeup is about 25 percent slower than a fastball because of the grip mechanics, not because the pitcher lobs the ball.

118. Pitcher Changeup Flip (Advanced)

Purpose: To practice throwing *changeup flip* pitches with proper mechanics (pitcher turns the throwing hand so the palm faces down at the release point and flips the hand up during the follow-through—some pitchers prefer the flip or finger grip to the palm grip because they feel it yields better control)

Equipment: Softball
Number of players: 1 or 2 (pitcher and catcher in full gear or 1 pitcher against a wall)
Number of repetitions: 25
Allocated time: 5 minutes
Parent-friendly drill: ✔
Cardio index: ♥ ♥ ♥

Flip grip at release—hand is turned over

1. A pitcher from the pitching rubber throws a live changeup to a catcher in full gear behind the plate. Consult local league rules for age-appropriate distance.
2. **Grip.** Start with the rise ball grip. Grip the ball with the fingers, not the palm.
3. The mechanics of the changeup flip and standard fastball are similar, but with the following adjustments:

   - The pitcher makes a long and aggressive stride to simulate a fastball but keeps her weight back like a rise ball.
   - At the release point (the throwing arm is already in front of the shoulders and hips), the pitcher leans forward and rolls her shoulders and hips forward and into a closed position. This will allow room for the pitcher to turn her throwing hand over and flip the pitch toward the catcher.

4. The catcher uses proper mechanics to catch the ball and throw it back to the pitcher.

Advanced Variation

Changeup Flip (Solo). The pitcher simply positions her body in release mode, grips the ball properly, and does wrist or elbow snaps into her own glove.

Hints

It's important to remember that the throwing arm must be in front of the shoulders and hips before the shoulders and hips roll forward and close. Shoulder injury could result if the arm comes in behind the shoulders and hips. This is one of the reasons the flip changeup is an advanced pitch. It's imperative that pitchers be able to feel when they are in a proper position versus one that is harmful to their bodies. Give your junior pitchers time to reach that level of cognitive awareness before allowing them to try this drill.

Changeups that sail high into the strike zone are easy to see and easy to hit hard. Changeups have to be thrown low in the zone to be effective. To do that, your pitcher has to keep her release point as low as possible. First, while she should keep her weight back somewhat in her power position, she should take care not to lean too far back, which will cause her to raise her release point. Second, she should lean slightly forward at the release point. She can think of an imaginary line in front of her, a "limbo rope," under which she has to release the ball. Once she releases the ball beneath this imaginary rope, she should flip the hand and arm up aggressively during her follow-through. This is designed to fool the batter into thinking "heat."

119. Pitcher Rise Ball (Advanced)

Purpose: To practice throwing rise ball pitches with proper mechanics (pitch spins backward and, properly thrown, rises up through the strike zone suddenly)
Equipment: Softball
Number of players: 1 or 2 (pitcher and catcher in full gear or 1 pitcher against a wall)

Number of repetitions: 25
Allocated time: 5 minutes
Parent-friendly drill: ✔
Cardio index: ♥ ♥ ♥

1. A pitcher from the pitching rubber throws a live rise ball to a catcher in full gear at the plate. Consult local league rules for age-appropriate distance.
2. In the *four-seam grip*, the pitcher's middle and ring fingers are on opposite sides of the smile seam of the ball. In the *two-seam grip*, the pitcher's middle and ring fingers are on opposite sides of the seams closest together. For either grip, the pitcher tucks her index finger, and her thumb is as usual opposite her middle finger.
3. The mechanics of the rise ball and standard fastball are similar, but with the following adjustments (to facilitate a lower release point and a rising trajectory).

   - The pitcher makes a long and aggressive stride but keeps her weight slightly back.
   - The pitcher collapses her back leg, further lowering her release point.
   - She grips the ball correctly and has her hand in a palm-down position during the windmill circle (when her arm is behind her head the palm will be facing out or away from the body), but at the release point, she quickly "turns the doorknob" (turns her hand from palm down to palm up) to release the ball.
   - She avoids overrotation and stands tall at follow-through.

Four-seam rise grip

Two-seam rise grip

4. The catcher uses proper mechanics to catch the ball and throw it back to the pitcher.

Advanced Variations

- **Rise Ball (Solo).** The pitcher simply positions her body in release mode, grips the ball properly, and does wrist or elbow snaps into her own glove. Her wrists should be wrinkled at the end of the snap.
- **Rise Ball Football.** Have the pitcher throw rise balls to the backstop using a youth-size squishy football; it's easy to check to make sure the ball is spinning (spiraling) in the correct direction.

Hints

Turning the doorknob with the right grip causes the ball to spin backward. This results in a decrease in pressure underneath the seams and causes the pitch to rise up through the strike zone. It's important to turn the doorknob quickly—the motion should not be long and lazy. Using the stride to build a hard opposite side is especially important for the rise ball because it helps to keep her weight back and lowers her release point. These mechanics are designed to help her deliver a pitch with sudden movement up the strike zone.

As far as the grip, your pitcher should experiment with the four- and two-seam grips and use the one she is most comfortable with. Michele prefers the two-seam grip because it gives her the greatest amount of break late and sharp through the strike zone.

In the first frame, Michele makes a long and aggressive stride but keeps her weight slightly back. In the second frame, Michele collapses her back leg, further lowering her release point, while "turning the doorknob" as she releases the ball.

120. Pitcher Drop Ball (Advanced)

Purpose: To practice throwing *the peel drop version of the drop ball pitch* with proper mechanics (pitch spins forward over the top and has a tendency to fall in the strike zone and generate a lot of ground balls)
Equipment: Softball

Number of players: 1 or 2 (pitcher and catcher in full gear or 1 pitcher against a wall)
Number of repetitions: 25
Allocated time: 5 minutes
Parent-friendly drill: ✔
Cardio index: ♥ ♥ ♥

1. A pitcher from the pitching rubber throws a live peel drop ball to a catcher in full gear at the plate. Consult local league rules for age-appropriate distance.
2. **Grip.** The pitcher's index, middle, and ring fingers are laid down across the smile seam of the ball, with the thumb opposite the middle finger.
3. The mechanics of the peel drop ball and standard fastball are similar, but with the following adjustments (to facilitate a higher release point and a falling trajectory):

Regular drop grip—
side view

   - The pitcher makes a slightly shorter stride compared to the fastball.
   - She bends her stride knee so that her body angle is slightly forward and her shoulder is slightly over her stride knee at release.
   - At the same time, the pitcher pulls up her shoulder to raise the release point.

4. The release itself is known as a peel. The ball rolls off the fingers—the finger action is similar to that of a jump shot in basketball but in the opposite direction. The pitcher releases the ball making sure the ball "peels" away with forward spin.
5. The catcher uses proper mechanics to catch the ball and throw it back to the pitcher.

Advanced Variations

   - **Drop Ball (Solo).** The pitcher simply positions her body in release mode, grips the ball properly, and does wrist or elbow snaps into her own glove. She should place her opposite hand on the ball to check to make sure the ball has a forward spin.
   - **Drop Ball Football.** Have the pitcher throw drop balls to the backstop using a youth-size squishy football; it's easy to check to make sure the ball is spinning (spiraling) in the correct direction.
   - **Flip Drop Pitch (Turnover Drop Pitch).** While the peel drop is the most common and perhaps easiest to learn of the drop pitches, very advanced pitchers can try another variation called the flip drop. The speed of the flip drop might be a bit slower than the peel drop, but

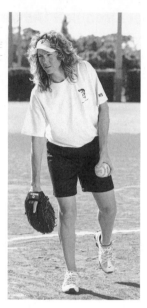

In the first frame, Michele bends her stride knee so that her body angle is slightly forward. This allows her to have her front shoulder slightly over her stride knee at release. Michele pulls up her opposite shoulder (second frame) to raise the release point.

very advanced pitchers can get the pitch to tail into the batter (kind of a drop/screwball combination pitch). To deliver the flip drop, the pitcher uses her index, middle, and ring fingers to grip the ball with the smile seam of the ball. This will give her a good turnover on the ball. The pitcher should experiment with putting her index and middle fingers together or apart to see which grip works best for her. When the hand comes into the release zone, the wrist should turn from palm up to palm down and flip the ball over, giving it downward rotation. The body position on the flip drop is the same as on the peel drop.

Hints

Make sure your pitcher pulls her shoulder up at the release point. This will raise the release point, making it easier to peel the ball away.

121. Pitcher Curveball (Advanced)

Purpose: To practice throwing curveball pitches with proper mechanics (pitch spins like a top and curves away from or toward the batter in the strike zone, depending on whether the pitcher or batter is right-handed or left-handed)
Equipment: Softball

Number of players: 1 or 2 (pitcher and catcher in full gear or 1 pitcher against a wall)
Number of repetitions: 25
Allocated time: 5 minutes
Parent-friendly drill: ✔
Cardio index: ♥ ♥ ♥

1. A pitcher from the pitching rubber throws a live curveball to a catcher in full gear at the plate. Consult local league rules for age-appropriate distance.
2. **Grip.** The pitcher uses either the four-seam or the two-seam rise ball grip.
3. The mechanics of the curveball and standard fastball are similar, but with the following adjustments (to facilitate the toplike spin):

Curveball grip

- The pitcher throwing a curveball starts with her normal stance on the pitching rubber, but instead of striding forward with her glove-side foot onto the power line—glove-side foot starting position indicated by point 1 (as she would do when pitching a fastball), she strides forward and steps to the far side of the power line—indicated by point 2. This is the "zig" of the zigzag movement.
- She then leans back over the power line, and as she completes her windmill circle, she "zags" or pulls her throwing arm across her hips (overrotates her hips back) and keeps her palm more or less under the ball. This is the "zag" of the zigzag movement that helps to make the ball curve.
- The pitcher snaps the ball at the release point with a toplike spin.
4. The catcher uses proper mechanics to catch the ball and throw it back to the pitcher.

Advanced Variations

- **Curveball (Solo).** The pitcher simply positions her body in release mode, grips the ball properly, and does wrist or elbow snaps into her own glove.

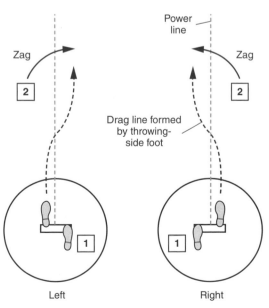

- **Curveball Fielding Response.** The momentum generated by the zig-zag makes it difficult for the curveball pitcher to field balls hit to her non-glove side. She will be slightly off center as she squares up during her follow-through. The coach can roll or throw a separate ball to her non-glove side immediately after she pitches to the catcher to get her used to backhanding balls hit hard to her non-glove side. The pitcher then either simulates a play to first base or uses the ball for the next pitch.

122. Pitcher Screwball (Advanced)

Purpose: To practice throwing screwball pitches with proper mechanics (pitch spins like a corkscrew in an outward tumbling direction—almost the opposite direction of a curveball—and curves away or toward the batter in the strike zone, depending on whether the pitcher or batter is right-handed or left-handed)

Equipment: Softball
Number of players: 1 or 2 (pitcher and catcher in full gear or 1 pitcher against a wall)
Number of repetitions: 25
Allocated time: 5 minutes
Parent-friendly drill: ✔
Cardio index: ♥ ♥ ♥

1. A pitcher from the pitching rubber throws a live screwball to a catcher in full gear behind the plate. Consult local league rules for age-appropriate distance.
2. **Grip.** The pitcher uses the same grip as the four-seam rise ball grip.
3. The mechanics of the screwball and standard fastball are similar, but with the following adjustments (to facilitate the corkscrew-like spin):

   - The pitcher strides open to the power line to help clear her hips. For right-handed pitchers, this means to the left of the power line, for left-handed pitchers, to the right of the power line.
   - The pitcher releases the ball by bringing her throwing arm inside (toward the center line of her body) and then out (away from her glove-arm side).
   - At the release point, she snaps the ball inside to outside so that it tumbles away.

4. The catcher uses proper mechanics to catch the ball and throw it back to the pitcher.

In the first frame, Michele releases the ball by bringing her throwing arm inside and then out. Is that Michele hitchhiking a ride to her next game (second frame)? Actually the second frame shows Michele snapping the ball inside to outside so that it tumbles away at the release point.

Advanced Variation

Screwball (Solo). The pitcher simply positions her body in release mode, grips the ball properly, and does wrist or elbow snaps into the air and then catches it. Throwing into your own glove is almost impossible while practicing the screwball solo, so toss the ball into the air, feel it leave the outside of the index finger, and then catch your own toss.

Hints

The screwball is hard on the elbow, so watch the pitch count to help minimize the chance for injury. Michele does not utilize the screwball very much because of the risk of elbow injury.

Pitcher Strength and Conditioning Drills

123. Pitcher Arm and Leg Strength (Advanced)

Purpose: Three drills designed to improve arm and leg conditioning and explosive strength
Equipment: Softball
Number of players: 1 or 2 (pitcher and catcher in full gear or 1 pitcher against a wall)

Allocated time: 15 minutes
Cardio index: ♥ ♥ ♥

1. **Long Toss/Regular Toss.** A pitcher executes drill 116, Pitcher Full Pitch Mechanics, (incorporating any type pitch) from alternating distances: 20 repetitions at 60 feet, and then 20 reps at 50 feet.
2. **Squat, Jump, and Pitch.** A pitcher squats, jumps, and immediately executes drill 116, Pitcher Full Pitch Mechanics, (incorporating any type pitch) from about 40 feet. Repeat 10 to 20 times.
3. **Weighted Balls.** A pitcher executes drill 116, Pitcher Full Pitch Mechanics, (incorporating any type pitch) using a commercially available weighted softball (heavier or lighter than regulation) from about 40 feet. When using the heaviest balls, have the pitcher throw into a net to avoid injuring your catcher and limit to less than 5 reps to avoid elbow injury to the pitcher.
4. The catcher (in full gear) uses proper mechanics to catch the ball and throw it back to the pitcher.

124. Pitcher Plyometics (Advanced)

Purpose: To improve explosive strength
Equipment: Softball
Number of players: 1 or 2 (pitcher and catcher in full gear or 1 pitcher against a wall)

Allocated time: 5 minutes
Parent-friendly drill: ✔
Cardio index: ♥ ♥ ♥

1. A pitcher executes single-leg bounds. With her full weight on the drive leg (and the stride leg in the air), the pitcher bounds or leaps forward as if driving off the pitching rubber and lands on the same leg. Do 1 set of 10 reps.

2. The pitcher executes drill 116, Pitcher Full Pitch Mechanics (incorporating any type pitch). Do 10 pitches from regulation distance to a catcher in full gear or into the backstop.

3. Repeat steps 1 and 2 one more time.

Hints

To build explosiveness in both legs, do single-leg bounds on the opposite leg (non-drive leg) as well. Do 2 sets of 10.

Pitcher as Fielder Drills

125. Pitcher Follow-Through (Intermediate)

Purpose: To practice finishing every pitch with the proper follow-through, ready to field hit balls
Equipment: Supply of softballs
Number of players: 6 (pitcher, infielders)

Number of repetitions: 5 ground balls for pitcher to field and throw to each bag plus home plate
Allocated time: 4 to 5 minutes per pitcher
Cardio index: ♥ ♥

1. A pitcher executes drill 116, Pitcher Full Pitch Mechanics, (any type pitch) from the pitching circle to a catcher in full gear at home plate.

2. As the pitcher releases the ball and follows through into an athletic stance, a coach about 10 feet away from home plate on either the first- or third-base foul line throws (or uses a fungo bat to hit) a simulated ground ball in the pitcher's area of responsibility.

3. The pitcher fields the ball and throws to first, second, or third base or home plate.

Advanced Variations

- Vary the speed, angle, and force with which the ground ball is delivered. Keep your pitcher guessing. Increase the speed of repetitions.
- Use a wild bounce ball (Z-Ball) for the drill.
- Throw a line drive every now and then to keep the pitcher alert.
- Throw two balls of different colors. The pitcher fields the ball of the color the coach calls.
- Position a second-base player and toss or hit hard grounders in the pitcher's area of responsibility. The pitcher fields the ball and throws to second base. The second-base player throws to first base for a double play.

Hints

This is also a drill for your infielders. Make sure the players are properly positioned and have the proper footwork at the bag to make the catch.

126. Pitcher Double Play

Purpose: To practice the pitcher's technique for turning a double play with a runner on first base
Equipment: 2 softballs, fungo bat
Number of players: 4 (pitcher, catcher, first-base player, shortstop)

Number of repetitions: 10
Allocated time: 3 minutes per pitcher
Cardio index: ♥ ♥

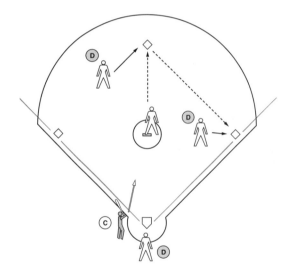

1. A pitcher executes drill 116, Pitcher Full Pitch Mechanics, (any type pitch) from the pitching circle to a catcher in full gear at home plate.
2. As the pitcher releases ball number 1 and follows through into an athletic stance, a coach about 6 feet away from the catcher hits ball number 2 (a ground ball) into the pitcher's area of responsibility.
3. The pitcher fields ball number 2 and throws to second base.
4. The shortstop covering second base makes the catch and throws to first base to complete the double play.
5. The first-base player tosses the ball back to the pitcher for the next repetition. The catcher tosses ball number 1 to the coach for the next repetition.

Advanced Variations

- Vary the speed, angle, and force with which the grounder is delivered.
- Hit a line drive every now and then to keep the pitcher alert.
- **Pitcher-Catcher Interaction.** Position a batter and a base runner on first base. The catcher must decide whether the pitcher will be able to turn the double play or just throw to first base for one out. The catcher yells to the pitcher which bag to throw to.
- **Slap Hit Double Play.** When a lefty slapper is the batter, the shortstop will be "in the hole" and "up the line," making it difficult to get to second base in time for the play. In this case, have your second-base player get to the bag and receive the throw from the pitcher and continue the double play.

127. Pitcher Basic Backup (Intermediate)

Purpose: To practice backing up in base hit and extra-base hit situations
Equipment: Softball, buckets
Number of players: 1

Number of repetitions: 10 to 15
Allocated time: 3 to 5 minutes
Parent-friendly drill: ✔
Cardio index: 💗 💗

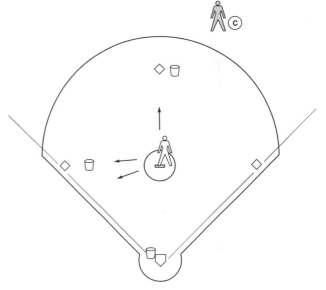

1. A coach holding a ball and standing in the shallow outfield calls out the game situation, for example, base hit to the outfield with nobody on base, or bases loaded extra bases hit, etc.
2. Station buckets (representing infielders) at the bags.
3. A pitcher in the pitching circle reacts and promptly moves into position to back up the appropriate base as follows:

   - If the ball is hit to the outfield with nobody on base, the pitcher backs up second base if it looks like a double.
   - If the ball is hit to the outfield with nobody on base, the pitcher backs up third base if it looks like a triple.
   - If the ball is hit into the gap with a runner on first base, the pitcher runs out the third-base line and, depending on where the coach (simulating catcher) calls for the ball to be thrown, backs up the appropriate base (third base or home plate).

4. The coach throws the ball to the appropriate bag.
5. The pitcher backs up the infielder (the bucket will make a catching error every time) and recovers the ball, making the play and/or a phantom throw for the secondary play if there is one.

Hints

Make sure the pitchers are taking the correct route to each bag and not interfering with base runners.

Pitcher-Catcher Interaction Drills

128. Pitcher Bunt (Intermediate)

Purpose: To practice working with the catcher to field bunts with runners on first and second base; helps pitcher work on footwork and setup for a good throw to proper base called by catcher
Equipment: 2 softballs
Number of players: 2 (pitcher, catcher)
Number of repetitions: 10 to 15

Allocated time: 5 minutes
Parent-friendly drill: ✔ In confined spaces, pitcher simulates full fast-pitch motion without the ball. Parent rolls the ball as the pitcher "releases" the ball. Pitcher fields and makes a phantom throw to the appropriate base.
Cardio index: ♥ ♥

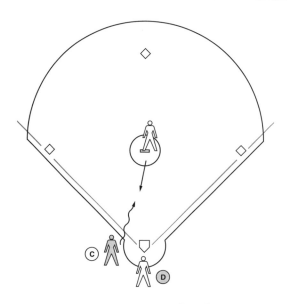

1. A pitcher executes drill 116, Pitcher Full Pitch Mechanics, (any type pitch) from the pitching circle to a catcher in full gear at home plate.
2. As the pitcher releases ball number 1 and follows through into an athletic stance, a coach about 6 feet away from the catcher throws or rolls ball number 2 (a ground ball) into the pitcher's area of responsibility.
3. The pitcher fields the "bunt" by running to the ball in the direction she wants to throw it. For advanced players, a right-handed pitcher approaches the ball directly if bunted to the first-base side and circles the ball if bunted to the third-base side. A left-handed pitcher approaches the ball directly if bunted to the third-base side and circles the ball if bunted to the first-base side.
4. After the approach, the pitcher plants her throwing-side foot next to the ball, picks the ball up, and pushes off her planted foot (with no extra steps) as she makes a phantom throw to the base called by the catcher.
5. The pitcher lobs ball number 2 to the catcher. The catcher tosses both balls to the coach for the next repetition.

Advanced Variations

- The catcher yells for the play at second or third. As the pitcher fields the ball, the catcher (realizing the second- or third-base player will not get to the base in time or the runner at second is not advancing) then yells "No, 1-1-1!" The pitcher who is getting ready to throw to second or third has to stop, reset her feet, and then throw to first.

- Station base runners at the plate and at the bases. Each runner will advance one base per drill repetition. The pitcher must work together with the catcher, and the pitcher will execute this drill to throw the appropriate runner out. Each runner should complete at least two trips around the bases to facilitate cardio exercise.
- **Pitcher Blind Bunt.** The coach stands behind the catcher and rolls balls to either side or between the catcher's legs. This is more challenging because the catcher will not immediately know where the ball is coming from or going. The pitcher fields the ball and makes the play if the ball rolls into her area of responsibility. The catcher fields the ball and makes the play if it rolls into her area of responsibility.
- **Pitcher Bunt and Run.** Have base runners "going" on some of the bunts as in a bunt-and-run play. This will challenge the catcher and give her little time to decide which base to have the fielders throw to.

129. Pitcher Pitchout (Intermediate)

Purpose: To practice throwing pitchouts
Equipment: Softball
Number of players: 2 (pitcher and catcher in full gear)

Number of repetitions: 5 to each side of the plate
Allocated time: 3 to 5 minutes
Parent-friendly drill: ✔
Cardio index: ♥ ♥ ♥

1. A coach indicates if the imaginary batter is right- or left-handed.
2. A catcher in full gear at home plate gives the pitcher her signal for the pitchout (a pitch thrown to the batter's box high opposite the batter's shoulder to enable the catcher to more efficiently throw an advancing runner out).
3. The pitcher in the pitching circle executes drill 116, Pitcher Full Pitch Mechanics, but rather than a fastball in the strike zone throws a shoulder-high fastball to the batter's box opposite the batter.
4. The catcher gets up from her crouch to catch the ball and throws the ball back to the pitcher.

Advanced Variations

- Station a batter in the batter's box (have your batter alternate right- and left-handed batting stances). This will simulate game conditions by slightly obstructing the catcher's view.
- Station first- and second-base players and a base runner at first base who may attempt to steal second base. The catcher will throw to the appropriate base depending on what the runner does.
- Have a batter "swing through" the pitchout as in a hit-and-run situation.

Hints

Try to have the pitcher throw to an area where the catcher can catch over her throwing shoulder, helping to decrease the amount of time she holds the ball from catch to throw in "and run" situations.

Playing Catcher

It's hard to avoid the catcher's stereotype of the large plodding athlete with feet of clay, tree trunks for arms, and a personality to match. While that image may work in Hollywood, the best catchers are able to think and move quickly to solve problems. In fact, ask any elite pitcher who the most important person on the field is to her, and without a doubt, she'll say the catcher. Catchers in youth softball must learn to deal with Murphy's Law, that is, excessively wild pitching and offenses geared to take advantage of pitching lapses by advancing bases often. As pitchers improve their accuracy through the middle and high school years, catchers start to learn the nuances of defensive and pitching strategy. As the only defensive player to face and therefore see all of the action, catchers are in a unique and privileged position to make a great impact on every play of the game.

The drills in this chapter are designed to reinforce the following skill sets for youth, middle school, and high school catchers:

- **Mechanics of catching.** The fundamentals of the catcher's skills.
- **Murphy's Law.** How to block wild pitches, etc., and then make the play.
- **Catcher as fielder and field general.** How to deal with pop-ups, bunts, steals, home-plate tag outs, and so on.

A Few Words About the Coach-Catcher Dynamic

Catchers love action. Sometimes youth and middle school age catchers get more action than they bargain for. Often everything goes wrong, and sometimes all in the same play: a wild pitch to the backstop and then a runner, or two, advancing home. What to do? Explain to your catchers that these situations are par for the course in junior softball, and that it's not the catcher's fault, or the pitcher's for that matter. Then reinforce these words of encouragement with the drills in this chapter. Playing catcher is not for the thin-skinned. But a combination of encouragement, repetition, and on-the-job training will eventually make the mistake-filled innings nothing but a distant memory.

Basic Mechanics of Catching

Catcher's Ready Stance

Make sure your catcher starts with the *ready stance*. She should do the following:

Katelyn is in a classic catcher's stance. She protects her throwing hand by tucking it behind her until she's ready to throw.

- Always wear full catcher's gear when playing or practicing, including the drills in this book.
- Squat, facing the pitcher, about 3 feet behind home plate, keeping her thighs more or less parallel to the ground and weight evenly distributed to prevent falling into the batter's box (and the bat's trajectory). Use common sense to increase the distance when the batter or the bat used is extraordinarily tall or long. Advanced catchers will develop the skill to adjust this distance based on where the batter stands in the batter's box (front, middle, or back).
- Stay square to the pitch because her gear is designed to protect the front of her body.
- Protect her throwing hand by tucking it behind her until she receives the pitch. This is the one exception to the rule that fielders should catch the ball with two hands. Your catcher should remember that the pitcher's priority is to strike the batter out, rather than deliver a throw the catcher can easily handle.
- Make herself as small as possible but provide a large strike target for the pitcher by keeping her open mitt out in front of her (arm stretched but not stiff).
- Make sure her glove-arm elbow is outside of her knees. This will ensure the maximum range of motion to enable her to receive any pitch.

Catcher's Throwing Mechanics

Now your catcher is ready for the pitch. As the ball is pitched, she should do the following:

- Receive the ball in her glove.
- Then in one smooth motion stand up, turning her body sideways to the target as she does so, while bringing her mitt and throwing hand to her throwing-side ear to accommodate a quick transfer of the ball to her throwing hand.
- Execute a proper overhand throw. The catcher must resist the temptation to throw sidearm; this will risk injury to the elbow and shoulders and cause the ball to take a curved path. With practice, your catcher

should be able to graduate from merely standing up and executing the throw to jumping up and executing the throw in any direction—that is, to any base.

- Keep alert and be ready for anything, including pitches thrown to either side or thrown too high or low.
- Keep her eye on the ball. With concentration and practice, your catcher will be able to properly track the ball into her mitt without flinching and regardless of what the batter is doing.
- Properly field any balls hit or bunted into her area of responsibility.

All of the drills in this chapter are designed to be used with any type of ball. Use softies or tennis balls (still with the player wearing full gear) until your catchers are ready for regulation softballs.

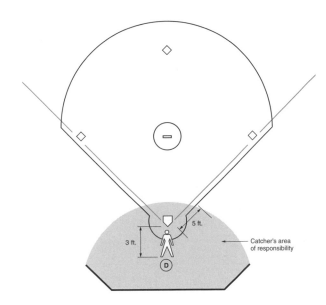

Chapter 7 Skills Matrix

Drill Number	Drill Title (Indented drills are "named" Advanced Variations)	Skills Reinforced ⟶					
		Catcher Mechanics	Framing	Blocking	Catcher Situation	Infielders Situation	Catcher Pop-Up Fielding
Catcher Mechanics							
130.	Catcher Strike Zone	●					
	Catcher Cross-Up	●					
	Catcher Framing	●	●				
Catcher Murphy's Law							
131.	Catcher Wild Pitch Block in Triangle			●	●		
	Catcher Mix-It-Up			●	●		
	Catcher Block No Hands			●	●		
	Catcher Wall Block			●	●		
132.	Catcher Wild Pitch with Runner at Third Base				●	●	
	Catcher Slide to Backstop				●		
133.	Catcher Drops Third Strike				●	●	
	Batter Strike 3 but Go!				●	●	
Catcher as Fielder and Field General							
134.	Catcher Pop-Up						●
	Catcher Two-Ball Pop-Up						●
	Catcher Pop-Up — Pick the Color						●
	Catcher Pop-Up — Umpire Obstacle						●
	Catcher Pop-Up Near Backstop						●
135.	Catcher Bunt First-Base Play				●	●	
	Catcher Bunt No Telegraph				●	●	
136.	Catcher Simulated Bunts				●	●	
	Catcher Bunt with Live Runners				●	●	
	Catcher Bunt Throw to Third				●	●	
	Catcher Bunt Second Option				●	●	
137.	Catcher Home Plate Tag Out				●	●	
	Catcher Block-the-Plate Tag Out				●	●	

Catcher Bunt Fielding	Catcher Backup	Catcher Throw to Base	Throwing	Catching	Baserunning	Simultaneous Arrive and Catch	Throw to Bag	Catcher Tag Out
			⚾	⚾	⚾		⚾	
			⚾	⚾				
			⚾	⚾	⚾			
⚾		⚾	⚾	⚾				
⚾		⚾	⚾	⚾				
⚾		⚾	⚾	⚾				
⚾		⚾	⚾	⚾	⚾			
⚾		⚾	⚾	⚾				
⚾		⚾	⚾	⚾				
			⚾	⚾	⚾			⚾
			⚾	⚾	⚾			⚾

(continued)

Chapter 7 Skills Matrix *(continued)*

Drill Number	Drill Title (Indented drills are "named" Advanced Variations)	Skills Reinforced ⟶					
		Catcher Mechanics	Framing	Blocking	Catcher Situation	Infielders Situation	Catcher Pop-Up Fielding
138.	Catcher "No One On" Infield Ground Ball Backup				⚾	⚾	
	Catcher Backup Errant Throw				⚾	⚾	
	Foul Line Fence Rebound				⚾	⚾	
139.	Catcher—Stealing to Second Base				⚾	⚾	
	Catcher Pickoff				⚾		
140.	Catcher Double Play Fungo				⚾	⚾	
	Catcher No Force Play				⚾	⚾	
141.	Catcher to First, Second, and Third				⚾	⚾	
	Catcher to Bases with Visual Obstruction				⚾	⚾	

Catcher Bunt Fielding	Catcher Backup	Catcher Throw to Base	Throwing	Catching	Baserunning	Simultaneous Arrive and Catch	Throw to Bag	Catcher Tag Out
	⚾		⚾	⚾	⚾			
	⚾							
	⚾							
		⚾	⚾	⚾	⚾	⚾	⚾	
		⚾	⚾	⚾	⚾	⚾	⚾	
		⚾	⚾	⚾			⚾	
		⚾	⚾	⚾	⚾		⚾	⚾
		⚾	⚾	⚾			⚾	
		⚾	⚾	⚾			⚾	

Catcher Mechanics Drills

130. Catcher Strike Zone (Beginner)

Purpose: To reinforce mechanics of receiving inside and outside pitches

Equipment: Catcher's gear, supply of softballs

Number of players: 1

Number of repetitions: 10 sets of 4 pitches (2 inside and 2 outside pitches)

Allocated time: 5 minutes per catcher

Parent-friendly drill: ✔

Cardio index: ♥ (drill involves lots of squats and rises)

Katelyn is in a classic catcher's stance and is about to receive a pitch. She protects her throwing hand by tucking it behind her until she's ready to throw.

1. A catcher in full gear assumes her ready stance behind home plate.
2. A coach about 20 feet away throws to either the outside or inside of the plate. For the purposes of our discussion, we'll assume a right-handed catcher and an imaginary right-handed batter.
3. For outside pitches, the catcher moves her mitt across the midline of her body to receive the ball backhanded, taking care not to turn the thumb of her mitt upward. The thumb of the glove of a right-handed catcher should be at about 3 to 4 o'clock. For a left-handed catcher, the thumb should be at 8 to 9 o'clock.
4. For inside pitches, the catcher receives the pitch in the proper glove-hand-side manner. The thumb of the glove for a right-handed catcher should be at about 2 to 3 o'clock. For a left handed-catcher, the thumb should be at about 9 to 10 o'clock.
5. In one smooth motion, the catcher picks up the ball to the ear and stands up quickly in the proper position to make the throw back to the coach.

Advanced Variations

- **Catcher Cross-Up.** Work on the catcher's body position on pitches that cross up the catcher. One way to do this is for the coach to set up for an outside pitch but throw an inside pitch. Encourage the catcher not to give up on the pitch. She should try to save the pitch and get the strike call whenever possible.
- **Catcher Framing.** Framing is the practice of taking a pitch just outside the strike zone and pulling it into the strike zone to make it look

like a strike. Stand about 10 feet away from the catcher, who is in her ready stance behind the plate, and toss balls up or down or at the corners of the strike zone. The catcher uses proper wrist movements to bring pitches just outside of the zone into the zone. For example, the catcher turns her glove to cup and lift low pitches back into the bottom of the strike zone. This drill also can be done barehand with softies or tennis balls.

Hints

Receiving outside pitches correctly will help the umpire call strikes for pitches close to the zone. For inside pitches, the catcher should avoid catching the ball outside her midline of her body; this will give the appearance of a ball even if the pitch is in the strike zone.

Catcher Murphy's Law Drills

131. Catcher Wild Pitch Block in Triangle (Beginner)

Purpose: To practice blocking low-thrown wild pitches in front of the catcher's body (like a hockey goalie—think "block" rather than catch!)

Equipment: Catcher's gear, supply of softballs

Number of players: 1

Number of repetitions: 4 to 5 for beginners and 8 to 10 for advanced players; 4 sets

Allocated time: 5 minutes per catcher

Parent-friendly drill: ✔

Cardio index: ♥ ♥

Katelyn has surrounded the ball and uses her legs, body, and glove to close all possible escape routes for the ball. Instead of trying to catch the wild pitch, she has correctly blocked it to prevent a bad situation (wild pitch) from getting worse (extra bases).

1. A catcher in full gear assumes her ready stance behind home plate.
2. A coach from 6 to 20 feet away throws a ball into the dirt in front or up to 2 feet to either side of the plate.
3. The catcher blocks the ball in front of her body so that the ball stays in the *triangle*. The triangle area has the apex at about chest level up the midline of the body, and the bottom points are the knees on the ground.
4. The catcher slides into position, drops to her knees, and blocks the ball by closing all possible escape routes as the ball arrives. She should do the following:

   • Touch her mitt to the ground between her knees
   • Keep her elbows close to her sides

- Cup her upper body in toward the ball (chin slightly down)
- Surround and trap the ball with her body

5. The catcher executes a proper overhand throw back to the coach. Advanced players can throw to the appropriate base designated by the coach.

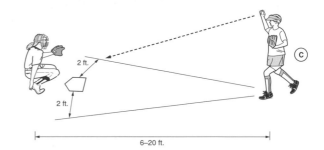

Advanced Variations

- **Catcher Mix-It-Up.** Mix it up by varying the speed, angle, and force with which the wild pitch is delivered. Throw a strike every now and then to keep the catcher alert. Or use a wild bounce ball (Z-Ball) for the drill. Have a batter in the box to take swings. This is designed to distract the catcher.
- **Catcher Block No Hands.** Reinforce the "block rather than catch" mentality by having the catcher execute the drill (1) with her hands clasped behind her back and blocking entirely with her legs and chest or (2) using a soft hands device.
- **Catcher Wall Block.** Have the catcher assume her ready stance facing a wall 10 feet away. Stand behind the catcher and throw the ball at the wall so that it bounces back in front of the catcher and have the catcher block the ball. Use tennis balls to increase velocity. The closer the catcher is to the wall, the more difficult the drill.
- Simulate a base runner stealing second or third base and have the catcher throw for the tag out.
- Throw two or three balls of varying color. Before throwing, call out the color ball the catcher should block.

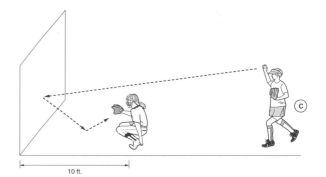

Hints

The catcher should try to block the ball straight down into the dirt in front of her body to avoid having the ball ricochet outside of the triangle. Keeping the ball inside the triangle will enable the catcher to see the field and make the play. Base runners will hesitate to advance when they see a catcher in control of the situation. Encourage your catchers to use their feet to quickly slide to the ball and to dive or backhand only as a last resort.

Remind your catcher to protect her throwing hand by keeping it behind her body. With experience, advanced catchers may move the throwing hand behind the mitt.

132. Catcher Wild Pitch with Runner at Third Base (Intermediate)

Purpose: To reinforce technique for pursuing and retrieving unblockable wild pitches and making the play as the runner from third base attempts to score

Equipment: Catcher's gear, supply of softballs

Number of players: 3

Number of repetitions: 3 for beginners and 5 to 8 for advanced players; 5 sets

Allocated time: 5 minutes per catcher

Parent-friendly drill: ✔ If you are short-staffed or don't have a backstop, a parent can initiate this drill by scattering balls (rather than throwing) about 10 to 15 feet behind the catcher.

Cardio index: ♥ ♥ ♥

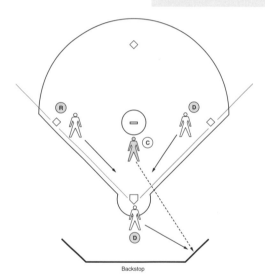

Backstop

1. A catcher in full gear assumes her ready stance behind home plate.
2. Position a player at first base and a base runner at third.
3. A coach from 6 to 20 feet away throws a ball past the catcher toward the backstop (too high, too far to the side, etc.).
4. The runner at third base decides whether to run.
5. The catcher pursues and retrieves the ball.
6. The catcher executes a proper overhand throw back to the coach or makes an underhand toss to the first-base player covering home plate, delivered at a height and position to enable the player covering home plate to tag out the base runner.

Advanced Variation

Catcher Slide to Backstop. Have more experienced catchers work on sliding on their shin guards as they approach the ball at the backstop. This will be quicker than running to the ball and bending over to pick it up.

Hints

Note that some coaches prefer the pitcher to cover the plate on wild pitches to the backstop.

The slide to backstop and throw technique is the best way to get the ball back to the plate to make the tag out. Watch your catcher's footwork. A drop step should be used as the first step to get to the backstop. Have your catchers join the outfielders as they execute the drop step drills in Chapter 2.

Make sure your catcher's gear fits well and is not in her way as she runs. Loose-fitting gear will slow her down when she is trying to get to the ball.

133. Catcher Drops Third Strike (Intermediate)

Purpose: To reinforce the catcher's technique for retrieving a botched catch of a third-strike pitch and throwing to first base for the out (batter is allowed to run to first base if the catcher drops a third-strike pitch)

Equipment: Catcher's gear, supply of softballs

Number of players: 2

Number of repetitions: 3 for beginners and 5 to 8 for advanced players; 5 sets

Allocated time: 5 minutes per catcher

Parent-friendly drill: ✔ Place several softballs at various locations a short distance behind, to the side, or in front of the catcher for her to retrieve and make the play to first base. The parent then assumes the role of first-base player when the drill begins.

Cardio index: 💜 💜 💜

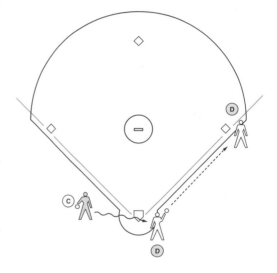

1. A catcher in full gear assumes her ready stance behind home plate.
2. Position a player at first base.
3. A coach standing several feet to the side of the catcher rolls a ball a short distance behind, to the side of, or in front of the catcher. This simulates a third-strike pitch that the catcher has caught but then dropped, allowing the batter to advance to first base.
4. Alternative: the coach about 20 feet away delivers an underhand toss to the catcher, who catches and then intentionally drops the ball.
5. The catcher retrieves the "dropped" ball.
6. The catcher executes a proper overhand throw to the first-base player, who is properly set up to receive the throw.
7. Some teams have the second-base player cover first base because the first-base player is chasing after the dropped ball as well. If so, first- and second-base players can take turns covering first base in this drill.

Advanced Variations

- **Batter Strike 3 but Go!** Have a batter attempt to advance to first base.
- Work different angles of the ball coming off the catcher's gear and mitt.

- Put a base runner on second or third base and have the catcher try to keep the runner from advancing while making the throw and getting the batter out at first base.
- Toss two different colored balls at the catcher and call out the color ball to go after.

Hints

Encourage your catchers to be aware of the game situation at all times. Being alert combined with being prepared will allow a catcher to readily handle these quick reaction situations.

When throwing to first base, the novice catcher should take a step or two inside the foul line and then throw. This will help her avoid hitting the base runner with the throw. If the ball is on the foul side of first base, she should throw to the foul side of the bag.

Catcher as Fielder Drills

134. Catcher Pop-Up (Intermediate)

Purpose: To practice fielding pop-ups and foul pops and throwing to the bases

Equipment: Catcher's gear, supply of softballs or tennis racket and balls

Number of players: 1

Number of repetitions: 3 for beginners and 5 for advanced players; 5 sets

Allocated time: 5 minutes per catcher

Parent-friendly drill: ✔

Cardio index: 💙 💙

1. A catcher in full gear assumes her ready stance behind home plate.
2. A coach about 10 feet away to the side of the catcher initiates the drill either by throwing a softball or using a tennis racket to hit a tennis ball high above the catcher's head, in any direction in the catcher's area of responsibility, including foul territory.
3. The catcher locates the ball and runs toward it.
4. If necessary to improve her vision, the catcher takes the mask off and throws it in the opposite direction so she doesn't trip over it.
5. The catcher catches the ball overhead, with her back to the infield.

Catcher's area of responsibility

~10 ft.   5 ft.

Backstop

Advanced Variations

- **Catcher Two-Ball Pop-Up.** Throw two balls in quick succession in the catcher's area of responsibility. The catcher executes proper technique to locate and field both balls.
- **Catcher Pop-Up—Pick the Color.** Throw two balls of different colors in quick succession in the catcher's area of responsibility. The catcher executes proper technique to locate and field the ball of the color called out by the coach.
- **Catcher Pop-Up—Umpire Obstacle.** After throwing or hitting the ball to begin the drill, the coach steps to where the umpire normally sets up. The catcher must get around the umpire to track and catch the pop-up.
- **Catcher Pop-Up Near Backstop.** Throw the ball close to or against the overhang of the backstop. This will force the catcher to focus on the ball, not the backstop or netting.

135. Catcher Bunt First-Base Play (Intermediate)

Purpose: To practice fielding bunts and throwing to first base for the out

Equipment: Catcher's gear, supply of softballs

Number of players: 2

Number of repetitions: 3 reps for 3 sets for beginners, 5 reps for 5 sets for advanced players

Allocated time: 5 minutes per catcher

Parent-friendly drill: ✔

Cardio index: ♥ ♥ ♥

1. A catcher in full gear assumes her ready stance behind home plate. Position a player at first base.
2. A coach 5 to 8 feet away simulates a bunt by rolling a ball in the fair territory portion of the catcher's area of responsibility.
3. The catcher hops out of her ready stance and runs to the ball in the direction she wants to throw it. In other words, right-handed catchers approach the ball directly if bunted to the first-base side and circle the ball if bunted to the third-base side. Reverse for left-handed catchers.
4. The catcher bends over to retrieve the ball.
5. The catcher executes a proper overhand throw to first base.

Advanced Variations

- **Catcher Bunt No Telegraph.** The coach stands behind the catcher and rolls balls to either side or between the catcher's legs. This is a more challenging variation because the catcher will not immediately know where the ball is coming from or going to.
- Station base runners at the plate. The batter will sprint to first base. The catcher will execute this drill to throw the runner out. The batter returns to home plate to wait her next turn.

Hints

When throwing to first base, the novice catcher should take a step or two inside the foul line and then throw. This will help her avoid hitting the base runner with the throw.

136. Catcher Simulated Bunts (Intermediate)

Purpose: To practice fielding bunts and throwing to the appropriate base for the out

Equipment: Catcher's gear, supply of softballs

Number of players: 4

Number of repetitions: 1 set of 10 balls

Allocated time: 3 minutes per catcher

Parent-friendly drill: ✔ If short-staffed or short on room, execute drill without second- and third-base players.

Cardio index: ♥ ♥ ♥

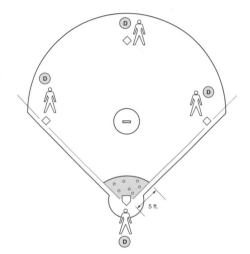

1. A catcher in full gear assumes her ready stance behind home plate.
2. Position players at first, second, and third base.
3. A coach places up to 10 balls at various distances in the fair territory portion of the catcher's area of responsibility. The locations of these balls simulate where bunts have been hit.
4. On the coach's cue, the catcher hops out of her ready stance and runs to a ball in the direction she wants to throw it.
5. The catcher bends over to retrieve the ball.
6. The catcher executes a proper overhand throw to first, second, or third base, as called out by the coach.
7. The catcher returns to her ready stance behind home plate and then quickly repeats this drill until all the balls have been thrown.

Advanced Variations

- **Catcher Bunt with Live Runners.** Station base runners at the plate and at the bases. Each runner will advance one base per drill repetition. The catcher will execute this drill to throw the designated runner out. Each runner should complete at least two trips around the bases to facilitate cardio exercise.
- **Catcher Bunt Throw to Third.** Challenge your advanced catchers by placing balls at difficult angles on the first-base line and asking them to make a good throw to third base.
- **Catcher Bunt Second Option.** Challenge your advanced catchers by having them pump (prepare to throw, but not throw) to second base, then reposition and replant their feet into proper throwing position for a strong throw to first base for the out. This will help in situations where the players become aware that the out at second is not possible.

Hints

When throwing to first or third base, the novice catcher should take a step or two inside the foul line and then throw. This will help her avoid hitting the base runner with the throw.

When throwing to second base, the catcher should make a quick line-drive throw. Novice catchers may need one bounce, but compared to a high arc throw, an accurate one-bounce throw will arrive at second both faster and in a better position for the player covering the base to make a tag out.

137. Catcher Home Plate Tag Out (Intermediate)

Purpose: To practice catching fielded balls thrown to home plate and tagging out a base runner advancing for the score

Equipment: Catcher's gear, supply of softballs

Number of players: 3

Number of repetitions: 10 throws to home for beginners, 10 throws for 2 sets for advanced players

Allocated time: 5 minutes per catcher

Parent-friendly drill: ✔ If practicing this drill in your backyard with your catcher, instead of a base runner, the parent stands on an imaginary third-base line and rolls a large exercise ball toward home plate, which simulates the base runner. The parent then throws a softball to the catcher to tag out the exercise ball.

Cardio index: ♥ ♥

1. A catcher in full gear assumes her ready stance behind home plate.
2. Position an infielder with a ball at first, second, third, or shortstop and a runner at third base.
3. The runner (wearing sliding gear) begins the play by sprinting to home plate on the coach's cue and slides into the plate with the proper technique.
4. The infielder attempts to throw the runner out with a quick line-drive throw to the catcher.
5. The catcher maintains a low center of gravity, receives the ball, and tags out the runner.

Advanced Variations

- **Catcher Block-the-Plate Tag Out.** Advanced catchers should try to block the plate and force the runner to slide around or behind the plate. This will buy some time for the catcher to receive the throw.

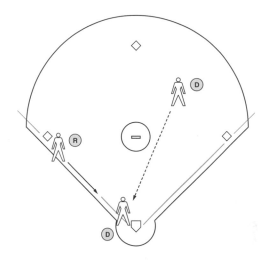

Safe or out? Katelyn applies the tag on Jenn as she does a bent-leg slide into home plate. Katelyn is blocking the plate with a low center of gravity and has two hands on the ball. Jenn protects her hands by having them up and behind her.

The catcher should brace herself for contact with the sliding runner by keeping a low center of gravity.

- Add a batter at home plate without a bat. This simulates an actual game situation by partially blocking the view of the catcher. The batter may take a pretend swing, but then should follow league regulations and quickly get out of the way in the proper manner when each repetition begins. This ensures the safety of the catcher and runner, not to mention the batter herself.

- Add a first-base player and a batter without a bat. The batter may take a pretend swing, simulate a hit, and advance toward first base. The infielder must decide where to throw—home plate or first base. If the throw is to home plate, the catcher makes the tag out and then decides whether to throw to first base. If the initial throw is to first base, the first-base player makes the out and then decides whether to throw to home plate.

Hints

This is a small group drill, but the coach may incorporate this drill into a team fungo workout involving the entire defensive unit.

The infielder should make a quick line-drive throw to the catcher. Novice fielders may need one bounce, but compared to a high arc throw, an accurate one-bounce throw will arrive at home plate both faster and in a better position for the catcher to make a tag out.

138. Catcher "No One On" Infield Ground Ball Backup (Intermediate)

Purpose: To practice backing up first base for "no one on base" infield ground ball
Equipment: Catcher's gear, supply of softballs
Number of players: All infielders

Number of repetitions: 3 reps for 3 sets for beginners, 5 reps for 5 sets for advanced players
Allocated time: 5 minutes per catcher
Cardio index: ♥ ♥ ♥

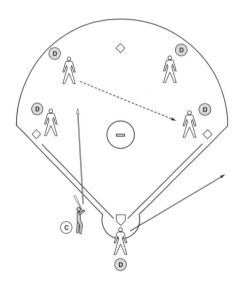

1. A catcher in full gear assumes her ready stance behind home plate.
2. All infielders assume their on-field positions.
3. A coach on the third-base line about 10 feet from the catcher tosses or hits a ball to simulate an infield ground ball hit outside the catcher's area of responsibility.
4. The appropriate fielder fields the ball and throws to first base.
5. In the meantime, the catcher (determining that there are no base runners to threaten home plate) runs outside the first-base line and in position about 20 feet behind first base.
6. The catcher determines her exact position behind first base based on the direction that the throw is coming from.
7. The catcher is ready to back up the first-base player in case of an errant throw or botched catch.

Advanced Variations

- **Catcher Backup Errant Throw.** Station another coach in the first-base coach's box. Have the first-base player take off her glove and assume the base runner role at first base (now there is no first-base player). An infielder fields the "infield ground ball" thrown or hit by the coach and throws to first base. The "invisible" first-base player can't negotiate the throw and the "errant" ball sails into foul territory. The catcher backs up and retrieves the ball and throws out the runner advancing to second base. This is a live simulation; the runner should try to beat the throw and slide into second base. The catcher will need to maneuver around the first-base coach.

- **Foul Line Fence Rebound.** Station only a second-base player and a runner at first base. A coach standing in the infield throws the ball at various angles at the foul line fence, simulating a variety of errant throws to first base. The catcher learns to predict bounce patterns in retrieving the ball. The catcher backs up and retrieves the ball and throws out the runner advancing to second base. Better yet, the catcher is so efficient in retrieving the ball that the runner decides not to go for it.

Hints

Have your catcher run sprints with her shin guards on, which takes some getting used to. Keep the catcher alert and every once in a while simulate a ball hit within the catcher's area of responsibility and see that she executes the proper play.

Softball Versus Baseball

Because of the angle of the throw to first base, right fielders are expected to back up first base on bunts. We do not recommend that softball coaches follow the baseball practice of sometimes having catchers back up first base on balls bunted outside the catcher's area of responsibility.

139. Catcher—Stealing to Second Base (Intermediate)

Purpose: To practice catching the pitch and throwing to second base for the tag out of the base runner stealing second base

Equipment: Catcher's gear, supply of softballs

Number of players: 3

Number of repetitions: 3 reps for 3 sets for beginners, building to 5 sets with increased arm strength; 5 reps for 3 sets for advanced players, building to 5 sets

Allocated time: 5 minutes per catcher

Cardio index: ♥ ♥

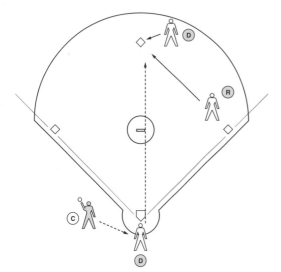

1. A catcher in full gear assumes her ready stance behind home plate.
2. Position a second-base player, as well as a runner at first.
3. A coach, from 5 to 10 feet to the side of the catcher, tosses a ball underhand to the catcher.
4. The catcher receives the ball.
5. The runner at first base, starting about two stride lengths from first base, attempts to steal. (Starting from this position simulates taking a lead as the pitcher releases the ball—consult with local league rules for when a runner can take a lead.)
6. The catcher executes a proper overhand throw to second base for the tag out.

Advanced Variations

- **Catcher Pickoff.** Add a pitcher, a first-base player, and a batter at home plate. Instead of the coach tossing the ball, the pitcher begins the drill by making an underhand medium-speed pitch to home plate. The catcher has the option to throw to first base to pick off any base runner with an overzealous lead. Make sure your catcher adjusts her footwork depending on the target of her throw.
- The pitcher also has the option to throw a pitchout to the catcher to begin the drill.
- Mix it up; don't let the catcher know if your runners will actually steal.
- Add steals to and pickoffs at third for advanced catchers.

Hints

The advanced catcher should throw to second base, rather than to the player covering second base. It is the responsibility of the player covering second base to get there to receive the throw. Of course, the novice catcher should use common sense; don't throw to second if it looks like nobody intends to cover second (system failure).

140. Catcher Double Play Fungo (Intermediate)

Purpose: To practice catcher-initiated double plays off the force play to home plate

Equipment: Catcher's gear, supply of softballs

Number of players: All infielders

Number of repetitions: 3 reps for 3 sets for beginners, 5 reps for 3 sets for advanced players

Allocated time: 3 to 4 minutes per catcher

Cardio index: ♥ ♥ ♥

1. A catcher in full gear assumes her ready stance behind home plate.
2. All infielders assume their on-field positions.
3. A coach hits a grounder to any of the infielders. Assume the bases are loaded.
4. The appropriate infielder fields and throws the ball to home plate.
5. The catcher catches the ball with her foot on home plate for one out (force play).
6. The catcher executes a proper overhand throw to first base for the second out.
7. When throwing to first base, the novice catcher should take a step or two inside the foul line and then throw. This will help her avoid hitting the base runner with the throw.

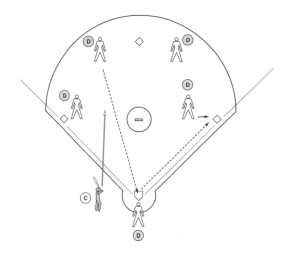

Advanced Variations

- Station base runners at home plate and at the bases. Each runner will advance one base per drill repetition. The players will execute this drill to throw the runner advancing to home plate out, and the catcher will then throw the batter advancing to first base out. Each runner should complete at least two trips around the bases to facilitate cardio exercise.
- Have the runners coming home slide into the catcher trying to break up the double play.
- Have the catcher throw to first base with the runner advancing at different distances to the bag. This will make the catcher have to decide whether she should make the throw.
- **Catcher No Force Play.** Station runners on second and third base, but not first base. The catcher throws to first base for the force out. The runners attempt to advance. The first-base player throws to home plate for the tag out. Since the runner at third base didn't have to run, it's not a force play at home plate, and the catcher has to tag the runner.

141. Catcher to First, Second, and Third (Intermediate)

Purpose: To practice catching the pitch and throwing to the bases

Equipment: Catcher's gear, supply of softballs

Number of players: All infielders except pitcher

Number of repetitions: 2 throws to each base for beginners, 4 to 5 throws for advanced players

Allocated time: 3 to 5 minutes per catcher

Cardio index: ♥ ♥ ♥

1. A catcher in full gear assumes her ready stance behind home plate.
2. The infielders assume their on-field positions.
3. A coach from the pitching circle throws a ball underhand to the catcher.
4. The catcher catches the ball with the proper technique.
5. The coach calls out the base the catcher should throw to.
6. The catcher executes a proper overhand throw to first, second, or third.
7. When throwing to first or third base, work all angles—the catcher alternates the following:

   - Takes a step or two inside the foul line and then throws to first or third base (this simulates plays of a bunt, mishit ball, or strikeout to start the throw around the horn).
   - Throws outside the foul line behind the batter to third base (this simulates a play to throw out a steal to third or a pickoff at third).
   - Throws outside the first-base line as when a ball has gotten away from her in foul territory (this simulates a dropped third strike and she has to make a throw to first base).

Advanced Variations

- **Catcher to Bases with Visual Obstruction.** Have a right-handed batter get in the way of the catcher trying to throw to third base. This will make her have to throw behind the batter. Have a left-handed batter get in the way of the catcher throwing to second base. Have the batter square to bunt and then pull the bat back into the line of sight of the catcher trying catch the pitch.
- Station base runners at the plate and at the bases. Each runner will advance one base per drill repetition. The catcher tries to throw the designated runner out.
- Don't have your runners steal on every pitch. Keep the catcher guessing and reacting.
- Work throws to second base with the second-base player covering some throws and the shortstop covering some throws.
- Work throws to third base with the third-base player covering some throws and the shortstop covering some throws.

Pregame Drills

It's about 60 minutes to game time. The team has had some productive practices using the drills in this book. Now it's time to put it all together.

First, make sure your players start with 10 to 15 minutes of *dynamic warm-ups*, which will help the team get ready to warm up their softball skills. It's important to warm up the body first before warming up for softball. Dynamic warm-ups include some light jogging, agilities (change in direction, foot speed, and explosiveness), plyometrics (jump training, used to develop muscles necessary for quick, bounding movements), and some light stretching. Most stretching should be done after the game or practice because stretching actually cools down the muscles, and we want to do that after our workouts are over. The starting pitcher and catcher should warm up separately about 30 minutes before game time under the trained eye of a coach knowledgeable about mechanics. Pitchers should always warm up their arms throwing overhand before starting to throw pitches.

The drills in this chapter are designed to reinforce the mechanical and mental aspects of *team* defense in a very compressed time schedule. Furthermore, most of the drills can be combined to enhance efficiency depending on how much time you have. The following sample pregame schedule also includes hitting drills, which will allow the players to find and keep their rhythm.

Sample Pregame Warm-Up Schedule

1. Dynamic warm-ups: 10 to15 minutes
2. One-Knee Throwing drill (drill 1) or Partner Throwing drill (drill 9): 3 to 5 minutes
3. Pregame Around the Horn (drill 142): 5 to 7 minutes
4. Any combination of the infield and outfield fungo pregame drills in this chapter: 5 to 10 minutes

5. Coach Pitch — Soft Toss drill (drill 76) or Coach Pitch — Front Toss drill (drill 80): 10 to 15 minutes

6. Dugout: Pregame pep talk

The pregame drills will refer to each defensive position by number as follows:

Player Position Key

1. Pitcher
2. Catcher
3. First base
4. Second base
5. Third base
6. Shortstop
7. Left field
8. Center field
9. Right field

Chapter 8 Skills Matrix

Drill Number	Drill Title (Indented drills are "named" Advanced Variations)	Skills Reinforced						
		Throwing	Catching	Fielding	Fielding Footwork	Pivoting	Infield Situation	Infield-Outfield Situation
142.	Pregame Around the Horn	⚾	⚾			⚾		
	Pivot Line	⚾	⚾			⚾		
143.	Force at First	⚾	⚾	⚾	⚾		⚾	
144.	Double Play Ground Ball	⚾	⚾	⚾	⚾		⚾	
145.	Double Play Fly Ball	⚾	⚾	⚾	⚾		⚾	
146.	Easiest Base	⚾	⚾	⚾	⚾		⚾	
147.	Play's at Home!	⚾	⚾	⚾	⚾		⚾	
	Outfield Do or Die	⚾	⚾	⚾	⚾		⚾	⚾
148.	Outfield Fungoes	⚾	⚾	⚾	⚾		⚾	⚾

Pregame Drills

For all pregame drills, the relief pitcher and/or backup catcher can participate while the starting pitcher and catcher warm up separately.

142. Pregame Around the Horn (Beginner)

Purpose: Pregame throwing and catching drill
Equipment: Softball
Number of players: Multiple players (in groups of 4)

Number of repetitions: 3 per turn
Allocated time: 5 to 7 minutes
Cardio index: ♥ ♥

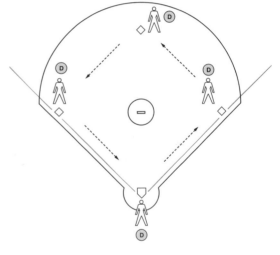

1. Four players assume positions at first, second, and third base and home plate.
2. Starting with any position, the players throw the ball around the bases (clockwise and/or counterclockwise).
3. After three trips around the horn, the next group of four players take their turn.

Variation

Pivot Line. This variation can be executed when space is tight or when the other team is taking infield practice. Simply form two lines (up to seven players per line about 30 feet apart) and have each player make a crisp throw to the next player in line. Be sure your players are pivoting in the correct direction (counterclockwise for right-handed players and clockwise for left-handed players) when throwing. After 10 or so times down the line, rotate your players to allow the "bookend" players a chance to pivot.

Hints

Reinforce proper pivot footwork and throwing angles. Throws should be gamelike and crisp. Don't limit this warm-up drill to your starting lineup, or even your infielders. Every player will benefit from this basic pregame warm-up drill.

143. Force at First (Beginner)

Purpose: Pregame situation drill
Equipment: Softballs
Number of players: 9 (all defensive positions)

Number of repetitions: As many as possible in the allocated time
Allocated time: 5 to 7 minutes
Cardio index: ♥ ♥

1. All defensive players assume their on-field positions.
2. A coach standing at home plate calls out "No one on base" and hits fungo ground balls of varying strength to any defensive position.
3. Infield players field the ball and throw to first base for the out.
4. Outfield players field the ball and throw to the appropriate cutoff, who throws to second base.
5. The player covering first or second base promptly throws the ball to the pitcher to stop the play.
6. The pitcher tosses the ball to the catcher for the next repetition.

Hints

Reinforce proper footwork and throwing angles. Lightly hit some balls toward first base; if the first-base player fields the ball, she needs to either tag the runner or throw to the player covering first base.

Make sure your outfielders throw the ball promptly to the cutoff, or if close enough to second base, directly to the player covering second base. This will help to prevent an extra-base hit. Once the player covering the bag catches the ball, she should throw it promptly to the pitcher to stop the action.

Encourage your infielders to get off the bag if necessary to catch or block errant throws.

144. Double Play Ground Ball (Beginner)

Purpose: Pregame double play situation drill
Equipment: Softballs
Number of players: 6 (all infielders)

Number of repetitions: As many as possible in the allocated time
Allocated time: 10 minutes
Cardio index:

1. All infield defensive players assume their on-field positions.
2. A coach standing at home plate calls out "Runner at first" and hits fungo ground balls of varying strength to simulate the following double play situations:

   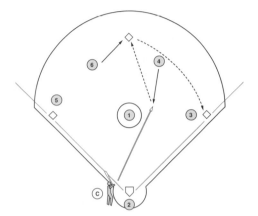

   - 4-6-3: fungo to second-base player's area of responsibility
   - 6-4-3: fungo to shortstop's area of responsibility
   - 3-6 (covering second)-4 (covering first): fungo to first-base player's area of responsibility
   - 5-4-3: fungo to third-base player's area of responsibility
   - 1-4-3: fungo to pitcher's area of responsibility

3. The player covering the last bag promptly throws the ball to the pitcher to stop the play.
4. The pitcher tosses the ball to the catcher for the next repetition.

Hints

Reinforce proper footwork and throwing angles. In game situations, double plays are not always possible. In 3-6-4, in certain situations the first-base player might go for the easy out and tag the runner or first base and forgo the double play. Or the player covering second base might not have enough time to throw to first. If any runners are left on base, it's crucial for the defensive player to get the ball back to the pitcher to stop the action. When runners are on second or third base, the defensive player may have to quickly jog the ball to the pitching circle and firmly hand the ball to the pitcher, all the while keeping an eye on the base runners.

Kids' Corner

Explain to your younger players that sometimes they have to *quickly* and *confidently* jog the ball back to the pitching circle because it's safer than possibly making an errant throw to the pitcher allowing the runners to advance. Young players sometimes have a tendency to jog without keeping an eye on the runners or to close the distance to the pitcher (which is good), but then stiffly toss the ball to the pitcher at close range (which can be even more inaccurate, not to mention dangerous, than throwing it from afar).

145. Double Play Fly Ball (Beginner)

Purpose: Pregame fly ball double play situation drill
Equipment: Softballs
Number of players: 6 (all infield positions)

Number of repetitions: As many as possible in the allocated time
Allocated time: 5 minutes
Cardio index: ♥ ♥

1. All infield defensive players assume their on-field positions.
2. A coach standing at home plate calls out "Runner at first" and hits fungo pop flies or line drives to 1, 4, 5, or 6.
3. The appropriate infielder catches the pop fly and throws to first base if the coach calls out "Runner going."
4. The player covering first base throws the ball to the pitcher to stop the play.
5. The pitcher tosses the ball to the catcher for the next repetition.

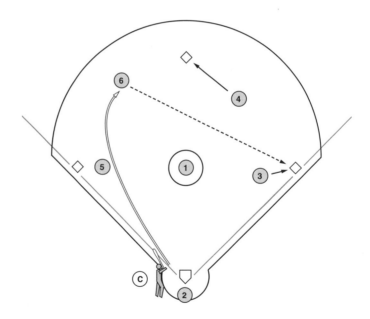

146. Easiest Base (Beginner)

Purpose: Pregame situation drill with runners at first and/or second and fewer than two outs
Equipment: Softballs
Number of players: 6 (all infield positions)

Number of repetitions: As many as possible in the allocated time
Allocated time: 5 minutes
Cardio index: ♥ ♥

1. All infield defensive players assume their on-field positions.
2. A coach standing at home plate calls out "Runners at first (and/or second), no outs" and hits fungo ground balls of varying strength to the infield.
3. The appropriate infielder fields the ball and throws to the closest base, or if close to the bag, tags the bag.
4. If the coach calls out "Runner at second" (meaning no runner at first), then assume the runner takes off for third, for a nonforce play at third.
5. The player covering the bag throws the ball to the pitcher to stop the play.
6. The pitcher tosses the ball to the catcher for the next repetition.

147. Play's at Home! (Beginner)

Purpose: Pregame situation drill (for example, bases loaded, less than two outs)
Equipment: Softballs
Number of players: 6 (all infield positions)

Number of repetitions: As many as possible in the allocated time
Allocated time: 5 minutes
Cardio index: ♥ ♥

1. All infield defensive players assume their on-field positions (infielders should play in a bit in order to get the play at home).
2. A coach standing at home plate calls out "Bases loaded, fewer than two outs" and hits fungo ground balls of varying strength to the infield.
3. The appropriate infielder fields the ball and throws to home plate.

Advanced Variations

Outfield Do or Die. Include the outfielders and call out "Play's at home," then hit fungo one-hops to the shallow outfield. The outfielders should execute the proper footwork to field the ball and immediately throw to home plate for the force play or tag out.

148. Outfield Fungoes (Beginner)

Purpose: Pregame situation drill for outfielders
Equipment: Softballs
Number of players: 9 (all defensive positions)

Number of repetitions: As many as possible in the allocated time
Allocated time: 5 minutes
Cardio index: ♥ ♥

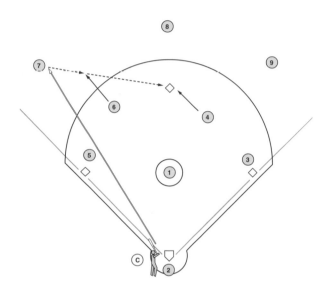

1. All defensive players assume their on-field positions.
2. A coach standing at home plate calls out the situation and hits fungo fly balls of varying depth to the outfield.
3. The appropriate outfielder fields the ball and throws to the correct target as follows (hitting the cutoff will depend on the outfielder's ability, the depth of the fly ball hit, and whether or not the ball is hit in the gap):

   - 7-6-4: for balls hit to deep left field or in the gap
   - 8-4-6: for balls hit to deep center field or in the right-center gap
   - 8-6-4: for balls hit to the left-center gap
   - 9-4-6: for balls hit to deep right field or in the gap
   - Outfielder directly to player covering second base for balls hit to the shallow outfield
   - 7-5 or 8-5: to force out or tag runners advancing to third base
   - 9-4-5 or 9-6-5: to force out or tag runners advancing to third base
   - Play's at home: execute Do or Die variation of this drill similar to the advanced variation for drill 147 for plays to home plate

4. The player covering second or third base throws (or quickly jogs and firmly hands) the ball to the pitcher to stop the play.
5. The pitcher tosses the ball to the catcher for the next repetition.

Hints

Young outfielders have a tendency to hold the ball for too long, sometimes because they are confused about where to throw ("Coach said always throw it to the cutoff" or "When in doubt, Coach said always throw it to second base"). Sometimes the cutoff doesn't show up, or sometimes the throw should be made directly to home plate. A big part of our job as coaches is to instill confidence in playmaking decisions through repetition. If the play is to home plate, then young players should throw to home plate. It doesn't really matter if the throw is a little wobbly or off target. Praise their *decision*, and work on their throwing mechanics during practice.

Index

About the Authors

Michele Smith is a two-time Olympic gold medalist (1996 and 2000) for the U.S. National Softball Team. A potent double-threat in pitching and offense, Michele is an active veteran and seven-time MVP of the elite Japan Pro Softball League, and helped lead her team, the Toyota Shokki, to seven league championships. A true ambassador for the sport of fast-pitch softball, Michele was selected as one of only six players worldwide to serve on the International Softball Federation task force formed to lobby for softball's reinstatement as an Olympic sport. She is the ESPN commentator for the Little League World Series and runs a longstanding coaching program for Little League. She runs her own softball clinics around the country through her company, Michele Smith Inc. (www.michelesmith.com). In recognition of her contributions to softball, Michele was inducted in 2006 into the American Softball Association Hall of Fame.

Lawrence Hsieh is a writer and corporate attorney. He is a graduate of the University of Chicago Law School and Cornell University. He attended Hillsborough High School in New Jersey where he was valedictorian and earned a varsity letter in basketball. Lawrence volunteers his time as a youth sports coach.